Spiritualism,
Madame Blavatsky,
& Theosophy

Mike Reiners
5/7/03

Spiritualism, Madame Blavatsky, & Theosophy

An Eyewitness View of Occult History

LECTURES BY
Rudolf Steiner

Selected and Introduced by
Christopher Bamford

Anthroposophic Press

The lectures and writings translated in this book may be found in the Rudolf Steiner Gesamtausgabe [GA]—the collected works of Rudolf Steiner—published by the Rudolf Steiner Verlag, Dornach, Switzerland, as follows: *Briefwechsel und Dokumente 1901–1925* (GA 262); *Spirituelle Seelenlehre und Weltbetrachtung* (GA 52); *Ursprungsimpulse der Geisteswissenschaft* (GA 96); *Der Christus Impul und die Entwickelung des Ich-Bewusstseins* (GA 116); *Erfahrungen des Uebersinnlichen. Die Wege der Seele zu Christus* (GA 143); *Die okkulte Bewegung in der neunzehnten Jahrhundert und ihre Beziehung zur Weltkultur* (GA 254); *Gegenwaertiges und Vergangenes im Menschengeiste* (GA 167); *Karma der Unwahrhaftigkeit, Erster Teil* (GA 173); *Die Geschichte und Die Bedingungen der anthropsophischen Bewegung im Verhaeltnis zur Anthropsophschen Gesellschaft* (GA 258). Translated with permission.

Published by Anthroposophic Press
Post Office Box 799
Great Barrington, MA 01230
www.anthropress.org

Book design by Will Marsh

Library of Congress Cataloging-in-Publication Data

Steiner, Rudolf, 1861–1925.
    [Selections. English. 2002]
    Spiritualism, Madame Blavatsky, and theosophy : an eyewitness view of occult history / by Rudolf Steiner ; edited with an introduction by Christopher Bamford.
        p. cm.
    Includes bibliographical references.
    ISBN 0-88010-495-3
    1. Spiritualism. 2. Blavatsky, H. P. (Helena Petrovna), 1831–1891.
    3. Theosophy. 4. Anthroposophy. I. Bamford, Christopher, 1943– II.
    Title.
    BP595.S894 S6813 2002
    299'.935–dc21

                         2001005056

10 9 8 7 6 5 4 3 2 1

Printed in the United States of America

Contents

Introduction

by Christopher Bamford

There are many ways of approaching Rudolf Steiner. The present collection places him in the spiritual streams in which he chose to begin his public esoteric work—spiritism (or spiritualism) and Theosophy. Such a choice does not, of course, tell the whole story. To begin to complete it, we would have to add, at the very least, as we shall see, Hermetism (or alchemy), Rosicrucianism, and Freemasonry, as well as German idealism and esoteric Christianity. Historically, these are Steiner's sources and, to some degree, Blavatsky's also. Nevertheless, Steiner's explicit choice of spiritism and Theosophy says a great deal—more than appears at a first glance. And though today this choice may seem a musty historical oddity, invoking a distant, less enlightened, more superstitious period than our own, careful readers of this collection will soon discover that it is, in fact, as relevant and vital now as it was then.

Much of this relevance is usually concealed from us because we forget just how much the spiritual movements—the spiritual revival—of the twentieth and now the twenty-first centuries owe to Madame Blavatsky and the Theosophical Society she founded. Although not yet counted with Marx, Nietzsche, and Freud as a creator of our time, Madame Blavatsky, no matter how wild her eccentricity or willful and capricious her natural freedom of spirit, deserves equivalent stature. Contemporary spiritual thinkers could not have accomplished what they have without her strenuous preparatory efforts. Much of what we think of as "New Age"—from Buddhism through "inner development" to channeling—was part of the original Theosophical mission. Despite the apparent differences in their individual teachings, the capacious being of Madame Blavatsky, deep as it is wide, lies behind most alternative "spiritual" teachers still read today—Gurdjieff, Krishnamurti, and Schwaller de Lubicz, for instance, to name but three. In fact, it is difficult to imagine anyone escaping her influence. The same is equally true of cultural figures like C. G. Jung (and the Eranos group), as well as contemporary figures like R. J. Stewart, David Spangler, or Caroline Myss. It was Madame Blavatsky (known as HPB), furthermore, who introduced world religions and world history into the theretofore parochial and tightly guarded confines of Western thought. It was she likewise who opened up the possibility of ecumenical and interreligious dialogue and laid the ground (with the philosopher Hegel) for a truly global theory of history as evolution of consciousness. Above all, it was her stubborn, independent, open-mind exploration that broke open the hegemony of the aging secret societies and began the process of tearing the veil of the temple and making esotericism part of cultural life, in two equally important ways. She made available—for rational reflection, speculation, and contemplation—long hidden spiritual teachings and doctrines, both Western and Eastern, about the universe and humanity's place and role within it. At the same time, she introduced and began to teach methods and practices of inner work by which any person of good intention willing to make the effort could achieve direct cognition of the realities she expounded, more theoretically, in her books. Thus, despite herself and her passionately held anti-Christianity, she was, perhaps without knowing it, of Christ's party.

All that said, one might sum up her achievement (and that of spiritualism, which, as we shall see, prepared the way for what she was able to do) by naming her the "prophet" or "mother" of what has begun to be called "post-religion spirituality." This is a tricky term, because it was not clear then, nor is it now, in fact, that religion—the Age of Religions—is over. To think so is perhaps only wishful thinking. It may be overly optimistic to believe that we have moved beyond religion to an age of spirituality in which each person has a personal, direct connection to the universe and the Godhead that translates into peace, compassion, justice, and mercy in social relations. It is by no means evident that the shared, communal institutions, rites, and rituals that have for untold millennia transmitted revelation and tradition in the form of wisdom and knowledge are obsolete. Certainly, much evil has been done in the name of the good, often with the best intentions. But we must never forget that to be human is to interpret, and any religion can turn on a new interpretation if it is radical enough. In this case—if the religions don't atrophy and fade away, but somehow manage to evolve—then the term "meta-religious spirituality" would perhaps be more appropriate. Rudolf Steiner himself was ambiguous on this question. On the one hand, Anthroposophy or spiritual science, like Theosophy, was whole in itself—sufficient for a complete spiritual life—and he clearly believed religions were dying (and, indeed, they seemed deader then than now). On the other hand, he was equally clear that Anthroposophy itself was *not* a religion—it was a "science," *a way of knowing*. But if one had a religion, the practice of Anthroposophy would only deepen, elucidate, and enrich it.

It is true, of course—whether or not the Kali Yuga, or Age of Darkness, ended in 1900, as Rudolf Steiner believed—that something "new" arose in the second half of the nineteenth century. Human beings had forgotten that beyond the countable, weighable, measurable universe lay other worlds. Spiritualism began to change all that. Suddenly the world revealed by sense perception, itself determined by the cognitive structures (ideology, prejudice) of science, became only the tip of an enormous, practically speaking infinite, iceberg. This was something obvious, but it had been obscured by three centuries of modern science. Such was the Good News proclaimed at the apex of materialism: the world is essentially spiritual. We live in a spiritual world. We are spiritual beings in a universe of spiritual beings. Materiality is the illusion.

Thus the realization dawned that, if the world *is* spiritual, we need only awaken to this reality to begin to explore it—to develop means of researching it—and so unite, as in the most ancient times, science and religion in a new universal mysticism. This was the mission of Theosophy. What was new in Theosophy was not so much the proclamation or the insights behind it, but the democratization of the teaching—it was available to everyone. In a sense, the reality had never been forgotten. Throughout dark ages of materialism, however, knowledge of it had remained the jealously guarded province of elitist occult and esoteric groups and secret societies. Then, during the Romantic period, beginning at the end of the eighteenth century and lasting about forty years, an attempt had been made to bring knowledge of the spiritual nature of reality out into the open and transform society, science, and religion in its light, but materialism (and opposing forces) won the day. Spiritualism, which began in upstate New York in 1848 and was to culminate in the profound revelation of esotericism and practice of Theosophy, was the ultimately successful response by the spiritual world to this impasse.

In his essay "Swedenborg, Mediums, and the Desert Places," W. B. Yeats, the Irish poet (who was also an occultist, magician, philosopher, and early Theosophist), told how he once withdrew in poor health to the West of Ireland. Here he helped his friend in the Celtic Revival, Lady Gregory, collect stories from country people. These stories, as living folk traditions often do, contained a great deal of wisdom and were filled with supernatural occurrences and miraculous powers. Listening to them, the poet felt he was beginning to live in a dream.

As "the ancient system of belief" unfolded before him, Yeats began to notice analogies between the informants' accounts and modern spiritualism. It seemed that a community of potential and practice existed between the Irish peasants and his own experiences when, as he wrote, "I climbed to the top of some house in Soho or Holloway, and, having paid my shilling, awaited, among servant girls, the wisdom of some fat old medium." As he says, "I did not go there for evidence of the kind the Society for Psychical Research would value, any more than I would seek it in Galway or Aran." His aim was simply, like Paracelsus, to compare beliefs. And the result? He discovered a continuity and network of kinship that reached from the ancient Mystery religions through Boehme, Swedenborg, and Blake to the spiritualist mediums and philosophers of his own time, and included the second sight of peasant people everywhere.

Andrew Lang (1844–1912), the Scots poet, folklorist, novelist, and psychical researcher, neatly corroborated Yeats's experience by publishing, in 1893, an edition of Robert Kirk's *The Secret Commonwealth*, subtitled *Of Elves, Fauns, and Faeries*. Yeats, in fact, owned a copy of this work and may well have been influenced by it. The Reverend Kirk, who was born in 1644, was a Scots minister and a linguist who translated the Psalms into Gaelic and other religious works into Highland dialect. He was also the seventh son of a large family—that is to say, he had "second sight." In June 1685, he was appointed to the family parish of Aberfoyle. Here he remained until his death in 1692, the same year he created the manuscript of *The Secret Commonwealth*, perhaps the most remarkable work of its kind ever written.

Interest in the clairvoyant capacities of the people of the Scottish Highlands had been at its height in the last twenty years of the seventeenth century. Scottish authors like Kirk, stimulated by scientific and philosophical curiosity about magic, were encouraged to put down whatever they could discover. And what was discovered was marvelous indeed. For Andrew Lang, the phenomena Kirk recounts, having lain dormant for two centuries, were evidently the stuff of contemporary spiritualism: rappings, teleportations, precipitations, poltergeists, and so forth. Lang was not alone in thinking so. W. Y. Evans-Wentz in his *The Fairy Faith in Celtic Countries* concurred in this assessment. And today, such fairy phenomena are assimilated to abduction and UFO phenomena. In a sense, the more things change, the more they remain the same—"There is nothing new under the sun." Yet, in the light of Yeats, Kirk, and Lang, we can begin to understand Steiner's veiled references to Scotland, as well his frequent reference to "atavistic clairvoyance." He means *second sight*, an inherited trait in certain families, which used to be, in country areas undisturbed by "scientific consciousness" or technological innovation, much more widespread than today.

The story, however, like all good stories, is more complicated. To understand it several strands must be unraveled—strands that are not just strings of historical connection but lineages or, more precisely, esoteric lines of filiation. Steiner's main concern was to make esotericism and the cult of symbolism, ritual, and practice that traditionally conveyed it accessible to the general public. Therefore he tried to move beyond the dualism of esoteric and exoteric. His later teaching is exemplary in this regard. At the same time, Steiner sought to ensure evolutionary continuity. At the start of his mission, therefore, he consciously and explicitly affiliated himself with those esoteric lineages and movements to whose transformation or flowering he sought to bear witness.

The history of these lineages, as Steiner never failed to emphasize, began long ago. Indeed, in a sense, it is a history without beginning, for it begins in the spiritual world. On Earth, however, it passes by Atlantis through great initiates into the great Mystery centers of prehistory. Thence, consciousness ever evolving, it metamorphoses into the temples, shrines, cults, and sacred sites—the Mystery religions—of antiquity. And these streams, Indian, Persian, Egypto-Chaldean, flow into the great pluralistic, multicultural maelstrom of Hellenism. At which point, suddenly and bafflingly, the incarnation of Christ erupts, transforming everything forever.

The full story is too complex to be told here in any detail—perhaps to be told at all. Nevertheless, several milestones or points along the way may be usefully noted.

Whether or not acknowledged consciously or known by name, the "Mystery of Golgotha"—Steiner's preferred designation for the Christ Event—transformed the world and human nature utterly and forever.

What had been outside the world was now in it. Matter was spiritual-ized. Living fire or spiritual leaven filled all things again and awaited only the love-filled recognition of the sons and daughters of God to be awoken and raised in the spirit to approach the kingdom. The Logos, the divine Word-Son, dwelling within and without, made this possible.

Throughout the early Christian centuries, Greek and Latin Church Fathers, early Gnostics, and alchemists of the Hellenistic period strove to understand what had come to pass and to create a new culture appropriate to it. Everyone had a part to play in this process—some of which went underground as the institutionalization of the Church under the aegis of the Roman Empire created a model of hierarchy and control that excluded certain streams as "heretical." Persia, Egypt, Greece, and Israel all played their part in this. From Persia arose the sense of the human mission to cultivate the Earth and transform evil. From Egypt, a dynamic and transformative cosmology in the shape of Hermetism; from Greece, philosophy (pre-Socratic, Platonic, and Aristotelian) and the remnants of the Mysteries; and from Israel, the personal and passionate relationship with the Living God.

Throughout the Middle Ages this vision encountered and then entered the human heart. True human feeling, residual clairvoyance, and the birth of new thinking came together to create a magnificent synthesis. True and embodied knowledge created a civilization. Con-sider the greatness of Romanesque and Gothic architecture, the growth of vernacular literatures (the Troubadour and the Grail cycles, for instance), the profound mysticism of such as St. Bernard, St. Fran-cis, Hildegard, Gertrude of Helfta, Margaret of Porete, Hadjewich, and Meister Eckhart, and the cognitive triumph of Thomas Aquinas. These are not signs of a dark and miserable time! Nor is this all. The sacred science of alchemy, Christianized, took hold and flourished. New precursors of a future spirituality planted the seeds of our time: Cathars, Templars, and the Brethren of the Free Spirit, the Friend of God from the Highlands, to name but a few. The new message was twofold, with two meanings—the local or particular and the cosmic or universal—in one. Exoterically, ordinary human beings came to feel that the embodied human heart made new and united to God in knowing could overcome evil and transform the world through love. The other side of this was that esoterically, the good news was dawn-ing that the world was in God as God was in the world—in the least atom of matter as in the greatness of the galaxies. The world was spiritual, a heavenly host, whose name (as the Valentinian Gnostics would say) is *anthropos*, Christ, or the fullness of human nature. In a word, it came to be realized that matter and consciousness were two sides of a single coin: the conscious heart.

It is clear from the above that one may speak of many renaissances. The very word *Renaissance* therefore requires specification. With the *Italian* Renaissance, which followed, we might say, the Renaissances of the ninth and twelfth centuries, reality struck. The foretaste of paradise was over. The journey would be long, perhaps indefinitely so. Many obstacles would call for human resourcefulness before the hard work of consciousness could take hold. George Gemistos Plethon brought the good news to the Council of Ferrara-Florence in 1439: what had been locally intuited was a global phenomenon with an ancient lineage. Zoroaster, Hermes, Orpheus . . . Min (the first King of Egypt), Minos, and Numa . . . and even the Brahman of India, the Magi of Media, and the Priests of Dodona—these were the ancient theologians, the *prisci theologi*, who had all taught the same thing: that the world is full of Gods whose nature is of fire. And the human task is the cotransfiguration of the Earth by this fiery Light of Glory, the all-luminous substance that is the true nature of human beings. Plethon also brought texts: Plato and the Neoplatonists (Plotinus, Iamblichus, Porphyry, Proclus), the *Corpus Hermeticum*, the Chaldean Oracles. These, in turn, translated by Marsilio Ficino, were read and poured over by indigenous magi such as Paracelsus, John Dee, and Giordano Bruno. The practice of alchemy—and other "occult sciences" like astrology and magic—deepened and became more widespread. The result was a call for a general reformation of all knowledge and being: a new way of knowing. At the same time, under the impact of the discoveries of Copernicus and Galileo, the first rays of modern science in the form of the search for abstract mathematical certainty combined with a pragmatic, empirical literalism could be sensed dawning on the horizon.

At the beginning of the seventeenth century, with Bruno dead at the stake, the battle lines were drawn. The Rosicrucian Manifestos of 1614–1617 announced the last struggle. In vain. Religious conflicts and the horrors of the Thirty Years War decided the issue: mechanistic, materialist science would become the outer form of the new civilization. The dream of the Renaissance was over. The Rosicrucians left

Europe for the East, perhaps the Baltic States, and the inner traditions of sacred science and the work of consciousness went underground, to emerge again later, like a message in a bottle, in Freemasonry and other secret societies. For a while, however, there was an attempt at some kind of collaboration. We see this, for instance, in the background to the Royal Society in England, behind whose ideas lay Rosicrucian ideals mediated by such as Comenius and Hartlib. It is evident, for example, in the alchemical work of Robert Boyle, the great founder of empirical chemistry. Boyle, like Newton, worked with alchemy all his life and understood the need for a higher, clairvoyant empiricism. For this reason, indeed, Boyle consulted with the Reverend Kirk, quizzing him about Highland "second sight." Kirk also spoke to him of the Mason "Word." For Masonry too appears to have originated in Scotland, where medieval guild initiations seem to have melded with a transformed Templarism—many Templars having fled to Scotland, already a Templar stronghold, after the destruction of the order by Philip the Fair between 1308 and 1314.

All these currents of inner wisdom then flowed through into the eighteenth century, carried primarily by the secret societies. Side by side, as rationalism and materialist empiricism flourished, the study and practice of ancient initiation metamorphosed and evolved, developed and unfolded by important pioneers such as Martines de Pasqually, Emanuel Swedenborg, Louis Claude de Saint Martin, Friedrich Christian Oettinger, Eckhartshausen, Cagliostro, and Franz Anton Mesmer. A whole history, known and thoroughly digested by Rudolf Steiner, and referred to between the lines of this collection, remains to be explored here.

Around the turn of the nineteenth century, a new dawn was felt, a third (or fourth) Renaissance: *Romanticism*. The inner side of Romanticism, from this perspective, is nothing but the transformation of the esoteric. Drawing on the rediscovery of direct experience, coupled with a renewed respect and deep reading of hermetic texts, these poets and seers proclaimed a new mystery cult of the everyday. A new science, a new religion, a new art—all available to all—were seen to be possible again. The good news was that the world was spiritual after all. We see this in great souls like Goethe, Novalis, Blake, Coleridge. We see it in philosophers like Franz von Baader, as well as the better known German idealists (Kant, Hegel, and Schelling); and above all we see it in those precursors of spiritualism, so-called "lesser" figures like Jung-Stilling and Justinus Kerner, who wrote the account of the "Seeress of Prevorst." For Rudolf Steiner, this moment marked the earthly reflection of the great "reopening" of the spiritual school of the Archangel Michael in heaven.

By the 1840s, the dream was over. Materialism seemed to have won the day. But just when humanity seemed to have reached the nadir, light—weird light—broke forth. Led by figures like Éliphas Lévi, esotericism, occultism, and magic reemerged gradually from the shadows of history to begin what would be a continuous ascent into the light of consciousness. At the same time, to the hour, the phenomenon of spiritualism erupted, shattering forever the complacency of the industrial age. With it, the "New Age" was born.

This is the point at which Steiner takes up the story. To understand his telling of it, the following should be borne in mind. Spiritualism itself was born in 1848 in the hamlet of Hydesville in Wayne County in the "Burned Over District" of Western New York. This region was called "burned over" because of the number of religious revivals (including Joseph Smith's discovering of the Book of Mormon) that had swept through it. Thence spiritualism, with its attendant and democratic culture of mediumcy and the primacy of women, spread like wildfire, first across America (where, by 1850, it could count over two million adherents), and then into Britain and continental Europe. However there was a difference between Anglo-Saxon "spiritualism" and Continental "spiritism." The Anglo-Saxon variant was concerned mostly with the "spirits of the dead," whereas spiritism, which began in France, under the aegis of Allan Kardec, and moved across into Germany and Austria, became something akin to a "religion of the spirits." (As a kind of animism, its major center is now in Brazil.) It was furthermore resolutely *reincarnationist* and, though universalist and even "Druid" in its origins, it was resolutely Christian in its moral and ethical fervor. But it had no method. Madame Blavatsky's great "Theosophical" contribution was both to link it to the perennial and esoteric wisdom traditions of the world and to incorporate into its program *a method* (meditation, ritual, and astral travel) whereby one could confirm its teachings for oneself. Rudolf Steiner's perhaps even greater contribution, as we shall see, was to remove the dust of the past and Blavatsky's prejudices and place both method and teachings squarely in the evolutionary development of human consciousness.

It is important to remember, however, that Rudolf Steiner did this as a Theosophist, within Theosophy. Anthroposophy, which he taught from the beginning, began as, and was for the first ten years of his public (and private) esoteric work, explicitly his contribution to Theosophy. On Steiner's part, this was a conscious deed, a historical decision freely made out of his own understanding of the spiritual world, given as a gift to the movement and impulse that he recognized as carrying the spiritual mandate of our time. During this period (1902–1913), he created an independent body of teaching based on his own spiritual research and written and spoken out of his own experience. But he always did so within the framework and context of the Theosophical movement whose world-historical mission he understood directly from the spiritual world. The emergence of Anthroposophy as a separate teaching—its radical separation from Theosophy enforced and rendered irrevocable by the momentous barrier placed around Central Europe by the First World War—came only as a final and humble submission to world destiny. The earthly circumstances of this separation were, of course, many and complex. The precipitating event—whether or not the young Jeddu Krishnamurti was the reincarnation of the Christ, the World Teacher; whether or not, that is, there could be a reincarnation of the Christ, which Steiner denied—was embedded within an extended, long-standing web of intricate and duplicitous personal and political struggle. Steiner resisted the inevitable as long as he could. He had honestly placed himself at the service of Theosophy—as late as 1907 he translated Madame Blavatsky's *The Key to Theosophy*—but in 1913 he realized that he had no choice but to place himself at the service of an Anthroposophy no longer connected to Theosophy. It was a costly decision, both in personal and cultural evolutionary terms. I am sure, however, that he made his peace with Madame Blavatsky and that on May 8, her death day, while no longer giving White Lotus Day lectures, he continued to acknowledge her contribution, to express his gratitude, and seek her counsel.

Prologue
A Personal Statement

(From the "Barr Document" for Edouard Schuré)

As is so often the case with servants of humanity and with saints, Rudolf Steiner's life and mission are almost indistinguishable and mutually illuminating. Every event in his life appears significant for his mission and no aspect of his mission is without biographical counterpart. In other words, biography is mission. Hence the value of the following autobiographical notes.

The notes were written for the French mystical writer, poet, and dramatist Edouard Schuré (1841–1926). Schuré was a member of the French Theosophical Society and since 1899 had been corresponding with Marie von Sivers (before she met Rudolf Steiner), who later became Marie Steiner. She translated several of Schuré's works, including THE GREAT INITIATES and the plays THE MYSTERIES OF ELEUSIS and THE CHILDREN OF LUCIFER.

Steiner first met Schuré at the Paris Theosophical Congress of 1906. Schuré wrote of this meeting: "For the first time I was certain that an initiate stood before me. For many years I had lived in spirit with initiates of the past, whose history and development I had attempted to describe. Here at last one stood before me on the physical plane." Steiner and Schuré became friends and coworkers. Thus it was that Steiner visited Schuré at his home in Barr, Alsace, from September 5 to 12, 1907. Schuré was planning to write a major introduction to the French translation of Steiner's CHRISTIANITY AS MYSTICAL FACT. To help him with this, Steiner gave a talk every evening. He also wrote down these notes, which were perhaps also notes for the talks that he gave. Schuré and Steiner remained friends until forced apart by the politics of the Great War. They reconciled in 1922.

The document is extraordinarily rich, with every sentence deserving amplification and commentary. All the strands that Steiner wove into his Theosophy are represented.

1

My attention was drawn to Kant at an early age.[1] At fifteen and six-
teen, I studied Kant intensively, and before going on to college in
Vienna I had an intense interest in Kant's early nineteenth-century
orthodox followers, who have been completely forgotten by official
historians of thought. . . . In addition, I immersed myself in Fichte
and Schelling.[2] During this period, and this is already due to external
spiritual influences, I gained complete understanding of the concept
of time. This knowledge was in no way connected with my studies and
was guided totally by my spiritual life. I understood there is a regress-
ing evolution, the astral occult, which interferes with the progressing
one. This knowledge is the precondition of spiritual clairvoyance.

Then came acquaintance with the agent of the M. [Master].[3]

Then came intensive study of Hegel.[4]

Then the study of modern philosophy as it developed from the
1850s onward in Germany, particularly the so-called theory of knowledge in all its branches. . . .

I did not meet the M. immediately, but first an emissary who was
completely initiated into the secrets of plants and their effects, and
into their connection with the cosmos and human nature. . . .

Officially, I studied mathematics, chemistry, physics, zoology, botany, mineralogy, and geology. . . .

. . . From early 1880 onward I started to work on Goethe's scientific
studies. . . .

I wrote introductions to Goethe's botany, zoology, geology, and
theory of color.[5]

Theosophical ideas can already be found in these introductions,
clothed in philosophical idealism.

They deal also with Haeckel.[6]

My 1886 *Theory of Knowledge* is like a philosophical continuation
of these introductions. . . .[7]

In all this, the public display of esoteric ideas was out of the question. And the spiritual forces standing behind me gave me only one
piece of advice: "Everything in the guise of idealistic philosophy."

. . . The first contact with Theosophical circles in Vienna at the end
of the 1880s had no *outward* consequences.[8]

In my last months in Vienna I wrote the little publication *Goethe as
Founder of a New Science of Aesthetics.*

Then I was called to the Goethe and Schiller Archive in Weimar, which was founded at the time, to edit the scientific writings of Goethe. . . .[9]

My next aim was to present the foundation of my world conception in purely philosophical terms. I did this in two books: *Truth and Knowledge*[10] and *The Philosophy of Freedom* (*Intuitive Thinking as a Spiritual Path*). . . .[11]

. . . Then the Nietzsche episode occurred. . . .[12]

. . . For a time I was considered to be the most uncompromising Nietzschean. . . .

1890–1897, I was in Weimar.

In 1897, I went to Berlin to edit the *Magazin fur Literatur*. . . . My next task was to bring a spiritual current to bear in literature. . . .

Gently and slowly I guided it into esoteric paths. . . .

In the meantime, a connection with the working classes had been established. I became a teacher at the Berlin Workers' Educational Institute. I taught history and the natural sciences. . . .

Eventually, in harmony with the spiritual forces that stood behind me, I could say to myself: "You have provided the philosophical foundation for a world conception. You have shown your understanding of current directions of thought by treating them only as someone who fully supports them. No one can therefore say, 'This esotericist speaks of the spiritual world because he is ignorant of the philosophical and scientific developments of our time.'"

By this time I had reached my fortieth year. Before this age, no one may present himself or herself as a teacher of esotericism in the sense of the Masters. (Every instance of someone teaching earlier has been an error.) . . .

2

In the early part of the fifteenth century, Christian Rosenkreutz went to the East to find a balance between the initiations of the East and the West. One consequence of this, following his return, was the definitive establishment of the Rosicrucian stream in the West. In this form, Rosicrucianism was meant to be a strictly secret school for the reparation of those things that would become the public task of esotericism at the end of the nineteenth century when material science would have found a provisional solution to certain problems.

Christian Rosenkreutz described these problems as: (1) the discovery of spectral analysis, which revealed the material constitution of the cosmos; (2) the introduction of material evolution into organic science; (3) the recognition of states of consciousness different from our normal one through the acceptance of hypnotism and suggestion.

Only when this material had reached fruition in science were certain Rosicrucian principles from esoteric science to be made public. . . .[13]

3

. . . When H. P. Blavatsky and H. S. Olcott founded the Theosophical Society in 1875 in New York, it had a decidedly Western nature. *Isis Unveiled,* in which Madame Blavatsky revealed a large number of esoteric truths, has just such a Western character.[14] But it must be said about this book that it often presents the great truths of which it speaks in a distorted or even caricatured way. It is like a face of harmonious proportions appearing distorted in a convex mirror. The things said in *Isis Unveiled* are true, but *how* they are said is a lopsided mirror image of the truth. They are true because the great initiates of the West, who also inspired the Rosicrucian wisdom, inspired them. The distortion arises because of the inappropriate way in which H. P. Blavatsky's soul received these truths. The educated world should have seen in *this* fact alone evidence that a higher source inspired these truths. For no one who rendered these truths in so distorted a manner could have created them. Because the Western initiators saw how little opportunity they had to allow the stream of spiritual wisdom to flow into humankind by this means, they decided to drop the matter in this form for the time being. But the door had been opened. Blavatsky's soul had been prepared so that spiritual wisdom could flow into it.

Eastern initiators were then able to take hold of her. To begin with these Eastern initiators had the best of intentions. They saw how Anglo-American influences were steering humanity toward the terrible danger of a completely materialistic impregnation of thinking. These Eastern initiators therefore wanted to imprint *their* form of spiritual knowledge, which had been preserved through the ages, on the Western world. The Theosophical Society took on its Eastern character under the influence of this stream. The same influence inspired Sinnett's *Esoteric Buddhism* and Blavatsky's *The Secret Doctrine.*[15]

Both of these also distorted the truth. Sinnett's work distorts the high teaching of the initiators through an extraneous and inadequate philosophical intellectualism, and Blavatsky's *Secret Doctrine* does the same because of her chaotic soul.

The result was that both the Eastern and the Western initiators withdrew their influence in increasing measure from the official Theosophical Society, and the latter became the arena for all kinds of occult forces that distorted the great cause. There was a short phase when Annie Besant entered the stream of the initiators through her pure and elevated mentality. But this phase came to an end when Besant gave herself up to the influence of certain Indians who developed a grotesque intellectualism derived from certain philosophical teachings, German ones in particular, which they misinterpreted.

This was the situation when I was faced with the necessity of joining the Theosophical Society. *True initiates stood at its cradle and that is why it is at present an instrument of current spiritual life, even if subsequent events have resulted in certain imperfections.* Its continued fruitful development in Western countries is completely dependent on the extent to which it shows itself capable of assimilating the principle of Western initiation among its influences. For the Eastern initiations must of necessity leave untouched the *Christ* as the central *cosmic* factor of evolution.

Without this Christ principle, the Theosophical movement will have no decisive influence on Western cultures, which trace their beginnings back to Christ's life on Earth. Taken on their own, the revelations of Oriental initiation would have to stand aside from the living culture in the West in a sectarian manner. They could only hope for success within evolution if the principle of Christianity were to be eradicated from Western culture. But this would be the same as eradicating *the essential meaning of the Earth,* which lies in the recognition and realization of the intentions of the *living Christ.* To reveal these intentions in the form of complete wisdom, beauty, and activity is the deepest aim of Rosicrucianism.

Regarding the value of Eastern wisdom as the subject of study, one can only say that this study is of the highest value, because Western cultures have lost their sense of esotericism, while the Eastern ones have preserved theirs. But equally it should be understood that the introduction of a correct esotericism in the West could only be of the Rosicrucian-Christian type, because this *latter* gave birth to Western life and, if it were lost, humanity would deny the meaning and destiny of the Earth.

The harmonious relationship between science and religion can flower only in this esotericism, while every amalgamation of Western knowledge with Eastern esotericism can only produce such unproductive mongrels as Sinnett's *Esoteric Buddhism*. The correct way can be represented schematically as:

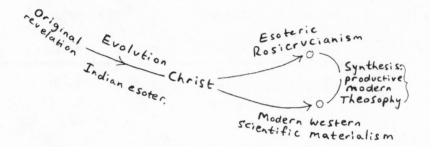

The incorrect way, of which *Esoteric Buddhism* and *The Secret Doctrine* are examples, would be represented as:

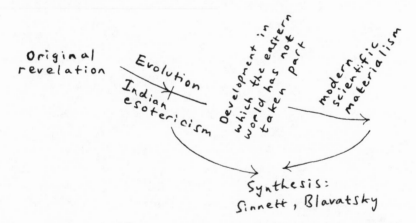

PART ONE

Spiritualism, Somnambulism, and Theosophy

1

Theosophy and Spiritualism

Berlin, February 1, 1904

PEOPLE HAVE ALWAYS ASKED questions about the soul's origin and destiny—questions that are today considered religious, theological, or theosophical. In earlier times, however, a science of daily life accompanied research into the spiritual world. Such questions were not then considered special. In those days, there were "knowers," who researched spiritual life and whose knowledge didn't concern just the facts and laws of outer nature and the science of material life. People who knew about natural phenomena and natural laws also knew the science of spiritual life. Spiritual guides were not one-sided then. Almost everyone had an overview of the whole realm of knowledge. No one would have dared make an authoritative pronouncement about any question, say, in the realm of zoology, without also knowing about the higher questions of spiritual life.

Things changed with the sixteenth century when religious questions and the contributions of the sciences separated. This opposition between faith and science, between religion and experience, reached its peak in the nineteenth century. Thus, many knowledgeable people place the beginning of the "scientific age" sometime in the 1830s—a period rightly identified as one of the most momentous in human history. People point with pride to the achievements of natural science in understanding natural laws and in controlling natural processes. It has rightly been said that the preceding millennia were no match for the nineteenth century in this regard. Especially in relation to the question of human nature and destiny, the landscape changed drastically.

One side effect of this powerful scientific development is that we have lost sight of spiritual life. The harmony that reigned between the two aspects of knowledge was lost. The harmony between a science interested in the outer facts of the material world and a science concerned with the realities of the soul is no longer available to us today. It is a curious fact that nineteenth-century science became completely powerless in relation to the great questions of existence—questions of the soul, the life of soul and spirit. It is remarkable, too, that, precisely in our time, our best scientists can be of no help regarding the higher "spiritual" sciences. When we ask scientists about problems of the soul, for instance, about human free will, they cannot give an explanation. Our age has been called materialistic. Our science, in other respects so perfect, restricts itself to whatever can be achieved by using only the outer senses, or what can be calculated, or made accessible through a combination of external perceptions. Knowledge of nature and knowledge of the life of the soul no longer go hand in hand.

Consider psychology, the "science of the soul." It is as if a great impotence had overcome it. Go from university to university, from professor to professor—what you will find there will be of no help whatsoever regarding the burning questions of our being. Characteristically, the so-called scientists of the soul have a slogan that is meaningful only in the reductionist way a slogan can be meaningful. Starting with the historian of materialism Friedrich Albert Lange, the formula "a science of the soul without the soul" has set the tone.[1] This slogan describes the condition of psychology in the second half of the nineteenth century; it expresses the idea that the human soul and its properties are nothing but the outer expression of the mechanical workings of sensory natural forces in our organism.

A clock consists of wheels and gears that help the hands move forward, so the movements of the hands result from strictly mechanical processes. Our psychologists treat our soul life, with its wishes, desires, passions, representations, concepts, and ideas in the same way: as if it were merely the result of physical processes comparable to the ongoing motion of the hands of a clock. For them our soul life has no basis other than the clockwork in our brain that modern science has so clearly described. There is nothing wrong with the scientific field of brain physiology. I am the first to acknowledge that it passes all the tests. But even if we may say that a clock is a set of mechanical gears, we still cannot forget *that where there is a clock, there is a clockmaker.* It would be as implausible to speak of a clock without a clockmaker as it is to speak of a science of the soul without the soul.

The latter is not just a formula, but in fact characterizes a whole spirit of research and thinking—the entire frame of mind of the nineteenth century, which looks at the soul and explains it as a mechanism, while eliminating the spirit. It is no wonder that those turn elsewhere who seek, out of a deep compulsion of the heart and soul, to answer such questions as: Where do human beings come from? Where are they going? What is the fate of the soul? It is no wonder that such people feel alienated from what is offered them under the label of psychology by those who should have a theory about the soul. For whatever we find in textbooks about the soul is nothing remotely like a teaching about the soul.

Nor is it surprising, then, that precisely at the time when official science became so impotent in face of their questions, those who sought knowledge about the spirit and the soul should seek to satisfy their thirst in *para-scientific* ways. Nor should it surprise us if such a para-science of soul and spirit takes its stand far removed from the modern science of materialism, which is deaf and mute—deafened to any approach other than its own, and mute when asked to speak of the soul. Even where there is good will, official science is impotent when it comes to the soul. This is so true that when it has come to a pitched battle between spiritualism and materialism, as for instance between Wagner and Vogt, the contest has ended to the benefit of the materialists.[2] In fact, unfortunately, the materialists' arguments against spiritualism are entirely valid, since, from the point of view of rigorous research, the spiritualists' argument is completely untenable. Even when scholars of good will working in the light of Weber's true spiritual science asked questions about the human soul, they proved to be ineffectual.[3]

To that extent, the phrase "a science of the soul without the soul" is more than a rhetorical phrase, for science has in effect lost the very concept of what the soul really is. If you ask for the opinion of the most famous psychologists of our time, you will find the same thing as you find with Wagner: psychologists have nothing to say, for they can no longer imagine what the soul is. Not only have they come up with the formula "soul science without the soul," but also the essence of the soul has altogether disappeared from their field of vision.

It is important to appreciate fully the significance of this fact if we intend to understand the development of the spiritualist, or spiritist, movements.[4] Ever since the beginning of the materialist era, which was greeted enthusiastically by some, and fought tooth and nail by others, there has been a countermovement: the spiritualist movement. Materialism and spiritualism belong together, as north and south poles belong together in a magnetic compass. If mainstream scientists can tell us nothing about the soul, people must turn to other research-ers for information. And since the question of the soul has such irre-sistible momentum, all the objections that could be made against spiritualism were in the end powerless in stopping it.

Today, then, I would like to examine what stand we, as Theoso-phists, should take toward the enthusiastic propagandists of spiritual-ism and toward the arguments of its opponents. I am working on the hypothesis that spiritualism is a necessary phenomenon. Whenever we study this question, we must be fully aware that it was not a coinci-dence but rather a necessary development; necessary simply in the manner of its appearance. At the outset, we shall have to disregard the fact that most people who occupied themselves with spiritualist mani-festations were dilettantes. We shall look instead at the fact that some significant and well-respected scientists and scholars have taken a sympathetic stand toward spiritualism. If you allow me, I would like to take a quick detour. Instead of looking at spiritualist phenomena, I would like to look at those who studied spiritualism and judged it favorably and who also exercised a significant influence in the realm of materialistic science. These scientists share many other people's dis-satisfaction with the concept of a "science of the soul without the soul" and have achieved much more than the strict materialists have.

We are certainly entitled to ask, Isn't it of considerable significance that a scientist of such impeccable credentials as the great English chemist Crookes has come out fully in favor of spiritualism?[5] Sir Will-iam Crookes is a scientist of unusual stature. He has made highly important contributions to the investigation of chemical laws and the chemical structure of the elements. He has not only had an impact in the field of research, but he also has considerable achievements in the realm of practical applications. This great scientist, then, has been involved in spiritualistic experiments. Some people have argued that his observations were not precise enough. The argument is of little significance and merely displaces the question. For the question in this case is not whether Crookes's experiments were precise, but rather whether Crookes, the great chemist, knew the extent to which nature obeys physical laws, how far those apply, and whether they constitute obstacles to a science of the soul gained by way of spiritualistic experi-ments. The question is whether high achievements in the natural sci-ences should prevent a person from attempting to gain scientific knowledge in the field of spiritualism. The real question is this: What does it mean for us to call Crookes a precise scientist if we question his experiments in the field of spiritualism? It is almost as if we have to construct a double Crookes: a morning Crookes and an afternoon Crookes as it were. In the morning, when Crookes busies himself with chemistry, he is thought to be of sound intellect; in the afternoon, when he devotes himself to his spiritualistic experiments, he is said to be insane. This is obviously absurd, but the academic scientists refuse to acknowledge it.

Another scholar is the English scientist Wallace, a founder of the theory of evolution.[6] Darwin and Wallace discovered the great idea of the theory of Darwinism independently of each other. In fact, if we study Wallace's books, we find that his way of approaching the question was even more remarkable than Darwin's. No one has questioned his contributions in this realm, but because he later expressed, orally and in writing, his opinion that spiritualist phenomena are real, he is, as it were, split in two. On one hand he fights for his scientific theory, and on the other he fights for his theory of the soul, which is of a similar nature to the one Crookes elaborated in his experimental teaching about the soul. This Wallace is then likewise spoken of everywhere as a poor deranged person, because he was interested in spiritualism and spoke approvingly of it. Intellectual dwarves absolutely refuse to consider the intellectual approach and inclination of these two great men.

The fact that a researcher in the field of spiritualism can also stand in the upper ranks of natural science, as is the case with these two figures, is what encouraged me to look at the issue as a matter of personalities. In fact, the main difference between the nineteenth century and all earlier centuries is that these highly important questions were treated like scientific questions. For these scientists, there is nothing in the least impossible about extending natural scientific research to the areas of soul and spirit. It is therefore not illegitimate to refer to them as authorities in these areas, for the question is not whether their observations were precise or not, but simply what they considered possible and impossible. The exactitude or incorrectness of an experiment can always be established later: it is possible to ascertain later, under different conditions, what was done wrong the first time around. The question then is simply this: Can one oppose this kind of "psychology" from a scientific point of view?

There is not yet a scientific psychology on record, and the weakest and most insignificant writings of nineteenth-century scientists have been their attacks on spiritualism. There may be a number of people here who disagree with me on this, but, if they are objective, they will concede one thing: even if the writings against spiritualism are correct, all of them till now have been trivial and unscientific; for it is possible to be right and still write stupid stuff.

Having established from a cultural historical point of view the necessity of the spiritualist movement, let us look a little at the differences between the spiritualist movement and other attempts to study phenomena of the soul.

You all know that a Theosophical movement has existed since 1875. Just as spiritualism has done for the last forty years, Theosophy has been busy establishing as a solid truth that the material world is not all there is, but that there are higher beings—real facts and beings—that cannot be reached and investigated solely by the external senses. Spiritualism has its own methods for investigating the existence of a spiritual, soul world. Theosophy is also interested in these higher worlds. It is a simple historical fact that, before they started working in a Theosophical manner, the founders of the Theosophical movement were part of the spiritualist movement. Helena Petrovna Blavatsky and Colonel Olcott, the great messengers of the Theosophical movement, came out of the spiritualist movement, and some people have quipped that the early Theosophical Society was a society of discontented spiritualists. In fact, all Blavatsky and Olcott were seeking was the truth about the spiritual realm, and they came to the conclusion that Theosophy was the right approach. What they changed was the method, the research techniques. I shall not go here into the reasons for the change.[7]

All spiritualist and religious movements seek to establish that there is a higher spiritual life, that something spiritual lives in the human being, that the human being itself is of a spiritual nature, and that life between birth and death is merely one part of the whole human life. In short, they want to establish that human beings are more than physical beings. This is what all researchers, whether Theosophic or spiritualist, seek to prove. This is what they share. It is the object of their common striving. And in attaining this goal, they encounter each other, so as to offer a necessary counterweight to the materialist stream. Truth cannot be attained on separate paths, but only in full unity, in harmonious striving, and for that we need to know not only the common goal, but also the common sources of both movements.

This is familiar to those who have been able to penetrate more deeply into the inner forces of the spiritual movement. What we see on the outside, all that lies immediately before our eyes when we look at the spiritual movements, takes place in the world of effects, not causes. The spiritual researcher knows that many of the things played out before our senses have their causes in much higher spiritual worlds. In a way, we move about in the sensory world like blind people, without the slightest notion of what is happening in the wings, where higher spiritual powers are pulling the threads. Thus the true spiritual scientist recognizes the common roots of spiritualism and Theosophy.

Anyone following human evolution with open, spiritual eyes knows that humanity's spiritual life is subject to evolution just as its physical nature is. There are huge differences in the gradations in sensory development as well as in the scale of spiritual development. There are highly developed natures in human beings—those who have found them can testify to that. Such great natures are the leaders of spiritual evolution. They are not only, as Schopenhauer said, an ideal Brotherhood holding hands over the ages. They also constitute an actual society of individualities working together and influencing each other.[8] The Theosophist is aware of their existence, and calls them the great Brotherhood of Adepts.[9] If we honestly believe in evolution, we must at least believe in this as a possibility; but those who have experienced it can testify that it really exists.

Materialism peaked around the middle of the nineteenth century. Higher beings then saw that a materialist tide was unavoidable, and that they would need to provide the counterforces. They were not in the least critical of this materialist movement, knowing that modern technology would make powerful, much needed progress in the process. This is why we should not fight the materialist movement. But the destructiveness of materialist science in respect to the soul demanded that a "counterpole" be provided—a spiritual stream to act as a counterpart to the material stream in humanity. In its first stage, this spiritual wave took the form of spiritualist phenomena. Human beings had to be shown that there was something other than what natural science could grasp with its means. Those Brothers—Adepts—who were able to read the signs of the times, who have always been the leaders of humanity, were also responsible for sending tidal waves of spiritualism upon humanity. Such Brothers work across the centuries. Unknown, misunderstood, neglected, they step forward as individuals to perform immeasurable deeds for humanity. As long as humanity in its greater mass looks for leadership among scientists who can provide no information about burning spiritual questions, these older Brothers can still lead spiritual humanity into the secret mysteries. They send their messengers into the world, messengers whom only occultists may recognize. Many people who study history run into these spiritual currents, which are inexplicable to purely materialistic research but become transparent when examined by the right spiritual scientist.

In the nineteenth century, things certainly changed. Precisely because the leaders of science abdicated their responsibility, it became necessary to provide visible proof for the existence of the spiritual world. It happened, however, that the three decades of the spiritualist movement from 1840 to 1870 brought to the surface very different interests than those that were intended. Please don't object that the wise leaders made an error since they should have anticipated those developments. This question must be approached differently. What happened was that the interests that attached themselves at first to the spiritual phenomena were interests of a purely personal, human nature. It turned out that people were most interested in communication with the dead, which was not what the messengers were meant to bring to humanity. The purpose of spiritualist phenomena was not the satisfaction of human curiosity, no matter how beautiful and noble. Instead, they were meant to bring humanity insights that properly applied would have led to a higher, spiritual life. Unfortunately, the movement fell prey to voyeurism, and research about spiritual matters was conducted in a manner unlikely to contribute to humanity's edification. This is why the Theosophical movement needed to be created.

Let me say briefly what this is all about. Purely natural forces do not create human beings. What constitutes human nature, the sheath of the soul and spiritual life, is not the product of purely physical forces. Wisdom created the world. Wisdom also created each individual human being. I can only sketch this out today. It would take a special lecture to develop it in detail.

You know that natural forces alone will not bring about so much as a clock, because human intelligence is required to effect the required combination. It is perfectly correct to say that when we investigate the human organism we find no God, no divine creation, merely natural forces. Even a little reflection is enough to make clear that you will not see the spiritual, creative forces. When you study a clock, likewise, you can explain it in a completely mechanical way, yet you are in the end faced with the necessity of asking about the human intelligence, the clockmaker who built it, whom you would never find inside the clock. This proves that the question is badly put. This comparison of the human organism with a clock is valid, of course, but it must be applied correctly. This means that just as a clock and its mechanism cannot happen without the spiritual influence of its maker, neither can the human spirit, the highest flower, the highest unfolding of the forces responsible for building the human organism, appear without the spiritual influence of its creator. The human soul, the highest that the spirit has created out of the physical body, required the creation within the human organism of a foundation for the flowering of organic life, the human spirit. Just think what was required—I am speaking metaphorically—to lay the foundation within this human soul for the flower of organic life, the human spirit.

It is easy to imagine that these so-called builders, these lawful builders of the organism, could have stopped building at a lower level, that they might not have bothered to put together the complicated human organism that the human soul needs. But let us go back to before the evolution of the human soul. We shall find that these beings are full of wisdom. It also becomes clear that the forces whose work created these beings are just as invisible to us human beings as the clockmakers are to the clock. Human beings know as little about spiritual powers, forces, and beings carefully working to prepare a dwelling place for the soul as the mechanical gears of the clock know about the clockmaker's spiritual activity.

Spiritual forces built our organism, and they are still at work within us. The very same forces that formed our organism in such a way that it breathes, its blood circulates, it digests, it concentrates tissues and forces in the brain, and it makes the brain a suitable tool for the soul—all these spiritual forces are still operating. But no more than we can see gravity or magnetism can we see the creative forces that are revealed in our passions, desires, wishes, and instincts—and just as little can we see the creative forces that work in building the organism. Try to imagine that the human being has not yet come to a point at which it is filled with what I have mentioned earlier as clear consciousness. Put yourself back into a time when these forces of consciousness had not taken possession of the human organism. Before our highly evolved brain could be formed in the course of evolution, other forms of the brain evolved. And these forms are still present in us, overlaid and regulated by the highly evolved brain of the contemporary human being. The spiritual makers of the world built up the human nature of desire and drive in ways that were unconscious to the human being. This is a nature human beings share with animals. Its flowering is the stuff of the soul. Even now, the spiritual beings that built us are active; they are beside us, within us, as real and effective as this lamp here is real and effective in the physical world. We move about in our physical world, and we know about the things of it because of our clear consciousness. Many beings live all around us, left over from earlier stages of being. Just as human beings have continued to evolve, specific beings have stayed and built their own spiritual world. But they are evolving also. Just as our consciousness has evolved up to our own level and clarity, so too does their evolution continue. It is impossible to deny our consciousness the possibility of further evolution. And when the human being evolves to an even higher level of consciousness than the present clear consciousness, we will again recognize the spiritual worlds that surround us at all times.

There are two ways to acquire knowledge about the spiritual world around us. The first is to research what happens to the human being when clear consciousness is switched off. This clear consciousness is like a light that spreads over the spiritual influences surrounding us. We don't see them because of the glare of our clear human consciousness. If we turn this off, however, we move closer to the spiritual beings that helped build us before we had it. In this way we learn that evolution does not just ascend, but also descends and moves in circles. Whenever we turn off our rational consciousness, we, as it were, move back to earlier stages of our evolution, when we were still more spiritual, whereas now we stand above that sphere. We really do come from a spiritual world, and this spiritual world has prepared the dwelling of the soul in the physical world. By turning back, as it were, the level that we have attained, we are in a certain way closer to the gods. This is one way; it is the way of spiritualism.

The other way, the way of modern consciousness, is the one that Theosophy chooses. Theosophy does not seek to investigate the spiritual world by turning off consciousness, but rather by developing it further, heightening it. The Theosophist's ideal is to obtain information about the spiritual world surrounding us while retaining the continuity of evolution, the emphasis on clear consciousness. This is the difference between Theosophical students and spiritualist mediums. Mediums bring us information from the spiritual world by acting as tools of the spiritual world. They hand themselves over as organs—intermediaries or mouthpieces—for the spiritual world. Theosophical researchers seek to take clear consciousness up to the heights where they will once again perceive the spiritual worlds. Theosophical researchers would consider it an insult to human autonomy—an obstacle to the human right of self-determination—to renounce the level of the clear consciousness that has been attained in the natural course of things. They do not wish to put themselves back into a condition passed through in earlier evolutionary stages.

The truths experienced in the state of "disconnected consciousness" are quite possibly incontrovertible; the correctness of the results of spiritualist experiments may be unquestionable. But this still leaves open whether it is right or advisable to use this method of investigation. The question there is whether it is in conformity with the laws of evolution and with the intentions of the cosmic powers to try to turn back the clock of nature, to undo steps that have already been taken. Nature does not advance arbitrarily, and human beings should not willfully turn back evolutionary developments that nature has already effected in them. We do not want to investigate truth out of pure curiosity, using incorrect, underhanded methods, but rather by using the way that the higher cosmic powers have shown us, the path on which our clear consciousness leads us. Therefore the striving of the Theosophical movement is not to listen to those who bring us revelations out of the unconscious or the subconscious, but rather to listen to those who speak out of the full, clear waking consciousness. Those who stand in the Theosophical movement and have direct experiences of truth have obtained that truth only through the use of the full, clear waking consciousness. Theosophists are not allowed to disconnect from their consciousness even for a moment. A greater development of consciousness, full, clear observation of the kind initiates have trained for, must be the object of a Theosophist's striving. If we attain that goal, we shall fulfill our human vocation.

Why should we put more trust in a medium speaking in a trance than in a person speaking out of the fullness of waking consciousness?

Trust is needed in any case. It is actually more comfortable to investigate by disconnecting one's consciousness, but it is worthier of the human being to adopt a method that preserves clear spiritual consciousness. This is why Theosophists have favored the latter path, so from the point of view of the Theosophical movement, any work out of the unconscious or subconscious is inadequate. The Theosophical movement, as we said, seeks to reach the spiritual world out of full consciousness, convinced that, as spiritual beings, human beings, because of their place in evolution, are to various degrees dependent on the body. Therefore Theosophy directs its attention to incarnated human beings who, while living in their bodies, can tap spiritual forces and attain spiritual vision by becoming temporarily independent of their physical organisms while fully conscious. The human being who is thus in control of the physical body has the possibility of collecting experiences of the spiritual world, not by going back to a time before clear consciousness had evolved, but rather by moving forward in time to evolutionary stages when consciousness will be higher than the currently average human consciousness.

The medium is a monument of the past. In earlier times, all human beings were mediums; all had a capacity for astral perception; all were able to perceive the spiritual world. Over time, our clear waking consciousness was formed out of this astral consciousness. When humans rise in the spiritual worlds, as all beings eventually must, we will once again step into this astral world, perceive in astral ways, clairvoyant again. But this is only a transitional stage: all evolutionary stages must be considered transitional. Our terrestrial course is a lesson that we must study thoroughly—that we must learn. We must not, therefore, be alienated from the world. We must not be hostile toward what is earthly, but rather live fully in the Earth. We must recognize in the terrestrial element the same forces, the same beings that we perceive in the spiritual world, for those spiritual forces are at work in our earthly world; they weave through the human soul and influence the life-forms of earthly reality.

This was behind the allegory of the bees used by the priests of the Ancient Greek Mysteries.[10] The allegory of the bees is meaningful for us, since it was the human soul that was being compared to the bees. Just as the bees are sent out of the hive to collect honey from the flowers, so the human soul is sent out of higher regions to collect experiences in the earthly realm. The bees' domain is the realm of the flowers; the human being's domain is the Earth. It would make no sense for either bees or human beings to look for other gathering grounds and other regions that either do not offer the material the gatherers need or contain suitable material in inappropriate amounts. This is why the Theosophical movement has made the allegory of the bees a metaphor of its work: the striving for more highly evolved knowledge and the development of clear consciousness are the focus of all its activity, as a way of ensuring human participation in spiritual worlds. The Theosophical movement's purpose is the higher evolution of humankind. If this succeeds, those interests will be awakened in the human being that lead us further along. The motive in trying to know more about the spiritual world is not simple curiosity. And what we learn must give us the strength, the power, to reach the goal assigned us by cosmic powers.

The spiritualist movement awakens in its followers the consciousness that the spiritual world exists. In this, Theosophy and spiritualism agree. But the methods used to attain this goal differ. The reasons why the Theosophical Society does not approve spiritualist investigative methods can be summarized briefly: It is very dangerous, at this stage of cosmic evolution, to disconnect human consciousness. Given the whole course of cosmic evolution, the human being must be active with this consciousness, on Earth. If we switch it off, we are delivered powerless, without will, without consciousness, to the spiritual powers. Let me make a comparison. It makes a difference whether I step into a robbers' den fully aware and in full control of my reason, or whether I enter it without this clarity of mind. This is true not only of the extreme case of the robbers' den. It is like that for the whole world. We must grasp the things that come toward us with full clarity. We must not make ourselves into powerless tools, even of the spiritual powers, for the latter could use us for all kinds of purposes. This is what has led to the curtailing of the cultivation of mediumistic activities. Leading spiritualists are increasingly sensitive to the insight that to contact spiritual beings, human beings must enter the spiritual world in full possession of their entire freedom. It can only be a matter of time before the methods of spiritual investigation developed by Theosophists are adopted by the spiritualists.

Theosophists and spiritualists both aim for clairvoyance. Theosophical students and spiritualist mediums are both tools, but the spiritualist medium is without will. Anyone who knows the dangers can describe what strong powers one has to encounter along the way—powers that have destructive or oppressive influences; powers that have useful influences, but also harmful ones. Things that were useful when human beings lived in their unconscious have become harmful. If we hand ourselves over powerless to the powers that built us up earlier, we become for better and for worse their instruments. Therefore it is important that we never allow our consciousness to be clouded. Clear consciousness has enabled us to discover great truths in our research, whereas the spiritualist medium is more or less condemned to fishing in muddy waters. Clear consciousness enables us to know not only what takes us to our goal, but also what prevents us from getting there.

Above all else, we must learn to find our way around the spiritual world. We must acquire the necessary information to make that possible, the information that is a precondition for knowledge of the spiritual world. If I want to be a good engineer, I had better study mathematics. If I want to be at home in the spiritual world, rather than be tumbled along helplessly, I must penetrate the fundamental Theosophical truths. What the Theosophists discovered in 1875 will bring more and more spiritualists to their side. The two currents need not fight each other, even if, as I showed, their methods are radically different. Rather they must find harmony. Let the followers of one movement bring what they have to offer and let the followers of the other bring what they have. Let both deposit it on the altar of humanity. In this way both movements can really help humanity, whereas fighting each other would only lead to humanity's losing track of the larger goal. Cooperation between the two movements, not fighting, is needed, and will lead to the common goal—to raise humanity out of the materialistic stream of the present.

This requires transmitting knowledge of the higher worlds—knowledge of eternity, of the soul's true nature, and of the possibilities afforded us to contemplate again the great spiritual forces of nature that show us the way. How few human beings there are with the self-knowledge to understand where we come from and where we are going, what the homeland of the soul is, which enables us to find what gives meaning to life! To gain all this, the human being must come to the conviction expressed by Johann Gottlieb Fichte when he said: "I do not need to be torn out of the earthly world to gain access to the supraearthly. I already live in it now. I live in it much more truly than I do in the purely earthly, for I am my own solid anchor, and eternal life, long since mine, is the only ground upon which I can develop my earthly life. *What they call the Heavens does not lie on the other side of the grave; it is already cast all over our nature, and its light shines in every pure heart.*"[11]

2

Theosophy and Somnambulism

Berlin, March 7, 1904

TODAY I WANT to expand some points I merely sketched out last time. More precisely, I want to speak about the phenomenon of somnambulism. This leads us into mysterious areas of human nature that from different perspectives have received the most diverse interpretations.

You all know the phenomenon of somnambulism or sleepwalking. The word designates a particular psychological condition, a particular alteration of a person's ordinary consciousness. This state is such that, though the person's "I-soul" may be active in some very specific ways, ordinary waking consciousness—the consciousness within which we operate in the natural world and which we use to perform our daily tasks—is not fully active. In other words, waking consciousness is repressed, virtually switched off. Whether we call this somnambulism, sleepwalking, sleep acting, or any other name, we understand by it a soul activity without the full involvement of ordinary waking consciousness: an activity arising from the depths of the soul and unilluminated by waking "I-consciousness." The human soul acts out of this dark depth, and from these depths brings up actions that are substantially different from what the person usually does. We know, too, that not every personality is suited to such a switching off of ordinary waking consciousness. We know that only those individuals who can be put in a kind of trance or dream condition can manifest this condition. Although these manifestations arise out of an individual's nature, the individual is in a subconscious or unconscious state.

Over the centuries, this somnambulistic state has been the object of a wide range of explanations. In Ancient Greece, for instance, we find priestesses or so-called oracles who could announce from their soul-depths all kinds of things in a state of extinguished waking consciousness. Future events were supposedly brought up from such deep soul knowing. The oracles might, further, be asked to decide, for instance, whether important matters of state, important legal decisions were justified or not. Briefly put, whatever they proclaimed was ascribed to divine inspiration. People believed that when the waking consciousness of the soul is extinguished, it stands under the influence of the gods and transmits divine messages. Not only did the individuals who could be put into that state enjoy the kind of honor bestowed upon the gods but, most importantly, the revelation that they transmitted was venerated as a divine message.

If we now move from Ancient Greece to the end of the Middle Ages, we find a completely different description and interpretation of these personalities. We see that these persons were then considered to be in alliance with all kinds of evil, demonic, or diabolical powers. We see that what they announced was considered destructive. It was something that could have only a harmful influence on human life. Persons with such gifts were persecuted for being witches—they were pursued because of their connections with the devil. Many of the most gruesome actions of the declining Middle Ages can be traced back to this interpretation of the sleepwalking state.

More recently, if we look at the beginning of the nineteenth century—actually at the last third of the eighteenth century—we find that people were starting to study "psychology," human psychological states. And we find some people who believed that the study of sleep-walking would give a key to understanding superior states in the human soul. They believed that when ordinary cerebral consciousness is switched off and the senses no longer receive input from the external world, human beings are capable of experiencing things about spiritual events and beings that we would not be able to perceive in our normal state, with usual sensory perception. Other researchers, however, merely saw these states as morbid conditions and considered it desirable that, as morbid states, they should be eliminated from the range of behavior considered normal. Actually, it was modern science with its materialistic faith that rejected any interpretation or explanation of these manifestations, and saw them as morbid, related somehow to insanity, altogether outside the norm. So much, then, for a few of the interpretations that have been given in the course of history.

Next we must ask, How is it possible to trigger such phenomena? We know many people spontaneously get into this state when their normal waking consciousness is turned off. They behave toward the outer world as if they were asleep; their ordinary senses seem not to be picking up anything of what happens in their environment: e.g., they don't notice a bell ringing next to their ears, they don't see a light burning nearby. At the same time, however, they are most delicately sensitive to very specific influences, for instance any words pronounced by a specific person. They see nothing, hear nothing, except for what one single person is saying, or one particular influence. In fact they are often able to sense what a particular person in the room is thinking. These things do happen with particular individuals every now and then—and quite spontaneously. We call such people sleepwalkers; they think, act, feel, perceive as if in a waking dream, a state of sleep, but a very peculiar kind of sleep, not at all to be compared with the common sleep we fall into to recover from the fatigue of the day.

We also know that these sleepwalkers have a heightened capacity for perceiving and sensing particular events, and that they can perform very particular actions, which they would be quite incapable of performing in a waking state. We have examples of their performing actions that are perfectly reasonable but require more than the ordinary orienting capacities of the waking state. We hear of them climbing on roofs and jumping over precipices without any sense of the danger they are in—precipices over which they would never even dream of jumping when "awake." They do things that they would be completely incapable of doing under ordinary conditions.

Such somnambulistic states can arise without any trigger at all. But they can also result from a person influencing the so-called somnambulist. A person can act so as to extinguish the waking consciousness of another—so that the resulting "somnambulist" is in an "artificial" sleepwalking state. When that happens, the "artificial" somnambulist acts just as a "natural" sleepwalker would act. Particular terms do not matter, but the influencing person is called a *magnetizer*, and the personality is said to be *magnetized*; people say they were put into a *magnetic sleep*.

What, then, is the meaning of these phenomena for spiritual life? What role do they play in the whole context of spiritual life? What can be learned from such phenomena? What do they tell us about the quality and nature of the human soul and the human spirit? Finally, are these manifestations really something completely abnormal, without any resemblance to things that happen in ordinary life?

It would be easy, and thus tempting, to agree with the view that these are abnormalities—but to do that would leave us hanging without any particular conclusion on the matter.

On the other hand, by taking a closer look at our ordinary experiences, we can try to find a gradual transition from ordinary life to these abnormal manifestations. I am thinking, for instance, of the phenomena of ordinary dreams, which everyone experiences almost every night. (Hardly anyone never dreams at all.) Dream phenomena will show, in a very elementary way, how we begin to approach these higher phenomena, which I have so far merely sketched out.

Dreams are often described as just fantastic images, empty imaginations passing through our dream consciousness. Those who think this are hardly inclined to take the curious manifestations of the dream world seriously. But there have always been more finely tuned minds inclined to study these fleeting images of dream consciousness more closely. They conclude it is true, at the lowest level, that unruliness and arbitrariness mostly rule dreams. It is as if we were looking at the shreds of waking consciousness, the memories and images that flitted through our consciousness in the course of the day. In other instances, dreams result from physical states occurring while we are asleep, or symptoms of specific illnesses, etc. This kind of dream is the lowest kind of dream, made up of images marked by their complete unruliness, their disorderly passing through the dream consciousness.

An attentive observer, however, cannot help noticing that even the most ordinary consciousness can have dreams besides these disorderly, arbitrary ones—dreams that have a very specific regularity. Let me draw your attention to some examples that give us a deeper insight in the regularity we can experience even in the ordinary state of dream consciousness. You are asleep, and a clock is ticking by your bed. You do not experience the ticking of the clock while you are asleep; instead, you dream that a regiment of soldiers is passing by your window. You distinctly hear the clatter of the horses' hooves. When you wake up, you become aware of having just heard the clock ticking, for it is still going on in your waking consciousness. You didn't hear it, however, as the ticking that your ordinary ears hear; instead it was transformed, metamorphosed into the metaphor of a cavalry regiment's clattering hooves.

Here is another dream. One Sunday morning a farmer's wife and her friend go to town. Entering the church, they see the priest climbing to his pulpit, and starting to preach. The two women listen for a while. Then something extraordinary happens: the priest turns into a wing, and then into a crowing rooster! This, by the way, is an actual dream. When the farmer's wife wakes up, of course, a rooster is really crowing. Again you can see what happened: The ear heard the rooster crowing, but did not at first interpret it as the rooster's call. Instead, the dream consciousness produced a metaphor out of what it had heard; the rooster's crowing was symbolically changed into the whole narrative I just told you.

Our dream consciousness can spin very dramatic stories. Sense impressions are not taken in immediately, but are transformed into symbols. Characteristically, dream consciousness is involved in creating dramas.

Here is another example—again an actual dream. A student dreams he is at the door of a conference room. Another student jostles him. This turns into an exchange of harsh words, leading to a duel. The student experiences the whole thing in the dream, all the preparations for a duel—a very long story indeed! Finally, the duel takes place at the agreed location; everyone, including the attendants, are there. The first shot is heard, the dreaming student wakes up. He has knocked over a chair that was standing next to his bed. He heard the chair falling, not as it really was, but symbolically transformed at lightning speed into this whole dramatic episode. This is the sleeping dream consciousness: a symbol-producing consciousness, whose symbolizing activity can be illustrated by countless examples.

We now ask ourselves, What is the relationship between ordinary waking consciousness and what happens in the soul when we are dreaming? Our usual waking consciousness has no part in these dream activities, for when consciousness enters the dream, another I arises, a "dream-I." Dreamers can see themselves; they can encounter themselves in a dream. We need to remember this: in the dream, there is a split between the dream-I and the real I, so that the dreaming individual can observe himself or herself quite objectively in the process of the various occurrences in the dream. The situations that take place in the dream are determined by dream consciousness and are completely integrated in the symbolic drama being played out.

When we dream about events from our own inner physical life, we are dealing with a higher level, if I may say so, of this dream consciousness. Again, I shall give you actual examples. Someone dreams that he is in a stifling cellar. There are spiderwebs on the ceiling and strange animals crawl about. He wakes up with a headache. The headache has expressed itself symbolically in the form of this oppressive cellar. Or someone dreams of being in an overheated room: he sees the glow of a red-hot stove, wakes up with his heart racing. Very specific organs, particular sensations, are symbolized during the dream in the form of particular events. In fact, observers in the field know that for a given person, a particular organ is stereotypically turned into a recurring phenomenon. Someone suffering from heart palpitations will have the same dream every time he has heart palpitations, as in the dream described, repeatedly dreaming of an overheated stove and things of the same kind. So external events are not the only triggers. Our physical body can also express itself metaphorically in the dream.

This is only one step away from a remarkable phenomenon in which dreamers—typically persons who already have a tendency toward some form of somnambulism—see themselves with some illness, sometimes expressed in a symbolic form, even though the actual symptoms may not appear until a few days later. In their dream consciousness, the sleepers assess their own inner condition. This, in turn, is just a step away from the next phenomenon, in which a peculiar kind of human instinct advises full-fledged sleepwalkers, through a dream, about a particular remedy, or some institution where they will go to get treatment. The dream in this case actually plays the doctor's role, advising about the illness and about the remedy. This happens to rare individuals with a prior predisposition to sleepwalking.

As you see, we are dealing here with a series of connected phenomena—from disorganized dreams to regular dream experiences obeying specific laws. All the things I have described here are to some extent dream experiences. Another step will take us to the phenomenon of dream actions.

The most common is people speaking in their dreams. This is a very common occurrence. We all know that sleeping persons will sometimes even give cogent answers to particular questions. At other times, what they say indicates that they have not fully understood what was said to them. Or, and this is something that comes out if we go about the matter systematically, they say that somehow the question was subjected to a symbolic transformation, the answer then being framed within that symbolic construct.

Now, there is only one step from speech to action. A dreamer, particularly if she has a somnambulistic disposition, gets out of bed, maybe sits down at a desk if she is a student, and opens her study books. It may also happen that a dreamer actually resumes writing what he or she had started writing before going to sleep, or in any case writes an actual text, etc. What we observe here is a passage to actual activity, from a simple perception or intention. Some individuals are very suggestible to hypnosis, yet do not go further than dream perceptions; others who don't get very far perceiving things in their sleep can perform complex activities like the ones described above.

Now, one characteristic of these dream actions by somnambulistic individuals is their compulsive, automatic character. Remember that in our waking life we do many things quite automatically: light strikes our eyes and we automatically close them. There are countless examples of this kind of action to which we don't give any thought at all. In the end, all that we do within our vegetative life-body, our digestion, our breathing, our heartbeat, are actions performed without our being conscious of them. Similarly, we perform reasonable actions in a "somnambulistic" state. For instance, under the spell of a particularly strong attraction we can act in an unquestionably compulsive manner.

We must now ask ourselves how we will account for such phenomena. Many people believe that in such activity we are eavesdropping on the soul independently of the body. Such actions, from this perspective, are proof that the soul can have perceptions independently of the bodily organs of eye and ear, and that it can act in the absence of conscious decision. But there are also many others who believe that in these activities the soul is expressing itself much more directly: that the soul in such states is loosened from the physical and acts immediately out of the spiritual sphere.

Let us now examine how these phenomena appear from a Theosophical point of view.

Theosophy shows us that human beings are not the singular, isolated beings they usually seem to be, but that countless threads connect us with the "Whole." Above all, Theosophy shows us that just as human beings have various things in common with the rest of nature, so they also have things in common with other worlds, things that are imperceptible to our ordinary senses. Therefore we shall best understand what I have been describing by looking at it in the light of Theosophy. Let me begin by briefly describing what Theosophy teaches us about human beings.

Theosophy considers the physical body with all its organs, including the nervous system, the brain, and all sensory organs, as only one part of the whole human being. This physical being includes tissues and forces that the human being shares with all the rest of the physical world. All the chemical and physical processes that play out in us are no different from the things that play themselves out in the physical and chemical processes of the outer world. Yet we must ask, Why do these physical and chemical processes play themselves out in our body so as to form one physical organism? Physical science cannot explain this. Physical, natural science can teach us only about physical and chemical processes, but it would surely be inadequate for natural scientists to call the human being a "walking corpse," just because their anatomical examinations show only the physical facts of the human body. Something must be there to hold the chemical and physical processes together, to assemble them into a form, as is the case in the human body. Theosophists call this "something" the other body of the human being, the *etheric double*. This etheric double exists in all of us. If we develop clairvoyant abilities, we can manage to see the etheric double body; it is the easiest thing for clairvoyants to see. If you are clairvoyant and a person stands in front of you, you can "suggest away" the habitual physical body. We routinely do this in ordinary life with things right in front of us to which we are not directing our immediate attention. In the same way, clairvoyants are able to direct their attention away from the physical body. But in the space the physical body occupied, there always remains a bodily "presence," a kind of outwardly identical double of beautiful luminous color, about the color of peach blossoms. This etheric double is responsible for holding together physical processes. At death, this etheric body, together with other higher bodies, leaves the physical body, and the physical body is handed over to the Earth, where it will perform only physical processes. That the physical body does not disappear in the course of life is due only to the presence of the etheric body.

Within this etheric body, and towering over it on all sides, is the third part of the human being, the so-called *astral* body. This astral body is a kind of portrait of our instincts, passions, desires, and feelings. A human being lives within the astral body as in a cloud. For a clairvoyant who can see such phenomena, the astral body is clearly perceptible, with the physical body and the etheric double existing within it. The astral bodies of persons who always follow their animal instincts, their sensory inclinations, have very different colors, quite different cloudlike formations from that of persons who have always lived a spiritual life. It is different again in egotists and in those who devote themselves to others in selfless love. In short, a person's soul life is expressed in this astral body.

The astral body also serves to mediate actual sensory perceptions. You can never look for sensations in the sensory organs themselves. What happens when the light of a flame meets my eye? This light exists in space outside of myself. The so-called etheric waves move from the light source into my eye, penetrate it, and cause particular chemical processes in the back wall of my eyeball. They change the retina and then implant these chemical events into my brain. My brain perceives the flame, receives the impression of imprinted light. If others were to observe the processes that take place in my brain, what would they observe? All they would see would be the physical events; they would witness something that happens in time and space, yet they would be unable to perceive the impression of light within the physical processes in my brain. This impression of light is something other than the physical imprint that is at the base of all these processes. The image of light that I must create for myself before I can perceive the flame takes place within my astral body. The person whose organ of sight is trained to perceive astral process sees quite precisely how the physical phenomena within the brain are transformed by the astral body into the image of the flame.

Within the bodies I have just described, within the physical body, the etheric double, and the astral body, within all of these, is the actual I—what we call our Self. This is that in which we are conscious of ourselves. Of this we say that we are it. This I itself has higher parts, which I will not say anything about today. It uses the higher parts of the human being as its tools.

Once we understand how the human being is put together, we also gain a way of looking at the phenomena we encounter in somnambulism. What is it that happens when we are in our usual clear waking consciousness? An impression of light is produced when etheric waves reach my eye. This impression is transformed by the astral body into an image of light, and this image of light becomes a representation. I become conscious of the image of light. Let us now assume that our I has been turned off. Such a shutting off occurs in ordinary sleep. I will not go into the question of where to look for the I when we are asleep, but when we look at a sleeping person, what are we looking at? In the true sense of the word, only one whose spiritual eyes are open can give us a report about it. Such a person would see very precisely how this I, joined with the astral body, has left the physical and the etheric bodies. Everyone knows in some way that when we are asleep the ordinary waking I, the real I is turned off, and the physical body and the etheric double holding it together are left to their own devices. In ordinary waking life, whenever we receive impressions from the outer world, the I—our consciousness—is always present. We do not interact with the outer world without the waking I that controls these impressions from the outer world. Presumably when a clock ticks next to me while I am asleep, it doesn't stop producing vibrations in the air, and those vibrations strike my eardrum. Now, do you think your ear is built differently in the daytime and in the nighttime? Of course not. All the things that happen to the physical body in the daytime keep happening when I am asleep. But what is missing? What is missing is the penetration of the individual person by the I-consciousness.

We can show in an experimental fashion the relationships between the parts of the human being that I have described. Let me present you with a simple experiment that can easily be performed with any sleepwalker. Let us assume the sleepwalker gets up in the middle of the night, sits at a desk, lights a candle, and tries to write in the light of the candle. Now do the following: illuminate the room very brightly, let us say with ten lamps set there (this was done in an actual experiment), and the person will continue to write as if nothing had changed. Now extinguish the one single flame, the small candle that he (or she) had lit himself, and he will stop writing, finding the room too dark. He will reach for a match, light the candle, and then go on writing, for now he can see again. As far as he is concerned, all the illumination around him does not exist. All that matters is the flame that he has perceived in his dream consciousness. Human beings, you see, need to penetrate their perceptual organs from the inside out in a very particular way, in order for outer impressions to make an impact. It is not just necessary for us to have eyes and ears, but also to enliven from the inside what the eyes and the ears transmit to us, in the way of images, representations—all of which ensures that things exist for us.

In the ordinary course of things, it is our I, our clear waking consciousness that by itself brings to the outer world, from inside us, all that is required for us to transform impressions into conscious representations. Now imagine this consciousness is turned off. What is left then? What is left are the physical body, the etheric double, and the astral body. The astral body can still convert into images everything it receives from outside, but these impressions will not be transformed into representations. So impressions are transformed into images that surround the person, sometimes in disorderly, irregular ways, or in regular ways if the I is along for the ride, as it were.

This is the kind of contact the astral body, the sleepwalker's soul, has with the outer world. This is also true of the ordinary dreamer. We must however distinguish between the two kinds of dreams I have described. We must distinguish unregulated, disorderly dreams that pass through the person's dream consciousness, from beautiful, dramatically symbolic dreams. In the case of the disorderly dreams, it is primarily the etheric body that is active and in contact with the external world. With symbolic, dramatic dreams, it is the astral body of the person that transforms the outer world into symbols, expresses it in the form of metaphors. Because in the current stage of evolution our waking I is realistically minded, and our waking consciousness relates to things by trusting in our combining, calculating reason, every sensation is combined with all others in a way that characterizes clear waking consciousness. But we could think of other ways, other states of consciousness. We might think that the human being sinks deeper into nature. Then our rational point of view ceases. This is again the case with higher levels of soul life. I will not go into this today, but we must look at the following. If the somnambulistic state is a heightened dream consciousness, how is it possible that we find regular actions, precise phenomena that have a soul character? It is possible to understand it only insofar as one does not consider the human being in isolation, but in relation to the whole rest of the world. We must be clear that what is present outside of us in the rest of the world is not the deadened reality of things strictly audible to the (physical) ear and visible to the (physical) eye: in the outer world, higher beings are at work, higher forces are active.

We do not usually ask ourselves why, when we look at the world, we find the very laws, concepts, and representations that we have reasoned our way to in some solitary twilight hour. Human beings do not, for the most part, think clearly about the most significant phenomena and manifestations, those that cast the strongest light on who and what we are. Think for a moment: Here is the mathematician in a study, thinking what a circle is, what an ellipse is. Without any recourse to field observations, he (or she) puts down on paper the laws of the ellipse, and he keeps studying until he knows what a circle is, what an ellipse is, etc. Later, still working on his own intellectual power, he discovers the law of the ellipse, planetary cycles, and other natural phenomena. The same is true in our spiritual life. The laws that our mind thinks in solitary study are the same laws that operate outside of us in the (natural) world, the same laws that rule the world. Granted that we call wisdom the things that human beings think, we find that outside of ourselves things are built in the same wise way, and human beings can observe them. In fact, if we look at the world in greater detail, we find that its own wisdom is superior in many ways to what the human mind can think and invent.

Take the beavers' achievements. Beavers are truly astounding; it isn't just that their constructions demonstrate an instinctive sense of architectural form that couldn't be more perfect. They show us something more. Beavers protect their hiding places by building dams that retain water and in very specific ways slow down or speed up its rate of flow. The dams are set against the force of the stream in a way that engineers would not be able to better. The layout of the dams is such that the slope of a dam and the angle at which it is set allow us to calculate quite precisely the speed and force of the water current. These dams are laid out in a way that engineers in their studies could not calculate better, using their science attained at the cost of a great deal of human thinking and effort.

Another example: Consider a very ordinary thighbone (femur). If you look at this through a microscope, you will see that it is not a compact structure comparable, say, to a piece of mortar. Instead, under the microscope the bone appears friable, a combination of delicate formations, assembled into a very fine structure of timbers and scaffolds. A network of very delicate bone fibers is built up; they knit together and support each other; and if you study this whole network of bone fibers, you find yourself looking at nature's remarkable wisdom in the construction of such an organism. If we wanted to build trestles that supported the individual parts of a wooden structure so that every application of force would have maximum effect, we could not do it any better than nature in its wisdom constructed this thighbone out of an infinity of minuscule bone fibers. We find in every single part of nature the kind of natural wisdom that a human being could only approximate after much spiritual effort. If we were able to pour our mind all over nature when we study it, and perceive nature from the inside, we would have to conclude that nature is not the result of accident, but the product of infinite wisdom. Try to imagine what it would mean if, instead of your calculating reason taking in the impressions of the outer world through the sensory organs, you had no senses, but your reason were spread evenly throughout all of nature. You would then perceive the very essence of things and not the effects of things on our senses; you would be standing in the middle of nature's wisdom—you would, in fact, be part of wise nature.

This is precisely what happens when our waking consciousness is turned off. What I just described is the kind of thing the sleepwalker does. As I said, one might think that our brain exudes, as it were, our reason—consciousness—which then penetrates all natural functions and facts, the wisdom of nature in all its manifestations and all its facts. But the fact that we possess such a clear, awake consciousness has the opposite effect—that of cutting us off from the rest of nature. This means that we need to receive the impressions of nature through the gates of our senses. Here is the flame, it makes an impression on my eye; the eye is a gate, through which the impression reaches my consciousness. My consciousness calls up representations of those perceptions. By the very fact of having sensory organs, I am separated from the outer world, and the world must first enter my consciousness by crossing the threshold of my sensory organs. In relation to the world, I am like one who has been standing in a meadow, able to look in all directions, and then steps into a small house. Of all the things in the meadow, I can now know only what I can see through a small window. It is the same with nature's wisdom in general, which we perceive in every bone, every plant, everything from the starry heavens to the smallest body parts. Wise nature has entered into our consciousness as into a single point and surrounded us with the shell of our organs and the gates of their senses. Our consciousness is cut off from the being outside of us, and can take it in only through the sense organs.

But if we shut off our conscious mind, contact with the outer world is reestablished. Then we really live again in connection with the outer world, for, unlike your "I" or your consciousness, your astral body is not separated from the rest of the world. Astral fibers reach out on all sides, and you participate in the life of the outer world. In fact, not just the life of physical nature, but also astral events—spiritual events— are continuously happening all around us. When our consciousness is shut off, we perceive them. Everything that we remember, think, and combine appears unmediated in the somnambulistic state, as if it were conducted to our inner being from external nature, from all the things that live outside of us. Just as you cannot see a single star in the day-time when the Sun is shining, even though the whole sky is covered with stars, because the light of the stars is obscured by sunlight, the same is true with our waking consciousness. The things that are hap-pening in our bodies, whether our physical bodies or our astral bod-ies, these things are like a weak light, which is overridden by the waking consciousness. If we shut off the latter, what happens in our bodies becomes visible, just as starlight becomes visible at night. Sleepwalkers are in that state, and we must be clear that in the sleep-walking state a person is actually in a closer, more immediate relation-ship with the rest of nature. To use a beautiful expression of the German philosopher Stilling, who lived around 1800: "When the Sun of clear waking consciousness sinks, the stars start shining in the sleepwalking consciousness."[1]

Now, we must ask ourselves: Can we really trust these appearances? They are true phenomena, they are a reality; but this reality is accessi-ble only when we exclude the organ humanity has evolved gradually in order to orient itself on the Earth—when we exclude clear waking consciousness. When this happens, a condition is induced in human beings in which something is revealed that is otherwise concealed, but which also pulls us down from a level we have already attained. For as Theosophists we know that the states we humans can attain in this way, which we think of as "higher" states, are actually states we had to go through on the way to our present human consciousness.

I cannot go into more details on this subject today; but just as the natural scientific theory of evolution shows us purely physical evolu-tionary developments, in the same way Theosophy shows us that human beings have gradually evolved to the stage we have attained. Our present consciousness, the consciousness we use to orient our-selves in our earthly environment, only appeared after humanity had spent millions of years undergoing a slow evolution through other states of consciousness. Before humans developed this clear waking consciousness, they had a kind of dream consciousness. In those days, human beings really saw all the proceedings around themselves in the form of symbols, just as our dreams still transform everything into symbols. Many of the legends that have been preserved come down from epochs when humans were still close to this dream conscious-ness and created these symbolic accounts. You can find more on this subject in the very interesting book of my deceased friend Ludwig Laistner, who collected legendary myths from the whole world, showing how they were developed by a symbol-producing human consciousness that had not yet awakened from dream consciousness.[2] Many legends can be traced back to this sleepwalking consciousness.

If we go further back, we come to more and more deeply sedimented states that were closer to nature and directly proceeded from physical development. The human being, when it first appeared as a wish of the Divine Being, was in a deep trance. All humankind was in a deep trance in those days, the kind of trance we now observe in sleepwalkers when they can be "magnetized" into a deep, so-called magnetic sleep. All these things were lived by human beings in earlier days, and now we are in the stage of clear waking consciousness. But this too is merely a transitional stage; it is the transition toward the reconstruction of this ability, henceforth operating out of the clear waking consciousness that had not yet evolved earlier.

This is where future human development will take us: to once again cast our mind out over all of nature, *to become clairvoyant in full waking consciousness.* Some individuals among us have already developed inner organs using specific methods indicated by Theosophy. They have speeded up the evolutionary process, and are really capable today of looking into the world of spiritual beings out of clear, waking consciousness.

Already now, there are some among us who are liberated from dependency on the sense organs, who, out of that clairvoyant contemplation, are in unmediated contact with the spiritual environment. They move among higher realities that are closed off from the ordinary consciousness, just as you and I move between the chair and the table. They perceive around themselves the spiritual world that surrounds us at every instant. These considerations gave birth to Theosophical theories. The sleepwalking state teaches somewhat similar lessons, for the things the sleepwalker sees by shutting off the waking consciousness are sometimes the same kinds of things the clairvoyants see while remaining in possession of their waking consciousness. But somnambulists cannot control what they see; somnambulists can never control the things they tell you about spiritual goings-on in their environment that bypassed the sense organs. They cannot even monitor whether or not what they perceive is really happening in the way they describe it.

Somnambulists can therefore fall prey to the most remarkable illusions. You might stand in front of a person, and claim to be such and such a person living in such and such a place far away. The somnambulist will believe it, will truly be convinced that you are indeed the person you are claiming to be. The somnambulist believes you, and therein lies the danger. Somnambulists can tell us things, not just the kinds of things whose truth can be easily verified, but things about the higher worlds. They may tell us things that we cannot verify with our senses, make claims about the so-called astral world or about higher spiritual worlds. Somnambulists may tell us that they perceive a certain dead person. Now it is true that somnambulists perceive *something;* they perceive a presence. But there is no knowing if it is really the deceased person that the somnambulists claim it to be. It could be a different being altogether, a being that actually has not the least relation to any earthly being. It could be a being living in the astral world that stepped into the earthly world. To make a long story short, in the absence of a controlling consciousness, somnambulists have no way of proving conclusively whether their impression is correct.

This is a danger for somnambulists, particularly whenever we step over the boundary of the astral world. I can only make some suggestions here. For instance, the astral world has completely different concepts than our earthly world of good and evil. Our earthly world's concepts of good and evil are adapted to our sensory circumstances. When the somnambulist has experiences in the astral world, concepts of good and evil are easily shattered. This is one reason why mediums who at first communicate only truths when they are in a trance lose their discernment over time, so that it becomes impossible later for them to distinguish between fraud and reality.

Anyone familiar with these higher worlds will have no trouble understanding that just because cross-examination of a medium shows that in a particular case the person was reporting things that are inaccurate, this does not prove that the medium is a fraud. It can be the case—as I observed myself in one case—that a person in a trance goes to a store and buys a pious picture. Her "I-consciousness" is shut off. Later, she emerges from her trance and has no idea how she has come by the picture. Upon returning to a trance state later, she produces the picture, explaining that she has received and brought it back from a supersensible world. The medium in this case had not the slightest idea that she herself had bought that picture, or how she had come by it. Strictly speaking, she was not being dishonest, even though the actual fact is a "put-on." The influences that can be exercised upon a person in a somnambulistic trance make it possible for a certain event itself to be a fraud; yet the medium is not personally a fraud, and may in fact be quite honest and of sound judgment.

This should show you that we have to adopt the Theosophical point of view when considering the problem of somnambulism. Theosophists and the Theosophical movement are convinced that access to the higher worlds, access to the worlds opened to us by somnambulists, should never take place without the presence of a clairvoyant *in full possession of a clear waking consciousness*. There must be a person who is capable of finding the way in the spiritual world as well as in the physical world.

Theosophy requires that whenever experiments are made involving mediums—experiments that in themselves may be quite commendable—they should only be done in the presence of a fully coherent clairvoyant who can oversee the whole proceeding and verify what is actually happening. Often, however, it is common for the medium and those making the experiment with the medium to be in no condition to oversee the experiment. It is by no means the case that all such mediumistic phenomena are dangerous, but it should be easy to see that they can be hazardous in the absence of a clear sense of orientation. Clairvoyants who work out of a sound waking consciousness know at each instant what is going on. They know what somnambulists are really seeing, how it matches what is being described. They know what influences are being exercised, even when somnambulists insist that they are free of any external influence. This is really the difference between spiritual science and other similar ventures. I do not wish to question in any way the truth of these other endeavors, but their reality must be validated in the same way any other endeavor's reality is. Theosophy does not feel an urge to oppose all experiments with somnambulists, for, finally, the conclusion is always the same: the conviction that there is a spiritual world at work all around us.

Theosophists will work in accord with other spiritual movements, considering them "sister movements," and will always be ready to give advice about the reality or truth of particular experiences. For itself though, the Theosophical movement will only consent to conducting experiments under the aegis of skilled clairvoyance. This is the case, too, in regard to spiritualist movements. According to Theosophy, occult research should never be undertaken otherwise than under the influence of individuals who know quite precisely and quite consciously what is going on. This is also true of spiritual healing, which must obey the same rules as physical healing, always with fully conscious supervision of the proceedings and of their implications.

This, then, is the point of view of Theosophy regarding somnambulistic events. The Theosophist point of view is equally removed from two extremes: it is not a superficial external condemnation of somnambulism as consisting merely in morbid, abnormal phenomena; it also stands apart from those who believe that (somnambulism represents) the only way to attain knowledge of higher spiritual worlds. Theosophy knows the origin of these phenomena, can explain them from a clairvoyant point of view. As for all those who see in those manifestations messages about spiritual life, Theosophy views them from a fraternal point of view, as seeking the same goal: to bring back a true knowledge of the spiritual world, to meet contemporary materialistic humanity with a spiritual, truly idealistic philosophy. This is a deep truth. A German visionary whom people do not normally know as a visionary, namely *Goethe*, has said that we should not rip the veils off nature with our instruments, our mechanical physical tools, but that instead it is the spirit that must everywhere seek the spirit:

> *Mysteriously in the light of day*
> *Nature allows her veils to be removed*
> *And what she does not willingly reveal to your mind*
> *Cranks and screws can't force out of her.*

Goethe did not doubt the revelation of the spirit around us. He was completely unambiguous in the passage in *Faust* where a philosopher is quoted as saying,

> *The spiritual world is not closed.*
> *Your mind is dead, your heart is dead!*
> *Wake up, apprentice, patiently bathe*
> *The earthly chest in the red dawn!*[3]

3

The History of Spiritualism

Berlin, May 30, 1904

TODAY, I WANT to address spiritualism, a subject that claims both enthusiastic proponents and the most violent opponents. Some of these oppose it in the harshest way. Others ridicule it, classing it with the darkest superstitions, or what they call "darkest" superstition. Still others simply try to brush it aside with empty, witty, derisive words.

In other words, it is not easy to speak about something that generally speaking seems almost instantly to arouse the most vehement passions today. Therefore, I must ask those of you who are followers of spiritualism not to condemn immediately any statement that I shall be obliged to make if it does not seem to agree entirely with your views. Rather, please remember that advocates of spiritual science share at least one common interest with spiritualists—namely, we both wish to investigate the higher spiritual worlds that transcend what we can hear with ears, see with eyes, grasp with hands in daily life. In this we are agreed.

At the same time, I must also ask the scientists among you to remember that the Theosophical movement in whose name I speak chose the motto—not merely as a label, as a phrase, but in the most serious sense—"No human opinion is superior to the truth." I would likewise ask you to reflect on the fact that even science has changed in the course of time, and that what is regarded today as scientifically established cannot be so regarded for all time.

And so, without taking sides one way or the other, and mindful of the fact that no human opinion is superior to the truth, allow me to speak briefly and sketchily about the evolution of the spiritualist movement.

First, I must emphasize that the founder of the Theosophical movement, Madame Blavatsky, as well as its great organizer, Colonel Olcott, themselves started in the spiritualist movement. Madame Blavatsky and Colonel Olcott were both thoroughly acquainted with spiritualism. They created the Theosophical movement (in 1875) only after they had first energetically sought the truth within the spiritualist movement, and had not found it. Theosophy does not seek to attack spiritualism. It is concerned with seeking the truth where it is to be found.

I want to call your attention to something else, too, which will surprise some people, but will probably not surprise others who are more accurately informed. Let me put it this way: You will never learn the last word about spiritualism or similar things from people who are obliged to speak about it as I do. As you know, there is in all science a precept that is justified by the scientific methods themselves. This is the precept that one's scientific findings must be presentable to a larger circle of hearers in a popular way. Anyone wanting to gain a more intimate knowledge of these findings, anyone wishing to know the more intimate truth, must undertake a longer course of study leading through the various methods with all the details. As a rule, scientific researchers cannot present in popular lectures what they have established in the inner sanctum of their laboratories, the privacy of the observatories.

If this is true in the case of physical science, it is even truer in the case of the great spiritual movements of the world. In spiritual research—speaking now of what the researcher acquires through spiritual insight—whoever has the right to utter the words is, in fact, under orders to withhold the last one. In spiritual matters, the final word is of a kind that scarcely ever permits public utterance. In questions relating to the spirit, therefore, you will never hear the last word from those who call themselves occultists—unless you are in a position and have the will to follow them in the closest, most intimate way. For those "in the know," however, the way in which a fact is stated will illuminate what is being spoken of not only between the lines, but perhaps even between the words.

After this introduction, let me proceed to the subject itself, which certainly has great cultural and historical significance, even for those inclined to treat it with derision. I shall address it from an angle that will shed light upon it, namely, from the point of view of the following questions: What is spiritualism seeking today? Is it seeking something new or something very old? Are the ways in which it is searching entirely modern, or have these very same paths been trod by humanity for hundreds, even thousands, of years? Answering these questions is the quickest way to discover the historical-cultural significance of spiritualism.

Without a doubt, what spiritualists are seeking *first* is knowledge of those worlds extending beyond our sensory world. *Second*, they seek the meaning of those worlds for the goal, the destiny, of humanity.

If we ask ourselves if these problems haven't been humanity's task ever since we have been upon Earth and striven for something, then we must answer, Yes! And since such problems are certainly among the highest of humanity's tasks, it would be absurd if something entirely new arose in the world regarding these questions. And yet, when we survey the spiritualist movement in ancient and modern times, it seems as if we are dealing with something quite new.

Spiritualism's strongest opponents appeal to the fact that it has brought something entirely new into the world. Others say that it has never been so necessary to fight this movement as at the present time. Therefore, our way of looking at this subject must have changed. This becomes immediately clear when we understand that humanity has reacted in three different ways to the questions that we designate today as "spiritualistic."

The first way can be found throughout antiquity, a way that was changed only in the Christian era. A second way was prevalent throughout the Middle Ages and lasted into the seventeenth century. Only in the seventeenth century, in fact, does what we are today justified in calling spiritualism really begin to take on a definite form.

In ancient times, the questions spiritualists wish to answer today were the province of the so-called Mysteries. Let me now, in a few sentences, try to make clear what the word *Mysteries* implies. In ancient times, wisdom was not proclaimed publicly as it is today. There was a completely different attitude to wisdom and truth. Throughout antiquity, people believed that to acquire knowledge of supersensible truths one had first to develop supersensible organs. Everyone understood that spiritual forces lie sleeping in all human beings. They knew that such spiritual forces are not developed in the average person, but can be awakened and unfolded by prolonged exercises.

Adherents of the Mysteries in fact described these stages of development as very difficult. It was generally felt that a person who had developed such forces and was able to research the truth in this way was related to the ordinary person as a seeing person is related to one

born blind. This is the kind of "vision" those within the holy Mysteries aimed at. Those within the Mysteries sought to achieve spiritually
something similar to what is achieved by the physician who operates
upon a person born blind so that he or she may see. A person who is
born blind and then operated upon begins to see the colors of light
and the forms of things.

Just so, ancient peoples understood that, for a person whose inner
senses are awakened, a new world appears, one that ordinary seeing
cannot perceive. Those consecrated in the Mysteries sought to create
from ordinary human beings a human being who had evolved to a
higher stage of evolution. Such a person they called an "initiate." Only
the initiate was thought to be in a position to discover anything about
supersensible truths by direct vision, by spiritual intuition. Ordinary
people could be given truths only by means of pictures. The myths of
antiquity, the legends about the gods and the origin of the world,
which seem to us today in a certain way as childlike, are nothing but
disguises of supersensible truths. Initiates communicated to ordinary
folk through *images* what they had been able to see of the temple Mysteries. All the mythologies—Greek, Roman, Germanic, and all the
myths of indigenous peoples—are only pictorial, symbolic representations of supersensible truths.

To be sure, you will perceive this fully only if, freeing yourselves
from the preconceptions of anthropology and ethnology, you devote
your attention to the spirit of these myths. Then you will see that a
myth like the Hercules myth represents a deep inner truth, and that
Jason's recovery of the Golden Fleece represents profound knowledge
that may be perceived in its truth.

With our own era, another way appeared. I can only roughly indicate the outlines of what I have to say. A certain fund of higher spiritual truths was established and made the special concern of the
religious communions, particularly of the Christian; and this fund of
spiritual truths was now removed from every sort of human inquiry,
was placed outside the realm of direct human effort. Those who have
studied the history of the Council of Nicaea (325 C.E.) will know what
I mean, and also those who understand the words of St. Augustine
when he says, "I would not believe in the truth of divine revelation if
the authority of the Church did not compel me to."[1] The belief that
established a certain body of truths took the place of the truths of the
ancient Mysteries that were preserved in pictures.

Now there followed the epoch in which those truths that were meant to give information about the supersensible world were no longer transmitted by pictures, but simply by authority. That is the second way in which the masses of the people and those who had to lead them were related to the highest truths. In ancient times the Mysteries transmitted them to the great masses through perception, that is, images. In the Middle Ages, they were mediated through belief, faith, and maintained by authority.

But besides those who had the task of maintaining these teachings in the great masses through belief and authority, there were in the twelfth and thirteenth centuries those who wished to develop themselves up to the highest truth *through their own direct, intuitive vision*. (There have been such in all ages, but they did not appear publicly.) These sought the truth in the same ways in which it had been sought within the Mysteries. Thus we find in the Middle Ages, besides those who were priests, also mystics, theosophists, occultists, who spoke in a language that is difficult or almost impossible for present-day materialists and rationalists to understand.[2] We find some who had pushed on to the Mysteries upon paths that elude sense perception. And those who as priests in the Mysteries had the task of spiritual guidance spoke in a language still more difficult to understand. Thus we hear of one who had the ability to send his thoughts across far distances; another boasted that he could change the whole sea into gold, if it were permitted. We hear that another speaks of being able to construct an instrument, a vessel, by means of which he could move through the air. . . .

We see, therefore, that, from the middle of the Middle Ages on, secret societies arose in Europe that led their members to the development of higher intuitive forces upon the same paths that had been followed by the ancient Mysteries. Within such societies, the path to the highest truths was taken according to the method of the Mysteries. I will mention only the most important and most significant of these societies, that of the Rosicrucians, founded by Christian Rosenkreutz.[3] This movement can be clearly followed historically into the eighteenth century. I cannot set forth in detail how it occurred. I can only give an example—the great representative of occult science in the sixteenth and seventeenth centuries, Robert Fludd.[4] For those of you who have insight into these realms, let me say that he shows in all his writings that he is acquainted with the paths that lead to the truth.

He demonstrates indeed that he knows how those forces must be developed that are of an entirely different sort from the forces by which we perceive illuminated objects of any kind. He shows that there are mysterious paths by which to come to the highest truths. He speaks also of the Rosicrucian Society in such a way that for any initiate the connection is clear.

To show you in what a veiled way these things were discussed in Robert Fludd's time, I wish to place before you just three questions, which he says that anyone who has reached the lowest stage of initiation must be able to answer with intelligence. These questions, and also their answers, will appear rather senseless to rationalists and materialists.

The first question that one wishing to rise in a worthy way to higher spiritual spheres must answer is this: *Where do you dwell?* And the answer is, *I dwell in the temple of wisdom on the mount of discernment.* To understand this single sentence, to have inner experience of it, means already to have opened certain inner senses.

The second question was this: *Whence does the truth come to thee?* And the answer is, *It comes to me from the Creative Spirit.* And now comes a sentence that cannot at all be translated into the German: *Most High . . . Almighty, Universal Spirit, Who has spoken through Solomon, and Who will instruct me in Alchemy, Magic, and in the Kabala.* That is the second question.

The third question is, *What would you build?* And the answer is, *I will build a temple like the original tabernacle, like Solomon's Temple, like the body of Christ, and—like something else that I cannot give utterance to. . . .*

I need not nor can I enter further into these questions. You see that for all who were not initiates in such societies what are called supersensible truths were veiled in a secret, mysterious darkness, and those who were not initiates had first to make themselves worthy, and had to have reached a high point morally and intellectually. Anyone who did not give proofs of this, whose inner being did not have the force to experience inwardly, was deemed unworthy, and was not admitted to initiation. It was considered dangerous to know these truths. It was known that knowledge is connected with power, with development of power of which the average person has no idea whatsoever. Only one who has reached that moral and intellectual height is capable of possessing these truths and this power without danger to humanity. It was said further that without having attained this height, one who was in possession of these truths and this power would seem like a child sent with matches into a powder magazine.

Throughout these times disclosures concerning phenomena such as were related everywhere in the folk traditions, and have been popularly talked about for thousands of years—phenomena such as spiritualism offers again today—were considered possible only for one who possessed the highest supersensible truths. What spiritualism recognizes today is nothing new, but something very old. In ancient times, it was simply said of such phenomena that human beings have the capacity to produce quite unusual effects. For instance, certain people cause the sound of knocking to be heard in their vicinity. Around other people, objects are made to move contrary to the laws of gravity, often without being touched. At other times, objects are caused to fly through the air without the use of physical force, and so on. Since ancient times it has been known, too, that there are people who can be put into certain states, today called *trance,* in which they speak of things of which they could never speak in waking consciousness. And it has been known that in such a state they can also give information about other regions not connected with our sense world. It was known that there are people who can communicate what they see in such supersensible worlds by signs or symbols. It was known too that there are people able to see distant events—people who see events miles away and are able to give information about them— people who through their gift of prophecy are able to foresee and foretell future events. All that is very ancient tradition. Those who believe they are able to accept it as truth consider it self-evident.

Such phenomena were regarded as true throughout the Middle Ages. They were, to be sure, looked upon by the Church of the Middle Ages as being evoked by means of evil arts. . . . But that does not concern us here. In any case, during the seventeenth and eighteenth centuries the path to the supersensible world was not sought by way of these phenomena. Up to those times no one maintained that by a dancing table or by a ghost appearing in some way, whether seen with eyes, or in trance, one can disclose anything whatever about a supersensible world. If someone had said that from here they saw a fire in Hanover, they were believed; but no one thought that from such a statement anyone could gain serious information about the supersensible world. Those who wished to make supersensible observations sought these through the development of inner forces in secret societies. Among people with insight it was considered self-evident that the supersensible cannot be sought in the other way.

Then came another moment in the evolution of the Western world, a time in which people began to seek all truth in the natural scientific way. The Copernican world conception appeared, and investigations in physiology. Then came the technical arts, the discovery of the circulation of the blood, the discovery of the egg cell, and so on. Humanity gained insight into nature by way of the senses. Any person who approaches the Middle Ages without prejudices, wishing to discover the medieval world conception in its true aspect, will soon be convinced that the thought of that time did not represent Earth, Heaven, and Hell as localities in space, but as something spiritual. It did not occur to anyone who had insight in the Middle Ages to advocate the worldview that today is attributed to the scholars of that time. It is not in this sense that the Copernican theory is something new. It is new in a quite different sense, in the sense that since the sixteenth century the criterion for truth became sense perception, what can be seen, can be perceived with the senses. The world picture held by people of the Middle Ages was not false in the sense in which it is often represented to be today, but it was a world picture that was not viewed with physical eyes. The physical aspect, perceptible to the senses, was a symbol for something spiritual. Dante too did not represent his Heaven and his Hell in the earthly sense; they were to be spiritually conceived.

Then followed a complete change in the point of view. The real psychologist of human evolution discovers that. The physical-sensible was exalted, and then little by little materialism conquered the world. Humanity unconsciously grew habituated to it. Only the investigating psychologist, hurrying behind evolution, is able to make a picture of it—human beings who are in it become used to such changes. The sense world becomes the real. Quite unconsciously it became a principle of human nature to admit only what is *seen* in some way, only what one can be convinced of through the evidence of the senses. People had no regard for those circles that spoke of initiation and led to supersensible truths upon secret paths. Everything had to be demonstrated to the senses.

How was it now with the supersensible world? How could the supersensible be found in a world in which the truth was to be sought only in sense effects? There were always isolated phenomena that were not explicable in the light of previously known nature forces—rare, so-called abnormal phenomena. These were phenomena that the physicist, the natural scientist, could not explain, and they were simply denied by anyone unwilling to admit the validity of what could not be physically explained. At the same time, people took refuge in those phenomena, which were now searched for. In the face of the urge to cling only to outer sense evidence, the impetus toward the supersensible took refuge in such phenomena. People wanted to know about what was inexplicable for the scientific critic—they wanted to know the facts.

When people began to seek evidences from another world in this way, that was the moment of *the birth of modern spiritualism*. We can even mention the hour of birth and the place in which it occurred. In 1716, a book by a member of the Royal Society, a description of the Shetland Islands, appeared. It gathered together everything that was to be learned about "second sight," that is to say, about what cannot be perceived with the ordinary eyes, but can be learned only by supersensible research. Here you have the forerunner of all that was done later from the so-called scientific side in the investigation of spiritualistic phenomena.[5]

And now we have arrived at the entrance to the whole modern spiritualist movement. The personality, from whom the whole spiritualistic movement originated, namely Swedenborg, is one of the most remarkable in the world. He influenced the whole of the eighteenth century. Even Kant took him into account.[6] The person who could call the modern spiritualistic movement into existence had to be as Swedenborg was. Born in 1688, dying in 1772, he was for the first half of his life a natural scientist who stood at the peak of the natural science of his time. He comprehended it fully. No one can attack Swedenborg as unlearned.

We know that he was not only an unquestionable expert of his time, but that he also anticipated many truths of natural science that the universities discovered only later. He was, therefore, in the first half of his life, not only accomplished from the natural scientific point of view, which would make all research according to sense appearance and mathematical calculation, but he was even far in advance of his time in this regard. Then he turned his attention completely to so-called visionary fancies. Whether you call him a seer or a visionary, what Swedenborg experienced in that realm was a quite definite group of phenomena; and even one who is only partially initiated in this field knows that Swedenborg was able to experience *only* this group of phenomena.

A few examples must suffice. Swedenborg saw a conflagration from a place sixty miles distant from Stockholm.[7] He immediately made this known to the people with him, and some time afterward it was learned that the fire had occurred just as Swedenborg had related it. Another example: A personality of high standing made a request concerning a secret that a brother had not entirely communicated before his death, because he died before finishing his statement. This personality turned to Swedenborg, requesting him to find his brother and ask what he had wished to say. Swedenborg performed the commission in such a way that the person in question could have no doubt that he had penetrated this secret. Still a third example shows how Swedenborg moved in the supersensible world: A scholar and friend visited him, but was told by the servant that he must wait a little while. The scholar sat down and heard a conversation in the adjoining room; but he always heard only Swedenborg speaking and no answer. The matter became stranger still when he heard the discourse continue in a wonderfully classical Latin, and especially when he heard Swedenborg talking in a familiar way about affairs of Caesar Augustus. Then Swedenborg went to the door, bowed, and spoke to some one of whom the friend saw nothing. He then returned and said to his friend: Pardon me that I have caused you to wait. I had exalted company— Virgil was with me.

People may think as they wish about such things. One thing is certain: Swedenborg believed in them; he took them for reality. I said that only a personality like Swedenborg could happen upon this kind of research. Precisely the fact that he was well grounded in the natural science of his time led him to his view of supersensible nature. He was a man who, in the time of the dawning of natural science, had become accustomed to admitting only the sensible, the visible. Thus, as a man who perceived the spiritual in the world, Swedenborg was dependent upon the sensible, the visible. Since he insisted upon recognizing as correct only what he could calculate and perceive with the senses, he brought the supersensible into the form it had to have for him. The supersensible world was drawn down into a lower sphere under the influence of the habits of thought of natural science. I shall not speak of the significance and of the kernel of truth in what Swedenborg saw.

I shall speak of the fact that as soon as one enters this region that serves as the basis of the Swedenborgian views, one sees what one is inclined to see. One sees what one has cultivated in oneself. A simple example may serve as proof of this.

When, in the second half of the nineteenth century, the spiritualistic wave began to spread, experiments were made—for example, in Bavaria. It was shown there that in experiments instituted in various places and attended by well-educated persons very different spiritual manifestations could occur. At one such meeting it was asked whether the human soul is received by inheritance from the parents, so that the soul too is inherited, or whether it is created anew in the case of each human being. In this society, the answer was given, "Souls are created anew." Almost at the same time in another society the same question was put and the answer was, "The soul is not created, but is transmitted from parents to children." It was found that in one society there were supporters of the so-called creation theory, and in the other society some scholars were present who were supporters of the other theory. According to their leaning, that is, according to the tendency of the thoughts that existed in those present, the answers were given. Whatever the facts may be, whatever may be the basis of these facts, it has been shown that what one gets as revelation corresponds to one's attitude toward these things. Whether it appears merely as intellectual manifestation or as vision is the same. What one sees depends upon one's own tendencies.

So it came about that this seeking for material supersensible proofs became straightway a child of the natural science of the materialistic age. And as matter of fact the principle became established that the supersensible world is to be sought just as one seeks the sense world. Just as anyone in the laboratory is convinced of the reality of magnetic forces or of light forces, so people wished to be convinced of the reality of the supersensible world by what takes place before their eyes. People had forgotten how to see the spiritual in a purely spiritual way. They had forgotten how to develop the belief in supersensible forces, and how to learn to recognize what is neither material nor analogous to the material, but can be comprehended only by spiritual intuition. They had formed the habit of letting everything come to them through the senses, so they wished to let these things also be transmitted to them in a material way. Research was conducted along these lines. So we see how the Swedenborgian tendency was continued.

What is shown to us offers nothing new. Spiritualism offers nothing new! We shall make a survey of this later and then understand better.

All the phenomena that spiritualism knows were explained in this way. Oettinger of southern Germany presented the theory that there is a supersensible substance that can be seen as physical phenomena.[8] Only (he says), supersensible matter does not have the coarse qualities of physical matter, does not have the impenetrable resistance and the coarse composition. Here we have the stuff of which materializations are made.

Then we have again one Johann Heinrich Jung, called Stilling, who published a detailed report about spirits and spirit phenomena, in which he described all these things. In this report he tried to handle everything so as to do justice, as a Christian, to the phenomena.[9] Because he was inclined to Christian belief, the whole world seemed to him to manifest nothing but truths of the Christian teaching. And because at the same time natural science asserted its rights, we see in his presentation a combination of the purely Christian point of view with the point of view of natural science. According to the method that we call occult, the phenomena are explained as the projection of a spiritual world into our world. You see all these phenomena described in the works of those who have written about spiritualism, demonology, magic, and so on, in which you can find much that goes even farther than spiritualism, as in the case of Ennemoser, for example. We even see carefully described how one can put oneself into a condition to perceive the thoughts of others who are in distant rooms. You will find such instructions in Ennemoser and in other works.[10] As early as the nineteenth century you find the teaching of reincarnation, or re-embodiment, in the works of a certain Mayer, who wrote a book from the standpoint of spiritualism about Hades as a manifestation of spiritualistic manipulations.[11] You will find there a theory to which spiritual science has brought us again, which shows us that ancient fairy tales are the expression of higher truths prepared for the common people. Mayer came to that view through physical manifestations.

In the work of Justinus Kerner, significant because of the moral weight of the author, we find all the phenomena that spiritualism knows.[12] We find there, for example, that the Seeress of Prevorst pushed away spoons and so forth lying near her. We are also told how this Seeress was in communication with beings of other worlds. Justinus Kerner describes all the communications she gave him. She herself told him that she saw beings from other worlds, who passed through her, to be sure, but she could perceive them nevertheless, and that she could even see such beings entering the room with other people. Of such things many may say that Kerner lived in fantasies, and that he allowed himself to be much imposed upon by his Seeress. I should like to say just one thing in this connection: You all know David Friedrich Strauss, who was a friend of Kerner's.[13] He knew how it was with the Seeress of Prevorst. You know too that his accomplishments took a direction that ran counter to the spiritualistic current. He says that the facts that the Seeress of Prevorst communicated are true as facts—there can be no discussion about that among those who know something about it. He considered the facts to be beyond all doubt.

Although at that time there were a comparatively large number of people who still had more or less interest in such things, this interest nevertheless began to wane. That resulted from the influence of the position taken by science. It was not inclined to look upon such phenomena as true evidence in the 1840s, when the law of the conservation of energy was discovered and with it the foundation of our physics was laid; when the cell theory was advanced; when Darwinism was in preparation. What appeared during that time could not be favorable to *pneumatologists*. They were therefore severely repulsed, and people forgot all that they had had to say.

Then came an event that indicated victory for spiritualism. The event took place not in Europe, but in the country where at that time materialism celebrated its greatest triumphs, where it had become customary in spiritual matters to regard as true only what hands can grasp. It happened in America, in the country where the materialistic habits of thought that I have indicated had been developed intellectually. It had its origin in those phenomena which, in the crudest sense, belong to those that must be called abnormal, to be sure, but which are physical nevertheless. The well-known knocking sounds, the connected phenomenon of table turning, the hearing of voices sounding through the air accompanied by intelligent manifestations for which there was no physical cause: these things in America, the country where great stress is laid upon outer appearance, indicated the supersensible in an obvious way. This view won an overwhelming acknowledgment that there is a supersensible world and that beings not belonging to our world are able to manifest themselves, to reveal themselves, in our sense world! It took the world by storm!

Andrew Jackson Davis, a man who dealt with these phenomena, was called upon to explain them.[14] He was a seer of the Swedenborg type, only he had not Swedenborg's depth. He had grown up as a farm boy, an unlettered American, whereas Swedenborg was an educated Swede. In 1848 Davis wrote a book entitled *The Philosophy of Spiritual Intercourse*. This work resulted from the most modern needs that had arisen in the modern struggle for existence, in which the only material to be admitted was what individuals wished to enlist for their personal egotism, to snatch for themselves as much as possible and so be as happy as possible. In this world, with habits of thought fixed only on the material, one could no longer have any inclination to a belief that leads away from the sense world. One wanted to see with the eyes, and to have a belief that satisfies the needs and desires of modern humanity. Most important of all, Davis says quite clearly that modern humanity cannot believe that a certain number of human beings will be among the blessed and others will be damned. That was what moderns could not bear—here an idea of evolution had to come in. Then Davis had a truth communicated to him that presents an accurate likeness of the sense world. Let me characterize it by an example.

When Davis's first wife died, he thought to marry a second time. He had scruples against it—but a supersensible communication made him change his mind. In this communication, none other than his first wife told him that she herself had married again in *Summerland*.[15] Therefore he felt justified in entering a second marriage here. In the first part of his book Davis tells us that as a farm boy he was brought up in the Christian faith. But he soon came to perceive that the Christian belief could offer no conviction. He understood that modern humanity must see into the What and the Why, and know whither the way leads. Davis says, "I was sent out to the field by my parents and there met a snake. I attacked it with the pitchfork but the prong broke off. I took the prong and prayed. I was convinced that prayer would help. . . . But how can I believe in a God who lets me have such an experience?" And thereupon he became an unbeliever. Through spiritualistic seances he took part in, he became qualified for the trance and became one of the most prolific spiritualist writers. He emphasizes in his writings that in the other world things appear about the same as in the sense world. It would be incredible that a good father should not concern himself about his children, since the father makes a long journey for this very purpose—and so on.

You see that the earthly world is carried over to the other world. For that reason this manner of thought spread like wildfire through the whole world. In a short time the followers of spiritualism were counted by millions. As early as 1850 thousands of mediums could be found in Boston, and in a short time it was possible to raise the sum of $300,000 to found a spiritualist temple. That such a fact has great significance for the history of civilization you will not deny. With the modern mode of thought, however, this movement had a prospect of success only when science took possession of it, that is, when science put faith in it.

If I were to give a lecture on Theosophy I could speak circumstantially about the fact that other, entirely different powers control the setting of the stage for spiritualistic phenomena. Behind the scenes profound occult powers are at work. But that cannot be my task today. At another time I will speak about those who actually set the stage for these phenomena. But this much is certain: If this occult power behind the scenes wished to assume that these phenomena profoundly convinced materialistically thinking humanity of the existence of a supersensible world, if this was to be believed for all time, then the scientific circles had to be won over. And these scientific circles were not so difficult to win over. Precisely among the most intelligent, among those who had the ability to think profoundly and logically, there were many who turned to the spiritualist movement.

In America there were Lincoln and Edison; in England Gladstone, the natural scientist Wallace, the mathematician Morgan.[16] Also in Germany there were a great number of outstanding scholars, who were indisputable in their fields, and who allowed themselves to be convinced of spiritualistic phenomena by mediums: for instance, Weber and Gustav Theodor Fechner, the founder of psychophysics.[17] To this group belongs also Friedrich Zollner, of whom only those who understand nothing about the subject can say that he had become insane when he made the famous experiments with Slade.[18] Then there is another personality, who is still underestimated: that is Baron Hellenbach, who died in 1887 and whose books will be a true source for studying the direction of this movement in the second half of the nineteenth century, especially among the more enlightened.[19]

A European impetus was given to the American movement, coming from a man who stood in the very midst of European culture, a pupil of Pestalozzi; and it was given at a time that is significant besides because of other discoveries. This person is Allan Kardec, who wrote his theory of the world of spirits in 1858, the same year in which many other works appeared that were epoch making for Western civilization.[20] Only a few of the works need be mentioned to indicate the great significance of the spiritual life of that time. One is Darwin's *Origin of Species;* another is a fundamental work in the psychophysical field by Fechner. A third is a work by Bunsen that acquaints us with spectral analysis and makes it possible for the first time to discover something of the material constitution of the stars. A fourth was the work of Karl Marx, *Capital.* The fifth was a work by Kardec, a spiritualistic book, but of a very different kind from the American works.

Kardec presented the idea of reincarnation, of the re-embodiment of the human soul. This French spiritualism had in a short time just as great a following as the American. It spread through France, Spain, and also especially through Austria. This form of spiritualism was in harmony with the ancient wisdom teachings of Theosophy. It was of such a nature that even men like Hellenbach could enter into it. And so Hellenbach, eminent in the field of social politics, who in the 1860s and 1870s played a leading role in important political affairs of Austria that shows at every step what a clear and acute thinker he was— Hellenbach advocated the form of spiritualism that Kardec founded, spiritualism in scientific form.

Also those who, unlike Hellenbach (or Gladstone, Wallace, or Crookes, who thought of the spirits of early Christendom in angel form), wished to speak not scientifically but only of the human being incarnating again and again, and of the projection into our sphere of unknown beings whose form Hellenbach leaves indeterminate—such personalities also helped in establishing scientific spiritualism in Germany. But even those who wished to know nothing whatever of another world could no longer avoid admitting the facts as such. People like Hellenbach, and even Eduard von Hartmann, wished to know nothing of the theories of the spiritualists, but the facts could not be denied.[21] They did not allow themselves to be disconcerted, either, during the period of unmasking. The most celebrated case was that of the medium Bastian by Crown Prince Rudolf and Archduke Johann of Austria, but the very mediums who had convinced our scientific circles were unmasked.[22] Anyone who has even a little insight into this realm knows how right Hellenbach was when he said, "No one will maintain that there are no wigs. Are we therefore to believe that there is no real hair because wigs have been detected!" And for those working in the occult field the statement is of value that it will be possible to prove with certainty that many a bank is a swindler's bank—yes, but has not this bank previously done honorable business also? The mode of judging spiritualistic truths hides behind such comparisons.

We have seen that the natural scientific and materialistic habits of thought since the eighteenth century—we can designate 1716 as the year of spiritualism's birth—have completely adapted themselves to modern thinking, even to the naturalistic views. A new form was sought which would make it possible to approach the higher supersensible truths—and all those who faced these facts tried to comprehend them in their own way. The Christian faith found in them a confirmation of the ancient beliefs of the Church. Even some orthodox people engaged in spiritualism in order to find in it good proof for their cause. Others, again from the point of view of material thinking, which judges everything only according to material conditions, benefited by it. Even those who were thorough scientific researchers, like Zollner, Weber, Fechner, and also some well-known mathematicians, like Simony, and so on, tried to approach the matter by passing over from three-dimensional to four-dimensional space.[23] The philosophical individualists, who could not believe that there is individual development in the spiritual world just as in the physical world, were led by profound investigation to see that this human mode of existence, the material mode—seeing with physical eyes, hearing with physical ears—is only one among many possible modes of existence. The advocates of a supersensible spiritualism, such as Hellenbach, likewise found their ideas confirmed in the spiritualistic facts. If you picture to yourself a man who understood how to submit to the peculiarities of each single medium, who knew how to accommodate himself to the most difficult conditions, so that it did one good to meet him, then Hellenbach was such a man. Even those who alluded only to a psychic force, which one does not and need not think very much about, even those advocates of a psychic force, like Eduard von Hartmann, or even individuals like du Prel, of whom I shall speak next time, all explained the facts in their own way.[24] There were many theories. It was a time in which a lack of clarity reigned in all fields, a time in which the phenomena could no longer be denied, but human minds proved to be utterly incapable of doing justice to the supersensible world.

At this time also the foundation was laid for a revival of the mystical way, a revival of the way that in earlier times had been followed in occult science and in the Mysteries, but it was revived in such a manner that it was accessible to anyone who wished to enter it. In order to reopen an understanding of this way, Madame Blavatsky founded the Theosophical Society. This research into wisdom, as it was carried on in the Mysteries and among the Rosicrucians in the Middle Ages, has been brought to life again through the Theosophical movement. The Theosophical movement desires to disseminate what has been sought in more recent times upon other paths. It is founded upon the ancient movements, but it relies also upon the most modern research.

Anyone who becomes intimately acquainted with the Theosophical movement will find that the way of Theosophy, or spiritual science, which leads to supersensible truths, is, on the one side, really spiritual, while on the other side it answers the questions: Whence does one come? Whither is one going? What is one's destiny?

We know that there had to be one mode of speech for the humanity of ancient times, another in the Middle Ages, and yet another for modern humanity. The facts of Theosophy are very old; but if you seek by way of spiritual science or Theosophy you will be convinced that when Theosophy is understood, embraced, and mastered, it will afford satisfaction for every demand of the modern scientific method. Those who would give up any of the scientific truths for the sake of Theosophy would be poor Theosophists. We need knowledge of the definite, clear kind that true science offers—yes—but not a knowledge that is limited to physical things, that is limited to what takes place between birth and death; we also need knowledge and awareness of what lies beyond birth and death. Unless spiritual science has the authorization to furnish that knowledge, it cannot do it, especially in a materialistic age. It knows that finally all spiritual movements must come together in a great common aim, which spiritualists will find at last in *spiritual science.* Spiritual science seeks the spiritual paths, however, in other, more comprehensive ways; it knows that what is of a spiritual nature cannot be attained in the physical world, nor by functions of a merely physical nature—let us say, by vision analogous to the physical. Spiritual science knows that there is a world into which one gets a glimpse only after going through a spiritual operation, similar to the operation upon a person born blind who is made to see. It knows that it is not in order for a modern person to say, "Show me the supersensible through the senses." It knows that the reply is, "Human being, lift thyself to the higher spheres of the spiritual world by becoming more and more spiritual, so that the connection with the spiritual world will be comparable to the connection with the sense world through the physical eyes and ears."

Spiritual science, or Theosophy, has the point of view that a believer of the Middle Ages, a profound mystic, Angelus Silesius, expressed when he said that the truly spiritual couldn't be sought in the same manner as the physical. In the seventeenth century he declared significantly that material arrangements, or anything analogous to the material couldn't attain the spiritual. Therefore he speaks the great leading truth pointing the way to the supersensible: "People wish to look at God with their eyes, in the same way they look at a cow and love it. They wish to look at God as if He were here or there. It is not so. God and I are one at the moment I know Him."[25]

We shall not behold the spiritual world by means of contrivances that would represent the higher world as one that is called supersensible, to be sure, but is still like the sense world around us. Nor shall we behold it by means of rapping sounds or other material performances of a perceptible nature; nor by means of such apparently supersensible contrivances as Angelus Silesius characterizes when he says, "Such people wish to see God just as they see a cow." Rather we shall see the spiritual through the development of spiritual eyes, just as nature has evolved for us the physical eyes so that we may see the physical world. Nature has finished her work and released us with outer senses through which the sense world is made perceptible to us. The path we must tread is to develop a perception of the spiritual order within the sense world, so as to be able to behold the spirit with eyes of spirit— we must tread this spiritual path independently and in harmony with modern evolution.

4

The History of Hypnotism

Berlin, June 6, 1904

... MANY PEOPLE BELIEVE that hypnotism is something modern, that science has been concerned with it for fifty years at most. Well, let me cite evidence from the seventeenth century. This is from a book that is little read today. It is by the Jesuit Father Athanasius Kircher. It was first published in 1646. Let me give you the words of this Jesuit Father in somewhat modern language. They may be found in a book that Goethe treated in detail in his history of the theory of color, because Kircher plays quite an important role also in the history of the theory of color.[1]

In his book, Kircher mentions something he calls *Actinovolismus*. It means something like "brilliant imagination." Kircher says:

This great force of imagination appears even among animals. Chickens, for example, as has been shown, possess a power of imagination so strong that, from the mere sight of a piece of string, they become motionless, seized with a peculiar stupefaction. The truth of this assertion is shown by the following remarkable experiment connected with the chicken's power of imagination. Lay a chicken, whose feet are tied together, anywhere on the ground. At first, it will struggle to get the fetters off by flapping the wings and so on. Finally, it will give up the vain efforts. Stroke the chicken with your hand, permit it to move after loosening the fetters, and you will find that the chicken will by no means fly away, even though you incite it to do so. The explanation is based on nothing but the lively power of imagination of the creature, which supposes the stroking to be its fetters. I have often made this experiment.[2]

About the same time, another German author, Kaspar Schott, reported something regarding this condition in animals in a book called *Pleasurable Entertainment of the Human Power of Imagination.*[3]

Schott, who was a friend of Athanasius Kircher, tells us that he gathered the fundamental facts for his book from numerous experiments by a French medical writer.[4] What he speaks of in his book is nothing but what we call "animal hypnotism."

You know that by hypnotism we mean a sleeplike condition into which a person may be brought by means of various methods. In this sleeplike condition people show various characteristics that they do not show in waking consciousness or ordinary sleep. For instance, you can prick individuals in hypnotic sleep with a needle, and they don't feel it. At a certain stage of the process, you can have the subject stretch out. The limbs become so rigid and fixed that you can then lay the person across two chairs, supported merely by the head and feet. Then the heaviest person in the room can stand on this rigid body. Those who have seen the experiments of the really extraordinary hypnotist Hansen in the 1880s know that after putting people into hypnotic sleep, Hansen, a truly heavy man, laid them with quite slight support on two chairs, and then stood on them![5] The hypnotized bodies behaved almost like boards.

Further, whoever has put the person into such a condition can give the subject so-called suggestive commands. You can say to a person you have put into such a state, "You will now stand up, go to the middle of the room, and remain there, standing as if spellbound. You will not go farther, you will not be able to move!" The person will carry out the order and then remain standing as if spellbound. That is just a beginning. You can say to the person, "Here in this room there is not a single person except you and me." He or she will say to you, even though the room is filled with people, "There is no one here; the room is quite empty." Or you say, "There is no light here," in which case the subject sees none. These are negative hallucinations. You can also suggest hallucinations of another sort. You can say as you put a potato into his or her hand, "That is a pear; take it, and eat it." And you can see that the subject thinks it is a pear. In a similar way you can give the subject water to drink and he or she will think it is champagne.

If, to create a vision-hallucination, you say, for example, "You will see a red circle on the white wall," the subject will see a red circle on a white wall. If, after this hallucination, you show the red circle through a prism, it becomes clear that the hallucination breaks, *exactly according to the prism's laws of refraction*; that is, exactly as the phenomenon would if it were not a hallucination. Visual hallucinations follow the laws of refraction; they follow other laws too, optical laws, but it would lead us too far afield to discuss these in detail. It is especially important to know that if we give a hypnotized person a command that is not to be carried out immediately, but only later, that too can happen. It is called post-hypnotic suggestion, and it can lead to strange things. I can suggest to a hypnotized person that a certain action be performed in three times ten days; but a great number of actions will have to be performed before that time. To survey the preliminary conditions necessary for this is perhaps possible only to the occultist; but have no fear about it, the person will nevertheless punctually carry out the given command in three times ten days.

These are phenomena that are denied by very few at the present time. Even scientists who have occupied themselves with these questions accept them. It is scarcely possible for anyone who has studied these things to deny the assertions I have made. What I am about to say is of course denied by many, but during the preceding decades we have seen such a large number of things conceded by physiologists and psychologists that we cannot know how much will still be added to the concessions already made.

Now I said that records of such abnormal states of consciousness are to be found even in the seventeenth century. I might also mention in regard to other phenomena that a knowledge of what we call the hypnotic state has existed among the occultists and occult researchers of all times. Of course, I cannot prove that the ancient Egyptians, and particularly the priest-sages of ancient India, had exact knowledge of *only* what I have mentioned here as the phenomena of hypnotism. These phenomena are very elementary: the sages knew much more. Indeed, the fact that they knew more prevented them from giving their wisdom to the masses. We shall see why. There is one odd fact, however. Kircher is said to have obtained his knowledge of these things indirectly from India.

During the centuries following the seventeenth century (when Kircher was supposed to have received his knowledge indirectly from India), outer science was not especially favorable to this sort of thing. This science nevertheless made great progress, especially in the field of physics and astronomy. This had great significance for human thinking. It accustomed people to seeking the truth, the actually knowable, only in the obvious reality. And thereby people formed the habit of not admitting what cannot be seen with eyes, grasped with hands, and comprehended by the calculating intellect. Historically, we are approaching the Enlightenment. This was the age when the average human condition became the fashion, the age when human beings wished to determine everything in the way they determined physical phenomena.

Experiments connected with physical phenomena must succeed if the hypotheses are correctly made; and anyone can make these hypotheses. In the realm of *hypnosis*, however, something else is necessary. Here the direct influence of life upon life is essential—the direct influence of human beings upon each other and other beings. The manipulations made with the chicken in the experiment that Kircher related in the seventeenth century had to be performed by a human being. In fact, all the experiments I have spoken of also have to be carried out by one living person upon another living person or being.

Now it might well be because human beings differ so much from one another that they have such varying qualities that are able to influence other living beings, especially other human beings, in quite different ways. And so it could also very well happen—because a human being is necessary in order to produce the phenomena of hypnosis—that one person does not have the qualities necessary for hypnotizing anyone, while another possesses these qualities. We need not be surprised if this is the case. We all know that a reciprocal effect takes place with the persons concerned comparable to that between a magnet and iron filings. The iron filings remain quiet if you put a piece of wood among them, but if you put a magnet among them, these splinters arrange themselves in a certain manner.

Now we must presume that human beings are so different from each other that one, like the magnet, can produce certain effects, and another, like the wood, can produce no effects. The purely intellectual explanation will never permit such a conception. The intellectual explanation takes for granted that one person is like another. The average standard is applied to people, and it is never conceded that someone may be an eminent scientist intellectually and yet have no ability, no qualifications whatever, to produce a state of hypnosis. It might be the case that less depends upon the hypnotized and more upon the hypnotist, who takes the active part. Perhaps qualities may even be called forth artificially in one person that exert such a powerful mastery over another that the phenomena we have spoken of appear—indeed, perhaps even much more significant phenomena appear. Intellectual explanations, which do not differentiate between human beings, will not admit this. However, those who occupied themselves with these things were convinced on this point even after the beginning of the Age of Enlightenment.

Anyone who follows the course of history will therefore find with regard to hypnotism an entirely different understanding of science than we have today. Often it was merely oral traditions that were passed on from school to school. In all of this nothing is ever said about the condition of the hypnotized persons, the condition of those who are to be hypnotized. That was not the important thing. On the other hand, methods are suggested that will qualify another person, the hypnotist, to call forth such inner powers that he or she may be able to exercise an influence upon others. In the occult schools of former ages, quite precise methods were taught by which one person could gain such power over others. But all the schools also required that the person seeking such power should go through a certain development that makes demands upon the *whole* being. Mere intellectual learning is of no use here; mere thinking and science cannot help.

Only those who know and use occult methods, who attain a high stage of *moral development*, who undergo the most varied tests in intellectual, spiritual, and moral relations, can rise above their fellows appropriately and become true priests of humanity. Such occult methods lead them to a stage of development at which it becomes impossible for them to use their power other than for the welfare of their fellows. And because such knowledge bestows the greatest power, because it comes about through the transformation of the whole person, it was therefore kept secret. Only when other approaches prepared the way did people acquire other opinions, other purposes, other intentions, concerning these phenomena. Thus, for hundreds of years, the traditions of occult science formed the basis of the subject, and nothing mattered but the following: What demands must one to whom such power is given fulfill? What methods are necessary in order that a person may gain such an influence over his or her fellows?

Thus the matter stood until the Enlightenment. Only at the beginning of that age could something be disclosed about these phenomena in popular scientific form—as Kircher did. Before that, no one who knew about the matter and the method would have dared speak about these in public. That would have occurred only through some indiscretion. Only when the saying "Knowledge is power" was no longer common knowledge did it become possible to discuss this knowledge, which is about nothing other than dominion of spirit over spirit. It is therefore not surprising that official science, which in content and method, as we know, is a child of recent centuries, had no idea what to do with these phenomena.

Scientists were especially perplexed when the phenomena appeared in a startling form at the end of the eighteenth century, through Mesmer, who was both slandered and exalted to heaven.[6] Mesmer brought the matter to an issue with the learned professions. The term "mesmerism" of course derives from his name. Mesmer was a rather peculiar personality, such as perhaps appeared in greater numbers in the eighteenth century than appears today. He was a personality who, as we shall see, necessarily had to be misjudged by many, but who was also in a position, because of his fearlessness, to bring this question to an issue. To an outsider it really looked like a desire for adventure, like charlatanry.

In 1756, a treatise by Mesmer on *The Influence of the Planets on Human Life* appeared, which scientists of the present time must look upon as a very fantastic thing. Preyer, Darwin's biographer, confronted this question without prejudice.[7] I choose Preyer as an example of how little the new science of the nineteenth century could do justice to what was written from entirely different hypotheses in the eighteenth century. Preyer, then, took up the works of Mesmer with complete goodwill, and could find nothing in them but empty words. Those who do not judge such things capriciously, but rather with expert knowledge of the subject, will understand this. They may indeed distrust those who believe they can defend Mesmer against Preyer. If one wishes to judge justly, the preliminary conditions for such judgment lie much deeper than is commonly believed.

Mesmer's first treatise will not, however, engage our attention, for it shows to observers with deeper insight nothing more than the fact that Mesmer was able to master the science of his time comprehensively and from a rather lofty standpoint. I wish to call special attention to this, so that it will not occur to anyone that Mesmer was a dilettante, or anything of the sort. When he wrote his doctor's thesis, Mesmer was, in fact, undoubtedly an unobjectionable young scientist, and you can find what he wrote in numberless theses by people who became quite clever and excellent scholars of the eighteenth century, and even of the early nineteenth.

In Vienna, in the last third of the eighteenth century, then, this Mesmer appeared on the scene with his so-called "magnetic cures." For these magnetic cures he at first made use of certain methods that were already in common use at the time. There was nothing deceptive about the method he used. By placing steel magnets on or near the affected parts of a sick body, alleged or actual alleviation or cure of pain was brought about. Mesmer used such magnets in his institution for a long time. But then he observed something quite extraordinary.

Perhaps he did not even observe it at all at that time—perhaps he already knew it, and only wished to use a more customary method as a means of concealment. That is to say, he stopped using the magnets. He said that the force came solely from his own body. He claimed that, as healing force, it was simply carried over from his own body to the diseased body under consideration. Healing was therefore the result of a reciprocal action between a force that Mesmer developed in his own body and another force that was in the diseased body of the other person. He calls this force *animal magnetism*. I am telling this story only in rough outline; to give it in a more detailed way would demand too much time.

Very soon—we will not discuss the results of his cure—Mesmer had trouble in Vienna and had to leave the city. He went to Paris. At first, he had quite extraordinary success there and was much sought after. However, professionals could not get over the fact that Mesmer earned six thousand francs a month. In fact, this attitude was to be expected on the part of an aspiring science, inclined to materialism; but of course it is something really distasteful from the point of view of the physician for anyone to earn so much.

You know that in the eighteenth century, when the Enlightenment was at its height, the waves of materialism rolled high in France. People were willing to admit the validity of nothing they could not see with eyes, grasp with hands, or calculate with the intellect. And you will understand that from the side of official science, which was more or less under the influence of the materialistic tendency, people took offense at things they could not understand. Mesmer's healings, therefore, became a public scandal. It was said that the illnesses must be only imaginary, not actual, so that hysterical people were cured only in their imagination, or the sick imagined they were freed from pain. In any case, Mesmer's method was questioned. The consequence was that, by order of the king, two corporate bodies were requested to give expert opinion about mesmerism. I should like to read to you from the report, so that you can see how the science of that time actually regarded these things.[8]

A woman who had been blindfolded was told that Mr. D. L. had been sent for and that he would magnetize her. Three authorized members of the commission were present, one to ask questions, one to take notes, and one to do the mesmerizing. The woman was not magnetized at first, but after three minutes she felt the influence, became rigid, rose from the chair, and stamped her feet. This was the *crisis*. This crisis was critical in Mesmer's cures—success was attributed to it.

A hysterical woman was brought to the door, and when she was told that the magnetizer was within, she began to shiver, to get cold: that was the crisis.

The commission ascertained that something strange was under consideration, which it could not anticipate; and it ascertained something concerning which it could scarcely have passed any judgment other than that Mesmer's whole procedure was fraud. Anyone who understood anything about it could have predicted to you that the probability was 95 in 100 that they would come to this conclusion, and that with their hypotheses they could arrive at no other solutions. Nevertheless the commission could have come to different conclusions! Is it then nothing at all that a woman outside the door, who merely grasps the thought concerning a person, comes into all the conditions related to us here about the woman in the room? First of all we must ask, and the commissioners should also at that time have asked themselves fairly and honestly: Could they from their point of view, from the rationalistic standpoint, have expected such an effect of thought? Would they have had with their materialistic means any possibility of explaining the effect of thought upon bodily conditions?

Even if we concede to the commission the right to condemn Mesmer, it can never be granted the right to drop the matter. The commission should have further investigated the matter, for a quite unique scientific question was under consideration.

I should like to call attention to another fact that is very interesting. A very large sum was offered to induce Mesmer to reveal his secret. It was also said that the sum was paid over to him, but that he kept the secret to himself, and did not tell it to others. By many that is considered fraud. But shortly afterward, there appeared throughout France so-called hermetic societies, in which the same arts were practiced to some extent. It was not said that he divulged his secret; nevertheless, there were those who used his methods. Anyone who knows something of these things knows that he communicated his secrets only to trustworthy persons. The fact that he did not publish his secrets in the newspapers reveals nothing at all. Connect that statement with the fact that those who actually know something about such things do not communicate them, since it is not a question of communicating, but of developing certain qualities that produce such effects.

Now you will comprehend whence the societies came. In this case the experiments are not at all the important factor; an unauthorized person should even be forbidden to perform the experiments. The only question of importance is the development of the hypnotist. Actually, the scientists of that time could hardly give any sort of explanation of these phenomena. Therefore the phenomena were finally given the death penalty, both by the French Academy and by the entire scientific world. But they came up again and again. Even in Germany such phenomena were continually discussed. Special newspapers were established for that purpose.

People who believed that such an influence could be exerted from person to person explained the facts by assuming that a fluid, a fine substance, passed over from the hypnotist to the persons hypnotized, and that this exerted the influence. But even those who did not deny this influence were not able to rise above materialism. They said to themselves that matter is matter whether it be coarse or fine. They could imagine what was spiritually effective only as something of a material nature. That these phenomena were interpreted in this way at that time is a consequence of the circumstance that the attempt to explain them was made in the materialistic age.

I cannot now describe in detail the different decades following Mesmer. I only want to mention that the phenomena were never entirely forgotten. People appeared again and again who took them seriously. There have even been university professors who have described them in detail and who already knew of various things that we class today under the concept "hypnotic phenomena." They knew of what we call verbal suggestion. They upheld as true much more than present-day science is willing to concede. One scientist asserted that he could read a book quite well with closed eyes, that he could read with the pit of his stomach, and in such a condition could read the words by merely touching the page of a book. It was asserted that by artificial somnambulism a person was able to see distant events, that is, become clairvoyant.

Thus the whole group of phenomena was brought under discussion again. It is strange that the scholars of the nineteenth century had to be forcibly reminded of these things. They were first brought to attention by itinerant hypnotists like Hansen, who traveled around in America during the 1840s, exhibiting phenomena before great public gatherings and getting paid for it. Such figures often produced quite tremendous results among their audiences, and were called "spell-binders." Justinus Kerner, in particular, called these people spellbinders, because they produced soul effects by merely staring, merely gazing.[9]

This focus upon the phenomena has its dangers, however, both because dangers exist for the persons undergoing the experiments and because certain frauds can be perpetrated upon the public in the most unbelievable way.

I want to cite one experiment that has often been made, which I know has caused people to be perplexed and deceived again and again in great public assemblies. The experiment consists in the following. A medium sits with blindfolded eyes. The showman concerned goes around in the audience and in the back of the hall says, "Whisper something in my ear, or ask a question, and we shall see whether the medium is able to know something about it. Or write for me on a scrap of paper a word or a sentence." Either one or the other is done, and after a very short time the medium, far removed from the showman, will speak the word that was whispered or written down. Nobody except the two people knows anything about it, and the showman concerned can produce the scrap of paper or ask the person in question whether the communication of the medium agrees. As a matter of fact, in many cases when I was present nothing but the following happened. The man who walked around was a very clever ventriloquist. At the moment when the word was to be spoken, the medium moved his lips. The entire audience was watching the medium's lips, and the showman himself spoke the word or the sentence referred to!

Thus, in the 1840s and 1850s hypnotism was again brought forcibly to the attention of scientists by itinerant spellbinders. Particularly, there was a certain man named Stone who made a great sensation and gave rise to much comment.[10] Before that, however, one scientist was brought to the point of closely studying these phenomena once more. From him, in the 1840s, we have treatises of a scholarly sort about these phenomena.[11] They allude chiefly to the fixation method, that is, staring at a bright object. Now this scientist immediately called attention to the fact that with all these phenomena it could not be a question of a particular, a specific influence passing from the hypnotist to the persons hypnotized. And this very experiment of fixation was for him so determinative because he wished to show that in these phenomena the chief matter of concern is an abnormal condition of the person undergoing the experiments. He wished to show that no reciprocal action occurs, but that everything that happens is to be conceived as only a physiological phenomenon produced by a mere brain process. He was concerned to show that mesmerism, which depends upon the mesmerist himself having special qualities, is an absurdity. This really set the fashion in which, from this time on, these questions were treated by official science during the entire second half of the nineteenth century.

With only a few exceptions the problem was taken up as if it could be treated as an ordinary experiment in natural science, that is, as if it were something that has significance only insofar as it can be reproduced, like any other experiment in natural science. The demand was now made of this experiment also, but the study was undertaken in a very unfavorable time. To indicate to you how unfavorable the time of the 1850s and 1860s was, I wish to cite something further, which is most significant for one who examines the progress of evolution of the nineteenth century, but which is as a rule overlooked by official science.

Long before Stone, long before the time of academic learning, a man who had been a Catholic priest appeared in Paris. He had gone to India, to the Brahmans, and now employed hypnotism and suggestion in Paris, that is, person-to-person suggestion for healing according to the methods he had learned in India. This man, whose name was Faria, explained all the phenomena in an essentially different way.[12] He said that only one thing mattered. This was the hypnotist's ability to reduce the mass of ideas of the person who was to be hypnotized to a condition of concentration or "collectedness." Once this collectedness or concentration was attained, that is, once all the ideas within a person were concentrated upon a definite point, the desired condition would appear. And then other phenomena would also appear, even the much more complex phenomena that Faria exhibited.

There you have for once an exposition and solution in accordance with the facts by someone who actually understood the matter. But he was not understood. He was simply disregarded. And that also is explicable. I have said that the Jesuit priest Kircher, who first discussed these matters and who also procured his wisdom from India, indicated the solution in the title of his book. Of this, however, scientists understood little, so that the well-informed Preyer could say as late as 1877, "If the Church traces these phenomena back to imagination, that only shows how much imagination the Church has." Preyer expressed his opinions strikingly about the Catholic priest who became a Brahman. It was always the case, however, that hypnotism was used for cures and for easing pain in operations. Those connected with Faria succeeded through spiritual influence in eliminating the sensation of pain in the person being operated upon. In 1847 chloroform was discovered, a remedy that materialistic researchers could justifiably believe in and say was capable of preventing pain during operations. With chloroform, other means of easing pain were lost for a long time. Only isolated researchers who actually thought occupied themselves with these phenomena during the succeeding years. At the same time, anyone who observes accurately will discover that physicians are very well acquainted with the methods belonging to this field and concede that behind the phenomena is something they do not understand. Those who have more insight warn against meddling with these phenomena at all, with this field so subject to deception that even great scientists can be fooled.

Certain scientists, for whom we must otherwise have the greatest respect, had this point of view. I will mention only the Viennese researcher Benedikt, who as early as the 1870s repeatedly alluded to these phenomena.[13] He is the same scientist who advanced the idea of so-called moral frenzy, which ordinarily is only little understood. It is not necessary to agree with his theory, nor with what he says about hypnotism and magnetism. As a young man he was already engaged more or less with mesmerism and believed there was some truth in it, but he never occupied himself with it in the same way as Liebeault and Bernheim, let us say, of the Nancy School. Benedikt opposed this school vigorously, and emphasized that even Charcot had given warnings concerning attempts to interpret these phenomena.[14] You will never be able to find a plausible reason for Benedikt's opposition to the whole theory of hypnosis. Nevertheless, his instinctive utterances take a remarkably correct direction. He says repeatedly that anyone who experiments in this field must clearly understand that those with whom he makes such experiments are just as able to deceive him— perhaps without being conscious of it—as they are able to be the means of bringing him some sort of truth. On the other hand, he also says that no solution at all is to be reached according to the methods by which science wishes to grasp these things.

Now we see—especially after an itinerant hypnotist like Hansen has again performed the most terrifying experiments before people, which were repeated successfully in part by scientists in the laboratory—how magazines seized upon the matter, how large volumes were written that were widely retailed by journalists, and how these things gradually became the questions of the day and popular articles were written about them, so that everyone might have instructions on these matters in their vest pockets.

It was especially the scientists of the Nancy School, Liebeault and Bernheim, who interpreted these phenomena scientifically. A characteristic quality had to be ascribed to them that would bring them into correspondence with other scientific phenomena and give them equal significance. So we see that the outer aspect, that which cannot be denied by materialists, was to be the determining factor for bringing about a state of hypnosis. Bernheim went so far that he excluded all methods and allowed only verbal suggestion. The word that I speak to the person in question acts in such a way that he or she comes into this state. Hypnosis is itself a result of suggestion. When I say, "You are going to sleep," or, "Your eyelids are closing," and so on, the corresponding mental image is called forth, and this produces the result.

By this means, then, materialism had happily disposed of the phenomena of hypnosis. Thus a fact that is known by everyone who knows anything of these things passed into the background—namely, that hypnosis depends upon the influence of one person upon another; that a person either has a natural talent for it or cultivates it by special methods, and thus develops into a powerful personality fraught with significance for his fellows. And this fact, that personal influence was exercised, had been entirely overlooked. The point of view of the average intelligence was allowed to prevail, according to which everyone is equal—a point of view that does not admit the possibility of human development to a certain high moral and intellectual completeness of training. In this way, what hypnosis depends upon was buried.

All the modern literature on hypnotism is written from this point of view. This is particularly true of the philosopher Wundt, who has no idea what to do with this phenomenon, explaining it by saying that a certain part of the brain becomes inactive.[15]

We have been led into a sort of blind alley. We shall not be able to find in the contemporary literature on this subject anything but a more or less large collection of simple, elementary facts. The explanation of hypnotism as the influence of one person upon another reveals more or less ineffectual, rather materialistic attempts at a solution. But we shall come to see, above all, that official science was not equal to these facts. Nothing is more unjustified than for the medical fraternity today to pretend that they understand these phenomena, while they advance the claim that these data should be solely the field of medicine, the prerogative of medicine. To those who have real insight it is clear that, from their present point of view, physicians do not know what to do with these data, and most important of all, that those people are right who point to the danger in such things. Not without reason have people like Moritz Benedikt warned against a scientific pursuit of the phenomena of hypnotism in the customary sense. Not without reason have they said that even a Charcot has to pay attention, because these states, which he as objective observer produces, can just as well attack him subjectively. Not without reason have they wished to protect science from such treatment of the problem as the Nancy School gave it, treatment that, for those with real insight, resulted in nothing except worthless attempts at records and explanations that actually prove nothing. With good reason Benedikt has pointed to the fact that in all the literature of the Nancy School it is not possible to distinguish between what is superficial and what is positive performance, whether someone has surrendered to self-deception or has been deceived.

That is the instinctive judgment of a man—that is, of this very Professor Benedikt—who is, after all, highly esteemed by certain individuals of the present day, especially by some profound physicians. This judgment is significant because it instinctively presents to us the true state of the case. Instinctively Benedikt indicates what really matters. The first point is—and Benedikt expresses this in clear words—

that these things must not be jumbled together with others in order to experiment with them. He therefore investigates only those data that come to him without his seeking. When someone passes into natural hypnosis, undergoing no change through the hypnotist, then the phenomena can be investigated scientifically. As soon as we exert an influence of this kind upon our fellow, then we exert an influence from person to person, from the force of one person to that of another. At that moment, we alter the condition of the other person, and then what matters is our own personality, what kind of person we are. This fact is known by those who are acquainted with higher methods that *science as yet knows nothing of.*

If you are a base person, in a certain sense a person of inferior worth, and you exercise an influence upon your fellows by means of hypnosis, then you do them harm. If you wish to exercise such an influence in a suitable way, so that vast cosmic forces are not injuriously tinged by it, then you must be well versed in the mysteries of the higher spiritual life. That is possible only when you have developed your power to a higher level. It is not a question of an experiment being performed here and there. Such phenomena are the same as those being constantly produced in our environment. *You cannot enter a room in which other persons are present without reciprocal action taking place analogous to what occurs—under other conditions—in hypnotic phenomena.* If such influences are to be consciously exerted, then one must first be worthy and capable of exercising them.

For that reason there will be healthy life in this field only when the ancient method is revived and it is no longer required to study these phenomena according to science. This would require that a person who has awakened the inner power, that is, who has the capacity to be a hypnotist, must first develop quite definite higher forces. This was well known in earlier times. The nature of these phenomena was known. What was important was the preparation of people so that they might properly bring about such phenomena. Only when our medical education is again of an entirely different nature, when the whole of humanity is again led to a higher moral, spiritual, and intellectual level, and when the human being has proved worthy, only then can a salutary development of this field be spoken of. For this reason, nothing is to be hoped for from the academic treatment of hypnotism and suggestion. There they are conceived in an entirely wrong way. They must first be considered again in the right way. If that comes to pass, then we shall see that these phenomena are really more wide-spread than is ordinarily supposed. We shall then understand much in our environment. We shall then know also that these phenomena cannot be popularized at all beyond certain bounds, because beyond these bounds they belong to the evolution of the inner human being. The highest power is not gained by vivisection of the spirit, but by the development of powers lying deep within us. The higher development of moral and spiritual powers is what will again make us worthy to speak in clear plain words about these subjects. Then we shall also again understand our forefathers, who never thought of displaying these things in their deepest significance before the profane world. Nothing else was meant when it was said, "No one who is guilty of a fault may lift the veil of Isis."

By this it was meant that one may know the highest truths only if one first makes oneself worthy of them. That throws a new light on the saying "Knowledge is power" and gives it a new significance. Yes, indeed, knowledge is power; and the higher the knowledge, the greater the power. The guidance of world history rests upon such power. The caricature of it is what science wishes to show us today. But a knowledge that wakens hearts, and a power that ventures to interfere with other hearts and with freedom, can be gained only through an insight that is at the same time a grace, before which we stand in awe. That our knowledge affects our whole human nature, that we stand before the highest truths and know that the truth we experience within us is divine revelation, which we look upon as something holy—that must stand before our spirit's eye as an ideal. We shall again experience knowledge as power when knowledge is again a communion with the Divine. Those who become one with the Divine in knowledge are called to realize the saying "Knowledge is power."

PART TWO

White Lotus Day Lectures

In Honor of the Anniversary of the Death of Madame Blavatsky

5

The Return of the Mysteries

Berlin, May 7, 1906

ON THE EVE of the day we call "White Lotus Day," we recall the great personality to whom we owe the beginning of the Theosophical movement. Fifteen years ago, on May 8, Madame Blavatsky left the physical plane. I do not, however, speak of a death day, but rather of a second, different kind of birthday. We recall the day on which an individual—who acted so meaningfully for humankind while in a physical body—was called to other spheres, to continue her work there. This day should awaken feelings and thoughts that lead us to become ever more aware of the kind of activity human beings are called to when they leave the physical world. This activity can be all the more meaningful if it can use more appropriate tools on the physical plane. Members of the Theosophical movement can be such tools. They are prepared for the task by the kind of spiritual truths they absorb throughout the year.

Every year on this day, we must feel a little closer to the individual who was called to announce, with unequalled selflessness, the great message to which the Theosophical movement is connected. Yet few among us have a sense yet of Helena Petrovna Blavatsky's significance for the world and for the future. Why is that? In the first century after Christ, a historical writer of unequalled significance lived in Rome. His name was Tacitus.[1] Tacitus knew of the spiritual movement upon which all of Western culture has been founded. Yet one hundred years after the foundation of that movement, all he had to say about it was that somewhere in the distant borderlands of the Roman Empire there existed an insignificant sect, supposedly founded by a certain Jesus of Nazareth.

Should it surprise us then, if scholars, professors, and wide circles of educated persons nowadays still know nothing of Madame Blavatsky's mission, or else have the most distorted notions and prejudices about her? Inevitably when something new, a great event, first appears in the world, it arouses contradiction, prejudice, and misunderstanding. It is a law of nature that what is confidently intended for the future overcomes what is small and insignificant only gradually and slowly. And what entered the world through Madame Blavatsky is not something that can be measured over the short term. What entered through her is an event inexpressible in today's language, which has become too dense for such things. Once we make real everything for which Madame Blavatsky laid the foundation, the entire realm of human feelings and perceptions—not just our understanding of the world, not just our grasp of things—will reach a new stage. We need consider only the transformation of the feeling world that is already taking place today among a few people, and will take place for many in the future.

To make myself better understood, I would like to paint a picture for your soul's eye. Let us go far back to the time of Ancient Greece. Whatever is left from that time in the way of wonderful artistic works, poetic creations, and scientific achievements—Homer's divine tones, Plato's deep-reaching thinking, Pythagoras's spiritual teaching—all that comes together when we consider the Greek Mysteries.[2] A Mystery School was school and temple simultaneously. It was withdrawn from the eyes of those who were unworthy of encountering the truth. Only those who had prepared themselves to encounter the truth with holy feelings were allowed to enter. When those who had not yet been initiated in the clairvoyant arts were admitted to the place from which all art, poetry, and the sciences proceeded, they could see the truth in images. But those whose slumbering spiritual forces had been awakened saw the truth in its reality: they saw the God descending into matter, incarnating and now resting in the realms of nature until the day of his resurrection.

To such neophytes, it was obvious that the kingdoms of nature—the mineral, vegetable, and animal kingdoms—contained in themselves the sleeping gods and that human beings were called to *experience in themselves* the resurrection of this God, to experience their own souls as a part of the Divine. Everywhere in the outer world, human beings saw something out of which they could awaken the slumbering divinity. They felt the divine spark in their own souls. They felt themselves as divine, and thus they acquired the certainty of their immortality. They understood how they worked and weaved within the infinite All.

Nothing can compare with the sense of elevation the neophytes experienced in the Mysteries. Everything was present—religion, art, and science. In the objects of pious veneration, the student experienced religion. Works of art awakened holy wonder. The riddles of the universe unveiled themselves to the student in beautiful images that induced piety. Some of the greatest who experienced it had this to say: "Only through initiation does the human being arise above mortality, and above the earthly to the infinite." Truly, a science and an art steeped in the holy fire of religious feelings present us with something that can best be described as *enthusiasm*, using here the literal meaning of enthusiasm: "to be in God."

With this image before us, letting our gaze sweep up to our time, we see that we experience these things—beauty, wisdom, and piety—as separate from each other. We also see that our culture has become abstract and rational, and has lost the living fire, the enthusiasm, it used to have. As a result, it has a shadowy quality.

This is why, at the turn of the nineteenth century, prominent representatives of our spiritual life, the Romantics, feeling misunderstood and lonely, looked back to times when humans still cultivated contact with spirits and gods. In the silence of the night, they felt nostalgia for the Greek Mysteries of Eleusis.[3] They were the last descendants of the Greek Mysteries. A profound German thinker, Hegel, the powerful master of thinking, tried to put into thoughts the images that students of the Mysteries contemplated. Hegel was one of those in whom these riddles of being had taken their abode. In his poem, he recreated for us the mood that overcame him when his thoughts wandered back to the old places of Greek wisdom. Let us listen to his poem.[4]

Eleusis
(To Hölderlin)

About me, within me, rest. The inexhaustible cares
Of busy humans are asleep, giving me
Freedom and leisure. I thank you, Night,
My liberator! The moon surrounds
The uncertain boundaries of the distant hills
With wisps of white mist. The clear line of the lake
Looks kindly down upon me. The day's tedious din
Seems years away from now.

The great meditative thinker, who can look into riddles of the world, encompass them in his thoughts, now turns to the Mysteries of Eleusis.

> *Your image, dear Friend, steps before me*
> *With joys and longings of days gone by*
> *Which soon give way to sweeter hopes*
> *Of future meeting. Imagination paints*
> *The ardent, the long-hungered-for embrace.*
> *The questions asked and answered;*
> *Intimate probings whether time has changed*
> *Countenance, look, and feelings—then the joy*
> *Of certainty, finding the pact maintained*
> *Firmer and riper now than then,*
> *That ancient pact no oath had bound us to*
> *To live for freedom and for truth alone.*
> *Never and never to make peace*
> *With the laws that rule sensations and beliefs!*
>
> *Now the mood that bore me lightly over hills and dales to you*
> *Compounds with dull reality.*
> *A tell-tale sigh betrays their discord,*
> *And with it flies away my fancy's happy dream.*
> *I look up to the eternal vault of heaven.*
> *To you, gleaming star of night!*
> *Oblivion of all wishes and all hopes*
> *Comes streaming down from your eternity.*
> *Reflection dies away in contemplation*
> *All that I labeled "mine" is here no more.*
> *I yield myself up to the Infinite,*
> *I am within it, I am naught else, I am All.*
> *Thought, soon returning, feels estranged,*
> *Trembles before the Limitless.*
> *Amazed, it cannot grasp*
> *Such depths of contemplation.*
> *Imagination links eternity*
> *To sense. Lofty Shades. Spirits sublime,*
> *Welcome! You, from whose brows perfection shines,*
> *You do not frighten. I feel: This also is my home,*
> *This austere radiance wrapped around you.*

In this way the philosopher calls out to the spirits, who really did appear to the students at Eleusis. Then he calls upon the goddess Ceres, or Demeter, who worked at the center of the Mysteries. For Ceres is not only the goddess of earthly fertility, but it is also she who quickens spiritual life.

Oh! If only the doors of your temple would part,
O Ceres, you who were once enthroned in Eleusis!
Drunken with ardor, I feel
The terror of your coming,
Even as your revelations dawn on me
—Then would I sing the sublime meaning
Of figured images, I would hear and understand
The hymns sung at a banquet of the Gods.

Alas, your halls are silent, Holy One!
Fled is the choir of Gods into Olympus.
Bare their polluted altars;
The genius of spotless magic that was here
Is fled from the grave of the unenlightened,
The wisdom of your priests is dumb.
No echo from their hallowed rites
Has been preserved for us. In vain the scholar's prying itch
Quests without the love of wisdom.
So possessed, they still despise thee.
Somewhat they hope to pin by grubbing after words—
Words that thy giant Meanings once informed.
In vain! They turn up only dust and ashes
And never find your life renewed.
What if in that deadened trash
They found some pleasure? The complacent ghouls
Were wrong: no vestige, not a trace remained
Of sacraments and images once yours.
Sons of initiation felt that high
Doctrine too full, too deep
To be bestowed in shriveled syllables.
The soul touched by eternity,
Immersed beyond the bounds of space and time,
By thought now unconfined, forgets itself,

Then back to consciousness once more
Awakes. Who seeks to speak of this
To others feels, even if he had the tongues of angels,
The poverty of words and is horrified
To find the sacred dwarfed by thoughts as small
As words will hold. His lips are sealed
Fearful before the sin of speaking.
What the adept forbade himself, wise laws
Enjoined on weaker minds: not to divulge
Anything that they saw, heard, felt throughout that holy night,
Lest the devotion of some better spirit
Be mischiefed by its noise; their pack of words
Might foster wrath with the Divine itself,
Were that so trodden in the mire
As even to be memorized, become
A toy, a Sophist's article on sale
For any shopper's coin,
Clothes for a fluent wordsmith, even a task
Imposed on careless schoolboys—till at last
It was left an empty thing, its living root
Only an echo heard through foreign tongues.
Oh never, Goddess, did your sons with greed
Bandy your Honor in the marketplace,
Rather wanted to guard it well
Within the arcane sanctum of the breast
Therefore not on their lips, but in their lives
You lived. In their deeds you live still.
This night I too discerned thee, Holy One.

Often your children by their life reveal you,
I scent thee as the Soul within their deeds!
Thou art the exalted mind, the constant faith
Which, still, though ruin reign, betrays not the Divine.

. . . This then is the time in which *Helena Petrovna Blavatsky's* mission is situated. Without diminishing the size of her personality, one may well say the job assigned to her soul was actually too big for her.

If we try to solve the riddle of why this particular woman was called to bring the message of Theosophy to the world, here is what we find.

She offered the only possibility, the only channel, through which the spiritual guides of Western humanity could communicate. People in official positions at that time had not the least understanding about the spiritual realities needed by humanity. The very concept of spirit had been lost. Any talk of spirit had a hollow ring. Such was the moment when this remarkable woman with her outstanding psychic-spiritual gifts was called from her youth to bring a message to the world. No scholar could do that for her.

From the very beginning, she saw the world completely differently from the prescriptions of nineteenth-century culture. From childhood, she could perceive spiritual beings in all that surrounds us. They were as real to her as anything we touch with our hands. And one thing above all characterized her since her earliest youth: her great respect and reverence for—her devotion to—sublime spirits. Without such devotion no human being can attain knowledge.[5] No matter how sharp a person's understanding, no matter what clairvoyant skills he or she may have developed, there can be no true knowledge without this sense of devotion. For true knowledge can only be *granted* to us by beings who have moved far ahead of humanity in their evolution. Everyone is willing to admit that individual human beings are at different levels of evolution. Although it may not be accepted quite so easily in our materialistic age, the existence of real differences is undeniable. But most people are convinced that they stand at the top of the pile of those who know. They do not quickly admit that there might be still higher beings, greater even than Goethe and Francis of Assisi. And yet this reverence is the foundation of all true knowledge. No one can attain true knowledge without the sense of reverence, which has completely disappeared from the leveling mood of our time.

This deep reverence has important consequences. We all come from spiritual worlds, from an earlier life in the spirit. The divine part of our soul stems from a divine foundation. For each of us, there was a point in time when we first looked out from the soul world into the sense world. In ancient times, human beings possessed an obscure, but clairvoyant, consciousness. Images arose from their souls, pointing to a reality all around them. Only later did sensory consciousness as we know it now arise. For each of us, there came a particular point in our evolution—as it did metaphorically for Eve in the story of Paradise—when the snake of knowledge said, "Your eyes will open, you will see good and evil in the visible outer world." The snake was always a metaphor for great spiritual masters. Everyone had such an evolved master. Each one of us has at one point stood with one whose mouth spoke the words, "You shall know the world of the senses." Given the proper reverence, all human beings encounter such a teacher when their spiritual senses open. Occult traditions call it "finding the guru again." Each of us must seek the great master whom we cannot find unless we have deep reverence, unless we know that there is something greater that rises above average humanity.

This deep reverence and the consciousness of the existence of a great master lived in Madame Blavatsky. That is why the great masters called her to transmit something to humanity. The guru rules in the hidden place and can be known only by those who have found their way there. Helena Petrovna Blavatsky, then, came with the right feeling to bring something new to contemporary humanity.

Anyone who looks briefly into those places where truth is shown can easily ascertain how fraught with obstacles the conquest of such a new thing is. People who do so and become even the least bit knowledgeable about the quest for truth come to a point when they will stop criticizing the great personalities, stop focusing on their mundane realities. Those with no concept of the role of great personalities in the world remain stuck with these mundane facts, but those who can see through things are thankful for these personalities' existence. This is the only possible way to look at a personality like Madame Blavatsky.

"Much admired and much scorned" is how this Helen appeared to the world, and there is hardly anyone about whom so many stupid, senseless things have been said and written. Scholars have claimed that she herself wrote the "Stanzas of Dzyan" in *The Secret Doctrine*.[6] Against the claim that they are transmissions of ancient texts, these scholars claim that Madame Blavatsky invented them and then falsely claimed them to have been transmitted to her from ancient times. We can certainly research this question. We can spend two or three years on the matter. But after we are done we will discover only that, compared to the great revelations contained in the stanzas themselves, everything discovered by modern research (no matter how interesting) appears trivial.

Indeed, assuming for a moment that Madame Blavatsky might actually have written these stanzas, shouldn't that increase our sense of reverence for her? No one who spends two or three years penetrating the deeper meaning of the stanzas will really care whether they were written thousands of years ago or in the latter third of the nineteenth century by Madame Blavatsky herself. In fact, if the second were the case, one's wonderment would if anything increase. The objections of the critics seem all the sillier, and merely show that they haven't understood a word of the stanzas themselves. This is just one example of the kind of obstacles Madame Blavatsky had to deal with. Besides this, of course, people have also pointed out that she had this or that fault. In all, there is hardly any sense of her true significance.

Madame Blavatsky has transmitted to humanity manifestations of the occult worlds. Anyone as familiar with the ways of the occult as Helena Petrovna Blavatsky knows the hazards to be encountered along these paths. We must realize how easily passions are aroused by the world of the senses and what precipices await us if we want to look into the occult worlds—as Madame Blavatsky had to do in order to write a book like *The Secret Doctrine.* Then we will stop concerning ourselves with the external details of this remarkable personality and her surroundings. Her strong nature was almost destroyed by the hostility of the world. In view of the receptiveness and sensitivity of her occult powers, it is easy to understand that, confronted with so much misunderstanding and so much false authority, she was by the end of her life a broken individual. *But what she brought to the world will live on in humanity and bear fruit in the future.*

Hegel's words, this mood of nostalgia, must spread ever more. It must fill our souls. It will find peace and satisfaction in what Madame Blavatsky brought to the world. And this must be ever more clearly formed. Helena Petrovna Blavatsky deserves our deepest respect, precisely when we look at her as a catalyst. She was only interested in authority in her capacity as a true student of the great spiritual powers that stood behind her. Likewise, we too can work in the true spirit of Theosophy only if we work in the spirit of these great beings. The spiritual life has become darkened, but it will regain strength as we understand better what Helena Petrovna Blavatsky tried to bring to the world with such courage, such energy. To gain a deeper understanding of the potential of this White Lotus Day we must look beyond all the historical chatter and make an effort to look at the essentials.

To truly understand the Theosophical movement would mean developing in us the awareness that the spirit of Madame Blavatsky continues to live for the well-being and progress of humanity. Then when we say that her spirit is immortal we will do more than mouth sentimental platitudes. We will instead be giving our selves to the life and effectiveness of her spirit in those places where it must be put to work. For that was really our founder's only wish—that the members of the Theosophical movement should become true tools for the transmission of the spirit, for her own spirit which she put selflessly in the service of this spiritual movement. The more the members of the Theosophical movement understand this spirit's selflessness, the more they will learn to grasp that *knowledge is a duty,* and the more concrete they will make the spirit of Helena Petrovna Blavatsky.

People keep repeating that the main things are love and compassion. Certainly love and compassion are the main things, but it takes *knowledge* to make love and compassion fruitful. We often find a feeling of complacency among those who think they are seeking the spirit. It takes just a second to say "love." But to acquire knowledge for the well-being and blessing of humanity requires an eternity. *To become fully aware that knowledge is the foundation of all truly spiritual work— this must be the work of the Theosophical Society.* It is our task to follow our founder unceasingly in a restless quest for knowledge. Little by little—not allowing ourselves to be stopped by a sense of comfort that refuses to learn, but would like to know everything right away—we can learn this from the work of Helena Petrovna Blavatsky. Beside that, everything else is idle talk. What we must learn, as a continuation of the work she herself had begun on the physical plane, is the striving for spiritual knowledge.

6

Remembering Madame Blavatsky

Munich, May 8, 1907

A DAY LIKE White Lotus Day—a day of remembrance—means much to those of us in the Theosophical movement who feel we belong to a spiritual movement. It means something quite different from a day of remembrance for others, for departed human beings who were firmly anchored in our materialistic culture.

Such a day is also a day of gathering together. What would Theosophy's teachings be if they did not enter into every fiber of our hearts and enrich our innermost life of feeling? If a soul has been separated from its physical body, that means for us only that a person's inner being has entered into a different relationship to us. It is just such a relationship to the founder of the Theosophical movement that we would especially like to enliven today. We want to be filled with a feeling for our *connection* with the founder of our movement. We want to become fully conscious that thoughts and feelings are invisible powers in our souls, that they are facts, that feelings are living forces.

This means that if we unite our thoughts with all that the name "Helena Petrovna Blavatsky" contains—if we unite ourselves with the spirit who left her earthly sheaths behind on May 8, 1891—then our feelings and thoughts are real forces and create a real, spiritual bridge to another form of existence. Across this bridge, another world then finds access to our souls. For those who can see clairvoyantly, such thoughts and feelings are living rays of spiritual light that shoot forth from human beings, and are then united in a point that meets with the spiritual being in question. Such a festive moment is a reality.

When our soul, dwelling in our body, wants to work on the physical plane, then it must form a body for itself. It must build and form matter and forces in such a way that it can express itself through them. If the matter and forces did not fit together then this soul could no longer live its life on the physical plane. It is the same for spiritual beings on the higher planes as it is here on the physical plane. If we want to understand Helena Petrovna Blavatsky correctly, we must realize that all of her efforts are now bound up with the proper progress of the Theosophical movement. It has been so since her soul freed itself from her physical body. Even now she is working as a living being within the Theosophical Society. If she is to be able to work, then matter and forces must be at her disposal. And where better could they be found than in the souls of those who understand her being within the Theosophical movement? As our souls take hold of matter and forces on the physical plane, so also does such a being take hold of the matter and forces in human souls in order to work through them. If those people who are members of the Theosophical movement were unwilling to place themselves at the disposal of this being, then she could not find expression on the physical plane. We ourselves must create a place in our souls for reverence, love, and devotion, thus creating the forces through which Helena Petrovna Blavatsky can work, just as our souls work through our bodies of flesh. We must become aware that we are truly creating something when, in this moment, we are loving and receptive. All the love and devotion that today stream up to the soul of Helena Petrovna Blavatsky are powerful forces that are called upon to connect with her.

We must understand correctly what Madame Blavatsky means in our cultural life. The nineteenth century will one day be described as the materialistic century in human history. People of the twentieth century cannot really imagine how deeply the nineteenth century was entangled in materialism. Only later, when human beings have become spiritual again, will that be possible. In the nineteenth century, materialism permeated everything, even religious life. Anyone who can look upon human evolution from higher planes knows that the 1840s were an extremely low point in spiritual life. Science, philosophy, and religion were in the grip of materialism—so much so that the leaders of humanity felt it necessary to gradually allow a stream of spiritual life to flow into humanity.

It is significant that in the spiritual life of the West as a whole no one as suitable as Helena Petrovna Blavatsky was found to return the stream of spiritual life into the world—the stream that would refresh humankind and begin to pull it out of materialism. In the light of this one fact, the impact of all the attacks against her swirling around in the world today fade away. For, among many other things, the Theosophical Society must teach us the feeling of positivity. We must acquire an attitude that seeks, above all, to see what speaks of greatness in a human being. Then, in comparison to this greatness, all the little faults that incite criticism must fade away. As with other great personalities, many things that were seen by her contemporaries with critical eyes have disappeared, but the great things she has accomplished will remain.

Let us learn to regard the mistakes of human beings as their own affair and the accomplishments of human beings as something that concerns all of humankind. People's errors belong to their karma; their deeds concern humanity. Let us learn not to be troubled by people's mistakes; they themselves must atone for them. Let us rather be thankful for their accomplishments, for the entire evolution of humanity lives from them.

This is the first year that we celebrate White Lotus Day—a day of remembrance for souls who have struggled free from the body and lift their experiences in another form up into the heights like a lotus flower—without Henry Steel Olcott, Helena Petrovna Blavatsky's associate.[1] He, too, has now left the physical plane. Colonel Olcott stood with us as the great organizer, as the form-giving power. To him too, then, we direct grateful, revering, and love-filled thoughts. These will flow into the spiritual world and we ourselves will thereby be strengthened. We should continue the celebration on the other days of the year as we send out our thoughts as rays of light, as we apply the strength we have received to the work that we call the Theosophical movement.

We will work in their spirit only if we are devoted to the spiritual life in an entirely nondogmatic, nonsectarian way. Helena Petrovna Blavatsky did not ask for blind faith. What can be asked of her followers is that they let themselves be stimulated by her spirituality. There is a spring of spiritual power in what Helena Petrovna Blavatsky left to the physical plane, a spring that will be a blessing to us if we allow it to influence us in a living way.

Letters on the page can stimulate us, but it is the spirit within that must become alive. One thing can be said of the writings of Helena Petrovna Blavatsky. Only one who does not understand them can underestimate them. Anyone who finds the key to what is great in these works will come to admire her more and more. That is what is significant about her works. The more one penetrates them the more one admires them. It is not the case that there are no mistakes to be found in them. But those who really take hold of life know, if they always strive to penetrate these works, that what is expressed therein could only have come from the great spiritual beings who are now guiding world evolution. This is how we must read *Isis Unveiled,* a book containing truths that, though sometimes caricatured like a beautiful face seen in a distorting mirror, are truly great.[2]

A critical spirit might perhaps think that these truths would have been better not to be distorted. But there is another way to view the matter. We place our own weak spiritual forces at the disposal of spiritual powers that wish to reveal themselves. We know that our own weak forces can produce only a distorted picture; but we know, too, that there is no one else who could do it any more accurately. Those who act in this way, by their devotion, make a great sacrifice for the world.

All renderings of the great truths are distortions. To wait until the whole truth could be manifested would be to wait a long time. Those people are selfless who devote themselves to the spiritual world and say, "It doesn't matter if people tear me apart; I must present the truth as I can." This sacrifice is much greater than a moral sacrifice. This is the noble sacrifice of the intellect—an expression so often misused by a wrongheaded conception of religion. It means yielding up the intellect for the instreaming of spiritual truth. If we are unwilling to offer up our intellect, then we cannot serve the truth. When we look toward Helena Petrovna Blavatsky with gratitude, we do so above all because she is a martyr in the sense just described, a martyr among the great martyrs for the truth. This is how we consider her when we gladly and willingly regard her as a model in the Theosophical Society. Therefore, when I speak about regions of the spirit inaccessible to her it will not profane this day.

I will speak about spiritual streams in the world that Helena Petrovna Blavatsky least understood on the physical plane. We serve her best by placing ourselves in the service of that to which she could find no access. She would much prefer to have followers rather than worshipers. Although much of what I say may sound opposed to her, nevertheless I know that we are acting according to her wishes; by taking this liberty we esteem her the most.

Our transition now to the Apocalypse is not something arcane.[3] It is not forced. For if we wish to understand more deeply the world mission of Helena Petrovna Blavatsky, then we must imagine evolution as consisting of two streams. The year 1841 was the low point of humanity's spiritual life. The opponents of spiritual life had, in 1841, the strongest point of attack in the evolution of humankind. These opponents did the groundwork necessary to prepare for many of the things described in the Apocalypse as prophetic visions of the future. The powers who, in 1841, found their moment for attacking the evolution of humankind prepared what is represented by the beast with the horns of the ram and the number 666, the beast with the seven heads and so forth. These powers, the elemental beings that found suitable soil at that time, have taken possession of a large part of humanity and are exerting their influence from that position. Otherwise, the adversarial powers that find expression in the two beasts would not reside in humanity, pulling it down. But against this downward pull another movement is drawing us upward. This upward movement is preparing all those who, entering into the stream of spiritual evolution, are to be "sealed." This stream found an instrument precisely in Helena Petrovna Blavatsky. We do not understand our time if we do not recognize the deep necessity for this spiritual stream. We are now in the fifth "sub-race" or culture of the "fifth root race" or root culture and are evolving toward the sixth and seventh. Then the sixth great root culture will arrive. This means that in the sixth epoch human beings who desire it will understand who Christ is.

This is to say that there will be human beings then who are Christ-filled, who have been *sealed*. In the ages of spirituality to come, the seals of human souls will be opened up, broken open. When it says that five wise virgins will have oil burning in their lamps and that the bridegroom will find illuminated souls, this means that a portion of humanity will have revealed to it the mystery that is still closed to humankind today. The book with the seven seals will be deciphered for a portion of humanity. The writer of the Apocalypse, John, seeks to point to this time through signs. He wants to proclaim this age prophetically. One sentence reads, "And a great sign appeared in heaven . . ." (Rev. 12:1). That means we are dealing with signs representing the great phases of the evolution of humanity. We must then decipher these signs. We remember that our present fifth root race was preceded by the Atlantean race, which was destroyed by a flood. What in turn will destroy the fifth race? Our fifth race has as its special task the development of egoism. This egoism will, at the same time, create what causes the downfall of the fifth root race. A small part of humankind will live toward the sixth main race; but a larger part will not yet have found the light within. Because egotism is the fundamental power in the soul, the war of all against all will rage within this larger part of humanity. As the Lemurian race found its end through the power of fire and the Atlantean through water, so will the fifth race find its destruction in conflict between selfish, egoistic powers in the war of all against all. This egotistic line of evolution will descend deeper and deeper. When it reaches the bottom everyone will rage against everyone else. A small part of humankind will escape this, just as a small part escaped during the destruction of the Atlantean race. It is up to every individual to find a connection to spiritual life in order to be one of those to go over into the sixth root race. Mighty revolutions stand before humankind. These revolutions are described in the Apocalypse. . . .

By understanding such a work we allow ourselves to be stimulated by the spirit who spoke through Helena Petrovna Blavatsky. What the Theosophical Society seeks to achieve must strike us like a trumpet proclamation sent to humankind. The more we understand the Apocalypse the more we understand the task of our movement.

7

Christ and the Further Development of Conscience

Berlin, May 8, 1910

TODAY, MAY 8, 1910, the Theosophical Society celebrates White Lotus Day, which is known to the outer world as the day of death of the one who activated the spiritual stream in which we stand. To us, however, it would seem more appropriate to select a different way of talking about today's festival, one that we take from our knowledge of the spiritual world.

We might speak of this day, for instance, as the day that we celebrate a transition from an activity on the physical plane to one in the spiritual worlds. Indeed, for us, it is not only an inner conviction in the ordinary sense, but the *deepening* knowledge that what the outer world calls death is only the passing from one form of work to another. We know that in death we pass from activities stimulated by the impressions of the outer physical world to activities stimulated by the spiritual world.

Today we remember H. P. Blavatsky and the leaders of her movement who have also passed into the spiritual realm. Let us, then, try to form a clear idea of what we must make of our spiritual movement so that it may represent a continuation of the activity she exercised on the physical plane. Let our work become a continuation of that activity and thus make it possible for her to continue her work from the spiritual world now and in the future.

On such a day as this it is only fitting that we should break away from our usual study of Theosophical life and problems. Instead, we should look in retrospect at the tasks and duties the Theosophical movement sets before us. This may lead us to see what this movement should become in the future, what we should and should not do. The Theosophical movement, as we are carrying it on, came into the world as the result of quite special circumstances and historical necessities.

You know that in the case of our movement it was not a question, as in other spiritual movements, of some individuals simply determining enthusiastically to follow certain heartfelt ideals or of trying to enthuse and induce others to form a society to carry these ideals into practice.

We must see our movement rather as a historical necessity of our present times. We must see it as something that was bound to come, regardless of what people felt about it, because it already lay in the womb of time, so to speak, and had to be brought to birth.

How, then, may we regard the Theosophical movement? We may think of it as a descent from the supersensible worlds, a new descent of spiritual life, wisdom, and forces into the sensory physical world. Such a descent had to take place for further human development to take place. Similar events in fact must occur repeatedly in the future. Of course, I cannot indicate today all the different impulses by which spiritual life has flowed down from the supersensible worlds to ensure that when human soul life grew old, as it were, it could be renewed. Such impulses have frequently occurred in the course of time. One thing, however, must be borne in mind.

In the primeval past, not long after the great Atlantean catastrophe, which various traditions record as the story of the Flood, the impulse occurred that may be described as the inflow of spiritual life into the development of humanity through the Holy Rishis.[1] Then came the stream of spiritual life that flowed into human evolution through Zarathustra or Zoroaster, and we find still another in the one that came to the old Israelites through the revelations of Moses. Finally, we have the greatest impulse of all in that mighty inflow of spiritual life that poured into the physical world through the earthly appearance of Christ Jesus.

This is by far the mightiest impulse ever given in the past, and, as we have repeatedly emphasized, it is greater than any that will come into earthly evolution in the future. At the same time, we have also stated repeatedly that new impulses must continue to come. New spiritual life and a new understanding of the old must flow into human development. Were it not for these new impulses, the tree of human evolution, which will grow green when humanity has attained its goal, would wither and perish. The mighty wave of Christ that poured into human development must, through the new spiritual impulses flowing into earthly life, be ever better understood.

As our own age, the nineteenth century, approached, the time arrived when human development again required a new intervention. New stimuli, new revelations had to flow again from the supersensible worlds into our physical world. This was a necessity, and it ought to have been felt as such on Earth—as it was indeed in those regions of the spirit from which the Earth is guided. It is shortsighted to ask, "What is the use of these constant fresh streams of perfectly new truths? Why should there be always new knowledge and life impulses? We have Christianity, and we can go on quite well and simply in the old way with that."

From a higher standpoint this point of view is really extremely egotistical. The very fact that such egotistical remarks are so frequently made today by the very people who believe themselves to be good and religious offers even stronger proof that our spiritual life needs to be refreshed. How often do we hear it said today, "What is the use of new spiritual movements? We have our old traditions that have been preserved from the beginning of recorded history. Let us not spoil these traditions by what those people say who always think they know better." That is an egotistical expression of the human soul. Those who speak in this way are unaware of this; they do not realize that they are anxious only about their own souls. They feel that they are quite happy with what they have. Therefore, they establish the dogma, which is dreadful from the standpoint of consciousness, "If we are satisfied with our way, those who come after us and must learn from us must find satisfaction in the same way. All must continue as we feel to be right and in accordance with our knowledge." One frequently hears that way of talking in the outer world. It does not come just from the limitations of a narrow soul; rather, it is connected with what we might call an egotistical bent of the soul. In religious life, souls may in reality be extremely egotistical while wearing a mask of piety.

Those who take the question of the spiritual development of humanity seriously must, if they study the world around them with understanding, become aware of one thing. They must see that the human soul is gradually breaking away from the method by which people, for centuries, have contemplated the Christ—that greatest impulse in the development of humankind. I do not as a rule care to refer to contemporary matters, because what goes on in the external spiritual life today is for the most part too insignificant to appeal to the deeper side of a serious observer. However, during the last few weeks it was impossible to pass a bulletin board without seeing notices of a lecture entitled "Did Jesus Live?" You probably all know that what led to this subject being discussed so widely, sometimes with radical weapons, were the views of a German philosophy professor, Dr. Arthur Drews, a disciple of Eduard von Hartmann, author of *The Philosophy of the Unconscious.*[2]

Professor Drews's book *The Christ Myth* has been made more widely known through the lecture "Did Jesus Live?" that he gave here in Berlin.

It is not my task to go into the particulars of that lecture. I will only put its principal thoughts before you. The author of *The Christ Myth* is a modern philosopher who may be supposed to represent the science and thought of the day. This philosopher searches through several ancient records that are supposed to offer historical proof that a certain person named Jesus of Nazareth lived at the beginning of our era. Then, with the help of what science and the critics have proved, he tries to reduce the result of all this to something like the following question: "Do the separate Gospels, as historical records, prove that Jesus lived?" He takes all that modern theology has to say and then tries to show that none of the Gospels, as historical records, prove Jesus ever lived. He also tries to prove that none of the other records of a purely historical nature are determinative, and that nothing conclusive concerning a historical Jesus can be deduced from them.

Now, everyone who has gone into this question knows that, considered purely from an external standpoint, the sort of observation Professor Drews practices has much in its favor and comes as a result of modern theological criticism. I will not go into details. What is of importance is that someone who has studied the philosophical side of science should assert that there is no historical document to prove that Jesus lived, because the only documents that are supposed to offer such proof are not authoritative. Drews and all those of like mind depend upon what has come to us from the Apostle Paul. In recent times there are even people who doubt the genuineness of the Pauline Epistles, but since the author of *The Christ Myth* does not go that far, we will not do so either.

Drews says that St. Paul does not base his assertions on a personal acquaintance with Jesus of Nazareth, but on the revelation he received in the event at Damascus. We know that this is absolutely true, but Drews concludes, "What concept of Christ did St. Paul hold? He formed the concept of a purely spiritual Christ, who can dwell in each human soul, so to speak, and can be realized within each individual. But St. Paul nowhere asserts that the Christ, whom he considered to be a purely spiritual being, should necessarily have been present in a Jesus whose existence cannot be historically proved. One cannot therefore say that anyone knows whether a historical Jesus lived or not—that the Christ concept of St. Paul is a purely spiritual one, simply reproducing what may live in every human soul as an impulse toward perfection, as a sort of God in the human soul.

The author of *The Christ Myth* points out further that certain conceptions of a pre-Christian Jesus, similar to the idea the Christians have of Jesus Christ, were already in existence, and also that several Eastern peoples held a concept of a messiah. This compels him to ask, "What then is actually the difference between the idea of Christ that St. Paul had [which Drews does not attempt to deny] in his heart and soul, and the idea of the messiah that already existed?" Drews then goes on to say, "Before the time of St. Paul, people had a Christ picture of a God, a messiah picture of a God, who did not actually become human nor descend so far as individual human nature. They even celebrated his suffering, death, and resurrection as symbolical processes in their various festivals and mysteries, but they did not possess one thing. There is no record of an individual human being having really passed through suffering, death, and resurrection on the physical Earth."

This then is more or less the general idea. The author of *The Christ Myth* then asks, "What, then, is new in St. Paul? To what extent did he carry the idea of Christ further?"

He replies, "The advance made by St. Paul on the earlier conceptions is that he does not represent a God hovering in the higher regions, but a God who became an individual human."

Now I want you to note this. According to the author of *The Christ Myth*, Paul pictures a Christ who really became human. The strange part is, however, that (according to Drews himself) St. Paul is supposed to have stopped short at that idea. He is supposed to have grasped the idea of a Christ who really became human, although, according to him, Christ never existed as such. St. Paul is therefore supposed to say that the highest idea possible is that of a God, a Christ, not only hovering in the higher regions, but having descended to Earth and become human. It never entered his mind that this

Christ actually did live on Earth in a human being. This means that the author of *The Christ Myth* attributes to St. Paul a conception of the Christ that to sound thinking is a mockery. St. Paul is made to say, "Christ must certainly have been an individual human being, but, although I preach about him, I deny his existence in any historical sense."

That is the nucleus around which the whole subject turns. Truly, one does not require much theological or critical erudition to refute it. One need only confront Professor Drews as a philosopher. His Christ concept cannot possibly stand. The Pauline Christ concept in the sense in which Drews takes it cannot be maintained without accepting the historical Jesus. Professor Drews's book itself demands the existence of the historical Jesus. It would seem, therefore, that a book centered upon a contradiction that turns all inner logic into a mockery can be widely accepted today. Can human thought really travel such crooked paths as these? If so, why? Anyone who wishes to understand clearly the development of humanity must find the answer to this question.

The reason is that what people believe or think at any given period is not the result of logical thought but of their feelings and emotions. They believe and think what they wish to think. In particular, those who are preparing the Christ concept for the coming age feel a strong urge to shut out from their hearts everything to be found in the old external records. Yet they also feel an urge to prove everything by such external documents. Considered from a purely material standpoint, however, these lose their value after a certain lapse of time. That time has already come for Homer and Shakespeare, and so it will come for Goethe also, when people will try to prove that a historical Goethe never existed. In the course of time, historical records must lose their value from a material standpoint.

What must we do, then, seeing that we are already living in an age when the thought of its most prominent representatives is such that they have an impulse in their hearts urging them toward the denial of the historical Christ? What is necessary as a new impulse of spiritual life? We must come to understand the historical Jesus in a spiritual way. Indeed, in what other way can this fact be expressed?

As we know, Saul became Paul at the event of Damascus. We also know that to him that event was the great revelation, whereas all he had heard at Jerusalem on the physical plane as direct information had not been able to change him. What convinced him was his Damascus revelation from the spiritual worlds. Christianity really came into being through that revelation, and through that revelation Paul gained the power to proclaim the Christ. Did he experience a purely abstract idea that might be contradicted? No. He was convinced by what he had seen in the spiritual worlds that Christ had lived on Earth, had suffered, died, and risen. As Paul quite rightly said, "If Christ be not risen, then is my teaching vain" (1 Cor. 15:14). Paul did not receive the mere idea, the concept of Christ from the spiritual worlds; he convinced himself of the reality of the Christ, who died on Golgotha. To Paul that was proof of the historical Jesus.

What then is necessary, now that the time is approaching when, as a result of the materialism of the age, the historical records are losing their value, when everyone can quite easily prove that these records cannot withstand criticism, and when nothing can be proved externally and historically? People must learn that Christ can be recognized as the historical Jesus without any external records whatever, that, by correct training, the "event" at Damascus can be renewed in each human being. Indeed, in the near future it will be renewed for humanity as a whole, so that it will be absolutely possible to be convinced of the existence of the historical Jesus. This is the new way in which the world must find the road to him.

It is unimportant that such a book as *The Christ Myth* contains certain errors. What matters is that it was possible to write it. It shows that quite different methods are necessary so that Christ may remain with humanity and be rediscovered.

A person, who thinks of humanity and its needs, and of how human souls express themselves externally, will not ask, "What do those who think differently matter to me? I have my own convictions and they are quite enough." Most people do not realize what dreadful egoism underlies such words.

It was not as the result of an idea, an outer ideal, or of some personal predilection that a movement arose through which people might learn that it is possible to find the way into the spiritual world and that, among other things, Christ himself can be found there. This movement arose in response to a necessity in the course of the nineteenth century. It arose so that possibilities could flow down from the spiritual worlds into the physical world, through which people could obtain spiritual truth in a new way, since the old way had died out.

I have repeatedly stressed that the first thing for us in our movement is not to take our stand on any external record or document, but to ask just what is revealed to clairvoyant consciousness when one ascends to the spiritual worlds. If, through some catastrophe, all the historical proofs of the historical Jesus of the Gospels and of the Epistles of Paul were lost, what would independent spiritual consciousness tell us? What do we learn about the spiritual worlds on the path that can be trodden any hour of the day by each and every one of us? We are told that in the spiritual worlds we will find the Christ even though we know nothing historically of the fact that he was on Earth at the beginning of our era.

The fact that must be established by a repeated renewal of the Damascus event is that there is an original proof of the historical personality of Jesus of Nazareth. Schoolchildren are not told they must believe the three angles of a triangle equal 180 degrees simply because it was stated as a fact in the past. They are asked to prove it. Just so, we today testify out of a spiritual consciousness not only that Christ has always existed, but also that the historical Jesus can be found in the spiritual worlds. We witness that he is a reality, and that he was a reality at the very time tradition says he was.

We have gone further in fact. We have shown that what we established by spiritual perception without the Gospels is to be rediscovered within them. We can then feel a deep respect and reverence for the Gospels, finding in them again what we found in the spiritual worlds independently of them, and we know that they must have come from the same sources of supersensible illumination from which we draw today. We know they must be records of the spiritual worlds.

The purpose of what we call the Theosophical movement is to make such a method of observation possible, to make it possible for spiritual life to play its part in science. The stimulus to bring this about had to be given by the Theosophical Society. That is one side of the question. The other is that this stimulus had to be given when the time was ripe for it. This is proved by the fact that today, thirty years after the birth of the Theosophical movement, the story of the non-historical Jesus still persists. How much is known outside this movement of the possibility of the historical Jesus being discovered in any way other than through external documents? What was begun in the nineteenth century continues, and the authority of religious documents is still being undermined. Thus, while there was the greatest necessity for this new possibility to be given to humanity, the preparations made for its reception were the smallest conceivable.

Do we in any way believe that our modern philosophers are particularly ready to receive this new possibility? How unprepared they are can be seen by the concept they have of the Christ of St. Paul. Anyone acquainted with scientific life knows that this is the great and final result of the materialism that has been developing for centuries. Although it asserts that it wishes to rise above materialism, the mode of thought prevailing in science has not progressed beyond what is in the process of dying out. Science as it exists today is certainly a ripe fruit but one that must suffer the fate of all ripe fruit. It must begin to decay. No one can assert that it could bring forth a new impulse for the renewal of its mode of thought or of its methods of reaching conclusions. When we think of this, we realize, apart from all other considerations, the weight of the stimulus given through H. P. Blavatsky.

No matter what our opinions of her capacities and the details of her life may be, she was the instrument through whom the stimulus was given, and she proved herself fully competent for the purpose.

We who as members of the Theosophical Society are taking part in celebrating such a day as this are in a peculiar position. We are celebrating a personal festival that is dedicated to one person. Now, although the belief in authority is certainly a dangerous thing in the external world, the danger is reduced through the jealousy and envy that play so great a part. Even though a few persons manifest reverence outwardly and rather strongly by burning incense, egoism and envy still have considerable power over them. In the Theosophical movement the danger of injury through the worship of personality and belief in authority is particularly great. We are, therefore, in a peculiar position when we celebrate a festival dedicated to a personality. Not only the customs of the time but also the matter itself places us in a difficult position, because revelations of the higher worlds must always come through a person. Personalities must be the bearers of revelation, but we must take care not to confuse the one with the other. We have to receive revelations through the medium of personalities. This raises the question of whether they are worthy of our confidence: "What they did on such and such a day does not harmonize with our ideas; can we, therefore, believe in the whole thing?"

In some sense, this reaction forms part of a certain tendency of our time that may be described as lack of devotion to truth. How often today we hear of some prominent person who may please the public for one or more decades. At first, what the person may do may be quite satisfactory because the public is too lazy to go into the matter. Some years later, if it should transpire that this person's private life is open to suspicion and not all that it might be, the idol is toppled. The point is not whether this is right or not. The point is that, even though the person may be the means by which spiritual life comes to us, we ought to acquire the feeling that it is our duty to prove this for ourselves. Indeed, we ought to test the person by the truth, rather than to test the truth by the person. That should especially be our attitude in the Theosophical movement. We pay most respect to a personality when we do not encumber him or her with belief in authority, as people are so fond of doing, because we know that the activity of that personality after death is transferred to the spiritual world.

We are justified in saying that the activity of H. P. Blavatsky still continues and that we, within the movement she instigated, can either further that activity or injure it. We injure it most severely if we blindly believe in her, swearing by what she thought when she lived on the physical plane, and blindly believing in her authority. We revere and help her most when we are fully conscious that she provided the stimulus for a movement that originated from one of the deepest necessities in human evolution. While we see that this movement had to come, we nevertheless ascribe the stimulus for it to her.

However, many years have gone by since that time. Now we must prove ourselves worthy of her work by acknowledging that what was started then must now be carried further. We admit it had to be instigated by her, but let us not ferret about in her private affairs, especially at the present moment. We know the significance of the impetus she gave, but we also know it only imperfectly represents what is to come.

When we recall all that has been put before our souls during the past winter, we cannot but say that what Madame Blavatsky started is indeed of deep and incisive importance. How immeasurable, however, is all that she could not accomplish in that introductory act of hers! What has just been said about the necessity in the Theosophical movement for a right understanding of the Christ experience was, for example, completely hidden from Madame Blavatsky. Her task was to indicate the seeds of truth in the religions of the Indian, Persian, Egypto-Chaldean, and Greek peoples. A comprehension of the revelations given in the Old and New Testaments was denied her. We honor the positive work accomplished by this personality, and we shall not refer to all that she was unable to do and that was concealed from her, which we must now contribute. Those who allow themselves to be stirred by H. P. Blavatsky and wish to go further than she did will say, "If the stimulus she gave in the Theosophical movement is to be carried further, we must attain an understanding of the Christ event."

The early Theosophical movement failed to grasp the religious and spiritual life of the Old and New Testaments, which is why everything in the early movement is wide of the mark. The Theosophical movement now has the task of making this good and of adding what was not given before. If we inwardly feel these facts, they will be experienced as a claim, as it were, made by our Theosophical conscience.

Thus, we visualize H. P. Blavatsky as the herald of a new light of dawn. What good would that light be, if it were not to illumine the most important thing that humanity has ever possessed? A Theosophy that does not provide the means of understanding Christianity is absolutely valueless to our present civilization. Should it become an instrument for understanding Christianity, then we would be making the right use of it. What are we doing if we do not do this, if we do not use the impulse given by H. P. Blavatsky for this purpose? We are arresting the activity of her spirit in our age. Everything is evolving, including the spirit of Helena Petrovna Blavatsky.

Her spirit is now working in the spiritual world to further the progress of the Theosophical movement. If, however, we sit before her and the book she wrote, saying that we will raise a monument to her consisting of her own works, who then is making her spirit earthbound? Who is condemning her to remain where she was when on Earth? We, ourselves. We revere and acknowledge her value if, even as she went beyond her time, we also go further than she did just as long as the grace ruling the development of the world continues to vouchsafe spiritual revelations from the spiritual world.

This is what we place before our souls today as a question of conscience. After all, that is most in accord with the wishes of our colleague H. S. Olcott, the first president of the Theosophical Society, who has also now passed into the spiritual world.

Let us inscribe this in our souls today since it is precisely through lack of knowledge of the living Theosophical life that all the shadowy sides of the Theosophical movement have arisen. If the Theosophical movement were to carry out its great original impulse unweakened, and with a holy conscience, it would possess the force to drive out all the harmful influences that have come in as time has passed, as well as others still to come. The one thing we must earnestly do is to continue to develop the impulse.

In many places today we see Theosophists who think they are doing good work and who feel happy to be able to say they are now doing things that are in conformity with external science. How pleasing it is to many leading Theosophists if they can point out that those who study the various religions confirm what has come from the spiritual world, while they fail to observe that it is just this unspiritual mode of comparison that must be overcome. Theosophy, for instance, comes into close contact with the thoughts that led to the denial of the historical Jesus. Indeed, there is a certain relation between them. Originally Theosophy ranked the historical Jesus with other founders of religions. It never occurred to Madame Blavatsky to deny the historical Jesus, though she certainly placed him one hundred years late. She did not deny his existence, but she did not recognize him either. Even though she instigated the movement in which he may someday be known, she was not able herself to recognize him. Here, the first state of the Theosophical movement comes strangely into line with what those who deny the historical Jesus are doing today.

Professor Drews, for instance, points out that the events that led up to the Mystery of Golgotha may also be found in the accounts of the old gods—in the cults of Adonis or Tammuz, where we find a suffering god-hero, a dying god-hero, and a risen god-hero. What is contained in these various old religious traditions is constantly being dragged out. We are told of a Jesus of Nazareth who suffered, died, and rose again and that he was the Christ. Then we are told that other peoples worshipped an Adonis, a Tammuz. The similarity between what happened in Palestine and the accounts of the old gods is constantly insisted upon.

These comparisons are also made in the Theosophical movement. People do not realize that comparing the religions of Adonis or Tammuz with the events that took place in Palestine proves nothing. I will show you by means of an example wherein such comparisons are at fault. They appear to be correct on the surface, but there is a serious flaw in them.

Suppose that an official living in 1910 wore a certain uniform as an outer sign of his official activity and that in 1930 a different man wore the same uniform. It will not be the uniform, but the individual wearing it that will determine the efficiency of the work he accomplishes. Now suppose that in the year 2090 a historian comes forward and says, "I have ascertained that in 1910 a man lived who wore a particular type of coat and trousers and that the same outfit was also being worn in 1930. Thus we see that these clothes have been carried over from 1910 to 1930, and so on both occasions we are confronted by the same person."

Such a conclusion would, of course, be foolish, but no more so than to say that in the religions of the Middle East we find in Adonis or Tammuz the same suffering, death, and resurrection as we find in the Christ. The point is not that suffering, death, and resurrection were experiences, but rather by whom they were experienced. Suffering, death, and resurrection in the historical development of the world are comparable to the uniform in the example given above. We should not point to the uniform we find in legends but rather to the individuals who wear it. It is true that individualities, in order that humans may understand them, have performed Christly deeds, so to say, which show that they too are capable of the accomplishments of a Tammuz, for instance, but each time there was a different being behind the acts. Therefore, all religious comparisons that hope to prove the correspondence between Siegfried and Baldur, Baldur and Tammuz, and so on are only a sign that legends and myths take similar forms in different peoples. In trying to gain knowledge of humanity, there is no more value in these comparisons than there would be in pointing out that a certain type of uniform is found at a later time to be in use for the same office. This is the fundamental error prevailing everywhere, even in the Theosophical movement. It is nothing but the result of materialistic thinking.

Madame Blavatsky's will and testament will be fulfilled only if the Theosophical movement can cultivate and preserve the life of the spirit. It must look to the manifesting spirit and not to books that someone may have written. Spirit should be cultivated among us. We must not merely study books written centuries ago, but must also develop the spirit that has been given us in a living way. Then the Theosophical movement will be a union of persons who do not simply believe in books or in individuals, but in the living spirit.

We will not then merely talk about Madame Blavatsky having departed from the physical plane and living on after her death. We will believe in what has been revealed through Theosophy in such a living way that our lives on the physical plane will not be made a hindrance to the further supersensible activity of her spirit. Only when we think about her in this way will the Theosophical movement be of use. Only when men and women who think in this way are to be found on Earth can H. P. Blavatsky do anything for the movement.

For this it is necessary that further spiritual research should be made. Above all, people should learn what was asserted in the last public lecture when I spoke of the fact that something approximating conscience came into being at the time of Jesus Christ. Such things do arise and are of significance to the whole of evolution. At a particular point of time conscience arose. Before that, it was altogether a different thing. It will be different again after the soul has developed further in the light of conscience.

Paralleling the appearance of Damascus, a great many people will experience something like the following in the course of the twentieth century. As soon as they have acted in some way, they will learn to contemplate their deed. They will become more thoughtful and will have an inner picture of the deed. Only a few will experience this at first, but the numbers will increase during the next two or three thousand years. As soon as people do something, a picture will be there. At first they will not understand it, but those who have studied spiritual science will know that it is not a dream but a picture showing the karmic fulfillment of the act. They will know that one day what is pictured will take place as the fulfillment, the karmic balancing, of what was done. This experience will begin in the twentieth century. People will begin to develop the faculty of seeing before them pictures of far-distant acts still to be accomplished. These pictures will show themselves as inner counterparts of people's actions, the karmic fulfillment that will one day take place. Then people will be able to say that they have been shown what they will have to do to compensate for what they have done. They will know that they cannot become perfect until the compensation has been made. When these inner pictures are experienced, karma will cease to be mere theory.

Such faculties are becoming more common. New capacities are developing but the old are the seeds for the new. What will make it possible for us to see the karmic pictures? It will come as the result of the soul having stood for some time in the light of conscience. It is not the soul's various external physical experiences that are of the most importance to it, but rather its progress toward perfection. By the help of conscience, the soul is now preparing for what has just been described. The more incarnations people have in which they cultivate and perfect conscience, the more they are acquiring that higher faculty through which, in the form of spiritual vision, the voice of God will again speak to them. This is the same voice of God that was formerly experienced in a different way. Aeschylus portrayed Orestes as having a vision of what was brought about by his evil actions. The new capacity developing in the soul is such that people will see in pictures the effects of their deeds for the future. That is the new stage. Development proceeds in cycles, following a circular pattern, and what people once possessed in older vision comes back again in a new form.

Through knowledge of the spiritual world we are really preparing to awake in the right way in our next incarnation. This knowledge also helps us to work in the right way for those who are to come after us. For this reason, Theosophy is not an egotistical movement. It does not concern itself with what benefits the individual alone but with what makes for the progress of all humankind. . . .

In this spirit let us endeavor to make ourselves capable of preparing a field in our movement in which the impulse of Blavatsky shall not be hindered and arrested, but shall progress to further development.

8

Ancient Wisdom and the Heralding of the Christ Impulse

Cologne, May 8, 1912

THE MEETING TODAY is an occasion that demands an introduction to our studies. It is the day known in the Theosophical movement as White Lotus Day, commemorating the yearly anniversary of the day on which Madame Helena Petrovna Blavatsky, the founder of the present Theosophical movement, left the physical plane. Very little effort is needed to touch a chord in every soul present here today in order to evoke feelings of admiration, veneration, and gratitude toward the individuality who came to the Earth in Helena Petrovna Blavatsky. By devoting herself to what she clearly realized to be the task of the modern age, she inspired people to turn their minds again to the ancient, holy Mysteries from which all the forces and impulses needed for human spiritual development have proceeded. . . .

I feel in full accord with the individuality of H. P. Blavatsky if, above all today, a few words of plain truth are spoken about her. It was characteristic of her that when she was fully herself she desired, above everything else, to be true. Therefore we can best honor her when we direct our grateful thoughts to her and speak a few words of unvarnished truth.

In her being as a whole, in her individuality, H. P. Blavatsky revealed what inner strength, what a powerful impulse was inherent in the spiritual movement we call the Theosophical movement. To substantiate this I need only refer to the first of her more important works, *Isis Unveiled*. Confronted with this book, ordinary readers will have the impression of a truly chaotic, bewildering confusion. Those who are aware of the existence of an age-old wisdom, guarded in the Mysteries and protected from profane eyes, will have the same impression. Yet they know that such wisdom is not acquired by external human effort but has been kept safe in secret societies. Certainly they will find much that is chaotic in this book, but they will find something else as well. They will find a work that courageously and daringly presents certain secrets of the Mysteries to the secular world *for the first time.* One who understands will be astonished at what an infinite amount of this wisdom has been correctly interpreted and will conclude that only an initiate could do that.

Nevertheless, the impression of chaos remains. This may be explained by the following reasoned consideration. The way in which *Isis Unveiled* is written shows that Madame Blavatsky could not possibly have produced what she had to give to the world out of her own outer personality, out of her own soul. The way in which she was incarnated in her physical body, the nature of her intellect, her personal characteristics, and her sympathies and antipathies show that she could not have written this book unaided. She communicates things that she herself was quite incapable of understanding. Anyone who thinks about this must come to the conclusion that higher, spiritual individualities used the body and personality of H. P. Blavatsky to communicate what, according to the need of the times, had to be inculcated into humanity.

Indeed the impossibility of attributing to her what she has given us is in itself living proof of the fact that those individualities who are connected with the Theosophical movement, *the Masters of Wisdom and Harmony of Feelings,* found an instrument in H. P. Blavatsky. Those who see clearly in such matters know that the knowledge did not originate in her but that it flowed through her from lofty spiritual individualities. Naturally, today is not the appropriate time to speak about these matters in detail.

Now the question might arise, and it often does, Why did those lofty individualities choose Madame Blavatsky as their instrument? They did so because in spite of everything she was the most suitable. Why did the choice not fall upon one of the learned specialists dealing with the science of comparative religion? We need think only of the greatest, most highly respected authority on Oriental religions, the renowned Max Müller, and his own pronouncements will tell us why he could not have proclaimed what had to be communicated through the human instrument of Madame Blavatsky.[1] When the religious systems of the East and Madame Blavatsky's expositions of them became known, Müller responded by saying, "If, somewhere in the street, a pig is seen and is grunting, that is not considered very remarkable, but if a human being walks along the street grunting like a pig, that is considered remarkable indeed." The implication is that one who is not prepared to distort the religious systems of the East in the style of Max Müller is like a person who grunts like a pig. In any case, the comparison does not seem to me very logical, for why should one be astonished when a pig grunts; but if a human being grunts, that would be a feat not everyone would be capable of. The comparison is rather lame, but that it could be made at all shows clearly enough that Max Müller was not the right personality.

So the choice had to fall upon a person of no particular intellectual eminence. This situation naturally had many disadvantages. Thus Madame Blavatsky brought all the sympathy and antipathy of her extremely passionate nature into the great message. She had a strong antipathy to the world conception that springs from the Old and New Testaments. She had a strong antipathy to Judaism and Christianity.

But to apprehend the ancient wisdom of humanity in its pure, primal form one condition is indispensable, namely to face the revelations from the higher worlds in a state of perfect emotional and mental balance. Antipathy and sympathy form a kind of fog before the inner eye. Thus it came about that Madame Blavatsky's perception became more and more enveloped in a kind of fog, and her mind remained clear only for so-called purely "Aryan" traditions. Here she looked into spiritual depths with great clarity, but she became one-sided as a result, so it came about that in her second great work, *The Secret Doctrine*, the early Aryan religion was presented in a biased form. Because of this antipathy, to look for anything about the Mystery of Sinai or of Golgotha in Blavatsky's writings would be useless. Hence she was led to powers who, with great forcefulness and clarity, could impart all *non-Christian* wisdom. This is revealed in the wonderful "Stanzas of Dzyan," which Madame Blavatsky quotes in *The Secret Doctrine*. But however wonderful they may be, *The Secret Doctrine* diverted her from the path of initiation in the physical world implied, although only in a fragmentary way, in *Isis Unveiled*. Bound as she was by a one-sided initiation, Madame Blavatsky could present in *The Secret Doctrine* only the aspect of spiritual knowledge inspired by the non-Christian world conception. Thus *The Secret Doctrine* contains the greatest revelations of this order that humanity was able to receive at the time. It contains themes that may also be found in other writings, namely in the so-called Mahatma Letters of the Masters of

Wisdom and Harmony of Feelings.[2] In these again we may find some of the greatest wisdom given to humankind.

But there are other sections of *The Secret Doctrine*—for instance, those dealing in great detail with the quantum theory. Anyone who truly understands must reckon the "Stanzas of Dzyan" and the Letters of the Masters among the highest revelations vouchsafed to humanity. But they must also conclude from the extensive sections dealing with the quantum theory that they are the work of a person incapable of laying down her pen and suffering from a mania for writing down whatever came into her head. Then there are other sections where a deeply rooted passionate nature discourses on scientific topics without reliable knowledge of the subject. Thus, *The Secret Doctrine* is a weird mixture of themes, some of which should be eliminated, while others contain the highest wisdom.

All this becomes comprehensible when we consider what was said by one of H. P. Blavatsky's friends who had deep insight into her character. He said that Madame Blavatsky was really a threefold phenomenon. Firstly she was a dumpy, plain woman with a magical mind and a passionate nature, always losing her temper. To be sure, she was good-natured, affectionate, and compassionate, but she was certainly not what one calls a gifted woman. Secondly, when the great truths became articulated through her, she was the pupil of the great Masters. Then her facial expression and her gestures changed; she became a different person and the spiritual worlds spoke through her. Finally, there was a third, awe-inspiring, supreme, regal figure. This occurred in the rare moments when the Masters themselves spoke through her.

Lovers of truth will always carefully distinguish in Madame Blavatsky's works what is essential and what is not. No greater service could be rendered to the one who is in our thoughts today than to look at her in the light of truth. No greater service could be done to her than to lead the Theosophical movement in the light of truth.

Naturally, in the beginning the Theosophical movement had to follow a particular course; but now it has become a matter of great importance that another stream should flow into the movement. It has become necessary to add to the Theosophical movement the stream that since the thirteenth century has been flowing from occult sources, sources to which Madame Blavatsky had no access.

So today we are doing full justice to the aims of the Theosophical movement not only by recognizing the religious creeds and world conceptions of the East, but by adding to them those that came to expression in the revelations of Sinai and in the Mystery of Golgotha.

And perhaps today it may be permissible to ask whether the scope of the Theosophical movement as a whole calls for the addition of what in the nature of things could not be given at the beginning— whether, in fact, an extremely questionable kind of specialization should be given out as truth through teaching and dogma?

I for my part say unreservedly that I know how great a wrong we would be doing to the spirit of H. P. Blavatsky now in the spiritual world if the latter course were taken. I know that it is not opposing but acting in harmony with that spirit if we do what it wants today, namely, to add to the Theosophical movement what that spirit was unable to give while in the earthly body. And I know I am not speaking against Madame Blavatsky but in complete harmony with her when I say the one thing I wish for is that our Western conception of the world shall come to its own in this Theosophical movement.

In recent years, knowledge and truths of many different kinds have become available. Let us assume that in fifty years' time everything will have to be corrected. Let us assume that not one stone will be left upon another in our spiritual edifice, as we picture it today, and that in fifty years' time occult investigation will have rectified everything fundamentally. Then my comment would be, Perhaps! But one thing will remain and should remain as the object of the main endeavor of our Western Theosophical movement. Namely, that it may truly be said that there was once a Theosophical movement whose one ideal in the field of occultism was to establish only what springs from the purest, utterly unsullied sense of *truth*. Our aim is that this may be said of us. We had better leave things still in doubt unsaid rather than deviate in any way from that course for which a pure sense of truth can take full responsibility before all the spiritual powers.

From this, however, something else follows.

Someone might feel called upon to ask why we reject this or that. Our answer is that our conception of tolerance (although others may have a different idea of it) is that we feel obliged to protect humankind from what could not hold its own before the forum of pure truth. Although our work may be misrepresented, we shall stand firm and try to fulfill our task by rejecting whatever must be rejected if we are to serve our purpose. Therefore, when anything conflicts with our sense of truth, we reject it, but only then. We obey no other sentiments or reasons. Nor will we indulge in trite phrases about equal rights of opinion, brotherhood, and so on, knowing that the love of people for one another can bear fruit only if it is sincere and true. It is fitting, particularly on this day of commemoration, that we should express this will to be inspired by the purest sense of truth.

Since new knowledge has been gained in the way I have indicated, much that can help to explain mysteries of the universe has come to light. Nothing is ever said to discriminate between the great cultures or religious movements of the human race. Has it not been said many times, when considering the first post-Atlantean epoch with the spiritual culture inspired by the Holy Rishis, that there we have something spiritually more sublime than anything that has followed it? Neither should we ever think of belittling Buddhism; on the contrary, we emphasize its merits, knowing it has given humanity benefits such as Christianity will be able to achieve only in the future. What is of immense importance, however, is that again and again we point to the difference that distinguishes Oriental culture from Western culture.

Oriental culture speaks only of individualities who, in the course of evolution, have passed through several incarnations. For instance, it speaks of the Bodhisattvas, describing them as individualities who pass through their human development more quickly than is usual. Thus Oriental culture is concerned only with what, as individuality, passes from incarnation to incarnation until in a certain incarnation such a Bodhisattva becomes a Buddha. When Bodhisattvas have become Buddhas—which can happen only on Earth—they have advanced so far that they need not descend again into a body of flesh. And so the further back we go, the more we find interest focused primarily on the individuality and less on the single incarnation. What is really in mind when speaking of the Buddha is not so much the historical Buddha, the Suddhodana Prince, but rather a *degree of attainment*, a rank that other Bodhisattvas also attain in the course of their successive lives.

In the West, however, it is different. We have lived through an epoch of culture that has nothing to say about the individuality who passes from life to life, but values only the single personality. We speak of Socrates, Plato, Caesar, Goethe, Spinoza, Fichte, Raphael, Michelangelo. We think of them only in the one incarnation. We do not speak of the individuality who goes from incarnation to incarnation, but we speak of the personality. We speak of *one* Socrates, *one* Plato, *one* Goethe, and so on; we speak only of a single life in which the individuality has found expression. Western culture was destined to stress the importance of the single personality, to bring it to vigorous, characteristic maturity, and to disregard the individuality passing from life to life. But the time has come when we must again learn gradually to recognize how the eternal individuality passes through the several single personalities. Now we find that humankind is striving to apprehend what it is that lives on from personality to personality. That will fire the imagination and illumine human souls with a new light of understanding. This can be illustrated by a particular example.

We turn our eyes to a figure such as the prophet Elijah. First of all we think of the prophet himself. But the essential significance of this prophet is the fact that in a certain way he prepared for the Mystery of Golgotha; he indicated that the Jahve impulse is something that can be understood and grasped only in the I. Elijah was unable to reveal the full significance of the human I, because for I-consciousness he represents a halfway stage between the Mosiac idea of Jehovah and the Christian idea of Christ. Thus the prophet Elijah is revealed to us as a mighty herald, an advance messenger of the Christ Impulse, of what came to pass through the Mystery of Golgotha. We see him as a great and mighty figure.

Now let us turn to another figure. The West is accustomed to thinking of him as a single personality. I refer to John the Baptist. The West sees him confined within his personality. But we learn to know him as the herald of Christ; we follow his life as the forerunner of Christ, as the man who first uttered the words, "Change the disposition of your souls, for the kingdom of heaven is at hand." He indicated the impulse that was to come through Golgotha: that divinity can be found within the human I, that the Christ I is to enter more and more deeply into the human I, and that this impulse is near at hand.

Now, through spiritual science, we learn the truth that is also indicated in the Bible, namely that the same individuality who lived in the prophet Elijah also lived in John the Baptist. He who as Elijah heralded the Christ was reincarnated as John the Baptist, again heralding the Christ in the way appropriate for his time. For us these two figures are now united. Eastern culture proceeds in a different way, concentrating on individualities and neglecting the single personality.

Passing on now to the Middle Ages, we find that extraordinary figure who was born—as if to give an outward indication of his special connection with the spiritual world—on Good Friday in the year 1483 and died in early manhood at the age of thirty-seven. This figure is a phenomenal influence through his gifts to humanity. I refer to the painter Raphael. He was born on a Good Friday as if to show that he is connected with the event commemorated on Good Friday. What, in the light of spiritual science, can the West experience through the figure of Raphael? If we study this figure in the light of spiritual science we shall discover that Raphael accomplished more for the spreading of Christianity, for the penetration of an interconfessional Christianity into human hearts, than all the theological interpreters, than all the cardinals and popes of his time. Before the eyes of Raphael's soul there may have risen a picture of the scene described in the Acts of the Apostles (17:22–31). A figure stands before the Athenians and says, "You people of Athens worship the gods ignorantly, with external signs. But there is the God that you can learn to *know.* This is the God who lives and weaves in everything that has life. That God is the Christ who suffered death and has arisen, thereby giving humanity the impulse leading to resurrection." Some did not listen; others thought it strange. In Raphael's soul this event came to expression in the painting, now hanging in the Vatican, that is incorrectly named *The School of Athens.*

In reality, this painting depicts the figure of Paul teaching the Athenians the fundamental principles of Christianity. In this picture Raphael has given something that seems like a heralding of the Christianity that transcends denominations. The profound meaning of this picture has not yet dawned upon people.

Of the other pictures of Raphael it must be said that whereas nothing has remained of what cardinals and popes did for humanity at that time, Raphael's work is only today becoming a vital force. How little Raphael was understood in recent times is shown by the fact that Goethe, visiting Dresden, failed to admire the Sistine Madonna. He had heard from the official at the Museum, who was only expressing the general opinion of the day, that there was something commonplace about the facial expression of the Child Jesus. He was also told that only some dauber could have added the two angels at the bottom of the picture, and that the Madonna herself could not be the work of Raphael, but must have been painted over. If we look through the whole of eighteenth-century literature we shall find hardly anything about Raphael. Even Voltaire does not mention him.

And today? Today, Raphael's pictures move people whether they are Protestants or Catholics or anything else. Today, we can see how a great cosmic mystery reveals itself to human hearts in the Sistine Madonna. We can recognize that through human hearts this mystery will carry its impulse into the future, when humanity will have been led to a broad and all-embracing interconfessional Christianity, such as we already have in spiritual science. This impulse will continue to work as a result of the fact that a wonderful mystery has inspired human souls through Raphael's Sistine Madonna. I have often said that when one looks into a child's eyes, one can know that what is gazing out of those eyes is something that has not come into existence through birth, something that reveals the depths of the human soul. One who studies the children in Raphael's Madonna pictures can see that divinity itself, an occult and superhuman reality, looks out of those eyes—something that is still present in the child in the earliest period after birth. This can be perceived in all Raphael's paintings of children, with one exception. The portrayal of one child is different, that of the Jesus Child in the Sistine Madonna painting. Whoever looks into the eyes of that Child knows that they already reveal *more* than can be embodied in a human being. Raphael has made this distinction to show that in this one Child, the Child of the Sistine Madonna, there lives something that is already experiencing, in advance, a reality of pure spirit, a Christlike reality.

Thus Raphael is a harbinger of the spiritual Christ who is revealed again by spiritual science. Through spiritual science, too, we learn that in Raphael there lived the same individuality who had lived in Elijah and in John the Baptist. We can understand that the world in which he lived as John the Baptist reappears in Raphael when we observe how his relation to the historic Christ Event is indicated by the fact that he was born on a Good Friday.

Here, then, we have the third harbinger after Elijah and John the Baptist. Now we understand many of the questions inevitably raised by those possessed of wider powers of perception. John the Baptist dies the death of a martyr before the event of Golgotha draws near. He lives through the dawn leading to the Mystery of Golgotha, through the time of prophecies and predictions, through the days of rejoicing, but not through the period of lamentation and sorrow. When this same mood manifest again in the personality of Raphael, do we not find it comprehensible that he paints pictures of the Madonna and of children with such deep devotion? Is it not obvious why he does not paint the betrayal by Judas, the bearing of the Cross, Golgotha, and the Mount of Olives? Any existing pictures of these subjects must have been commissioned, for the essential being of Raphael finds no expression in them. Why are such pictures alien to him? Because as John the Baptist he did not live to experience the Mystery of Golgotha.

Thus, as we think of the figure of Raphael, we think how he has lived through the centuries and is still living today. We think of what remains of his work and what has already been destroyed. We reflect that all material things must eventually perish. Then we know well that the living essence of these pictures will have been taken into human souls before the pictures themselves will have perished. For centuries yet, reproductions will of course be available; but what alone gives a true idea of Raphael's personality, of what he was, what his own hands accomplished, will crumble into dust. His works will perish. And nothing on our Earth can preserve them.

Yet it is clear to us through spiritual science that the individuality in Raphael bears what has been achieved in one incarnation into the next. And we learn that this same Elijah-John-Raphael individuality appears again in the poet Novalis.[3] We take his first proclamation, which, like a radiant sunrise, reveals a new and living concept of Christ, and we say to ourselves that long before Raphael's works will disappear from the outer world, the individuality in that personality returned to bequeath his gifts in a new form to humankind. How good it is that for a time Western culture has paid attention only to the actual personality, that we have learned to love a personality simply from the fruits of a single life! And how immeasurably enriched must our souls feel when we learn that the eternal part of a human being passes from personality to personality.

And however different these personalities may seem to us, the concrete facts that spiritual knowledge provides about reincarnation and karma somehow bring us understanding also. Humanity will profit more from details that can throw light upon individual cases than from general concepts. On this basis much that is attainable only through intuitive vision and occult investigation can be brought to bear on these matters. Then, finally, we will be able to turn our gaze to the Mystery of Golgotha itself and remind ourselves that in the thirtieth year of the life of Jesus of Nazareth the Christ entered into Jesus and lived through the Mystery of Golgotha.

When it is maintained nowadays that the Christ cannot incarnate in a physical body, it must be said that that has really never been asserted. For the physical body into which the spiritual Christ entered at that time was the sheath of Jesus of Nazareth. In that case it was not as it is with other individualities who build up their bodies themselves. The Christ descended into the body that had been prepared by Jesus of Nazareth. True, there was then union, but we cannot really speak of a physical incarnation of Christ. To one who has knowledge, these matters are self-evident.

We know that through this Christ Impulse, as it streams into the different civilizations of humankind, something has come to the Earth, has flowed into humanity, for the benefit of all humanity. What went through death is like a seed of corn that multiplies and can make its way into individual human souls and spring to life. As we know that the body of Jesus of Nazareth had received the Christ Being who, by passing through death, united himself with the Earth, let us now ask, What will be the outcome of this when the Earth has reached its goal and comes to its end? Christ, who united himself with the Earth, will be the one reality on Earth when it has reached its goal. Christ will be the Spirit of the Earth. In fact, he is already the Spirit of the Earth—only then human souls will be permeated by him, and humanity will form a whole with him.

Now another question arises. We have learned that a human being in earthly form is to be regarded as *maya*. The form disintegrates after death; what appears outwardly as the human body is an illusion. The external form of the physical body will no more remain than the physical bodies of plants, animals, and minerals will remain. Physical bodies will become cosmic dust. What is now the visible physical Earth will completely vanish, will exist no longer. And what then of etheric bodies? They have meaning and purpose only as long as they have to renew the life of physical bodies, and they too will cease to exist. When the Earth has reached its goal, what will remain of all we behold? Nothing at all will be there, nothing of ourselves, nothing of the beings of the other kingdoms of nature. When the spiritual is set free nothing will be left of matter but formless dust, for the Spirit alone is real. But something will then have become a reality, something that in times gone by had not been united with the Earth at all, with which human souls will now unite—namely, the Christ Spirit. The Christ Spirit will be the one and only reality that can remain of the Earth.

But how does this Christ Spirit acquire his spiritual sheaths? In the Mystery of Golgotha he descended into the sphere of Earth as an Impulse, as the Soul of the Earth.

It does not happen in the same way as in human beings, but the Christ too must form for himself something that can be called his sheaths. Christ will eventually have a kind of spiritualized physical body, a kind of etheric body and a kind of astral body. Of what will these bodies consist?

These are questions that for the time being can only be hinted at. When the Christ descended to the Earth he had to provide himself with something similar to the sheaths of a human being: a physical body, an etheric body, and an astral body. Gradually, in the course of the epochs, something that corresponds to an astral, an etheric, and a physical body will be formed around the originally purely spiritual Christ Impulse that descended at the Baptism by John. All these sheaths will be formed from forces that have to be developed by humanity on Earth. What kind of forces are they?

The forces of external science cannot produce a body for the Christ because they are concerned only with things that will have disappeared in the future, that will no longer exist. But there is something that precedes knowledge and is infinitely more valuable for the soul than knowledge itself. It is what the Greek philosophers regarded as the beginning of all philosophy. I mean *wonder* or *astonishment.* Once we already know, the experience that is valuable to the soul has really already passed. People in whom the great revelations and truths of the spiritual world can evoke wonder nourish this feeling of wonder, and in the course of time this creates a force that has a power of attraction for the Christ Impulse, which attracts the Christ Spirit. The Christ Impulse unites with the individual human soul when the soul can feel wonder for the mysteries of the world. Christ draws his astral body in earthly evolution from all those feelings that have lived in single human souls as wonder.

The second quality that must be developed by human souls to attract the Christ Impulse is a power of *compassion.* Whenever the soul is moved to share in the suffering or joy of others, this is a force that attracts the Christ Impulse; Christ unites himself with the human soul through compassion and love. Compassion and love are the forces from which Christ forms his etheric body until the end of earthly evolution. With regard to compassion and love, one could, to put it crudely, speak of a program that spiritual science must carry out in the future. In this connection, materialism has evolved a pernicious science, such as has never previously existed on Earth. The very worst offense committed today is to correlate love and sexuality. This is the worst possible expression of materialism, the most devilish symptom of our time. Sexuality and love have nothing whatever to do with each other. Sexuality is something quite different from and has no connection at all with pure, original love. Science has brought things to a shameful point by an extensive literature devoted to connecting these two things that are simply not connected.

A third force flowing into the human soul as if from a higher world, to which we submit, to which we attribute a higher significance than that of our own individual moral instincts, is *conscience*.

Christ is most intimately united with conscience. Christ draws his physical body from impulses that spring from the conscience of individual human souls.

The reality of an utterance in the Bible becomes very clear when we know that the etheric body of Christ is formed from feelings of compassion and love: "What ye have done unto one of the least of these my brethren, ye have done it unto me" (Matt. 25:40). To the end of the Earth's evolution, Christ forms his etheric body out of compassion and love. He forms his astral body out of wonder and astonishment, his physical body out of conscience.

Why do we speak of these things at the present time? Because one day a great problem will have to be solved for humanity, namely, how to present the figure of Christ in its relation to the various domains of life. This will be possible only if many things that spiritual science has to say are taken into account. When, after long contemplation of the Christ as conceived by spiritual science, an attempt is made to present the figure of Christ, his face will be found to contain something that can, indeed will, baffle all the arts. The countenance will express the victory of the forces that are contained only in the face over all other forces in the human form. When human beings are able to fashion eyes that radiate only compassion, a mouth not adapted for eating but only for uttering true words that are the words of conscience, when a brow can be shaped whose beauty lies in the molding of the arch spanning the position of what we call the lotus flower between the eyes—when it becomes possible to accomplish all this, it will be understood why the prophet says, "He hath no form nor comeliness"

(Isa. 53:2). What is meant is that it is not beauty that counts, but the power that will gain victory over decay: the figure of Christ in which all is compassion, all love, all devotion to conscience.

And so spiritual science passes over as a seed into human feeling, into human perception. The teachings that spiritual investigation can impart do not remain mere teachings; they are transformed into life itself in the human soul. And the fruits of spiritual science will gradually mature into conditions of life that will appear like an external embodiment of spiritual knowledge itself, of the soul of future humanity. . . .

PART THREE

Hidden Aspects
of Occult History

9

Materialism and Occultism

Dornach, October 10, 1915[1]

YOU WILL HAVE realized from recent lectures that contemporary materialism, the materialistic way of thinking, is not a consequence of arbitrary human free will but of a certain historical necessity.

Those who have some understanding of the spiritual process of human evolution know that human beings generally participated in spiritual life more in earlier centuries and millennia than they have during the last four or five hundred years. We know too with what widespread phenomena this is connected. At the very beginning of the evolutionary stage we call Earth, the inherited clairvoyance of the Old Moon stage continued to work in human beings. We can envisage that in the earliest ages of earthly evolution this faculty of ancient clairvoyance was still very powerfully active. As a result, the range of humanity's spiritual vision in those times was wide and comprehensive.

This ancient clairvoyance then gradually diminished to the point at which the great majority of human beings had lost the faculty of looking into the spiritual world. The Mystery of Golgotha came to take its place. And yet a certain vestige of the old faculties remained. Evidence of this may be found, for example, in the knowledge of nature that existed among the alchemists until the fourteenth and fifteenth centuries, and even the sixteenth and seventeenth centuries. Such alchemical knowledge was very different in character from modern natural science. To some extent, it was still able to rely, if not upon clear, imaginal clairvoyance, then at least upon vestiges of inspirations and intuitions. The alchemists, when they were honorable and did not seek egotistic gain, still worked to some degree with the old inspirations and intuitions, applying and elaborating them. While they were engaged in their outer activities, vestiges of the old clairvoyance still stirred within them, although no longer accompanied by any reliable knowledge. But the number of people in whom these vestiges of ancient clairvoyance survived decreased steadily. . . .

From all this you will realize that the nearer we come to our own period, the more we are faced with a decline of old soul forces and a growth of tendencies in the human soul toward observation of the outer, *material* world. After slow, gradual preparation, this tendency reached its peak in the middle of the nineteenth century. Although it is not generally realized today, it will be clear to people in the future that the materialistic tendencies of the second half of the nineteenth century had peaked by the middle of the century. Materialistic tendencies had by then developed their greatest strength. Now, the consequence of every tendency is that certain talents develop on its basis, and the really impressive greatness of the methods evolved by materialistic science stems from these tendencies of the soul to hold fast to the outer, material, sensory world.

We must think of this human evolutionary phase as being accompanied by another phenomenon. If we carry ourselves back in imagination to the primeval ages of humanity's spiritual development, we find that humanity was in a comparatively fortunate position regarding spiritual knowledge. Most, in fact all, human beings then knew of the spiritual world through direct vision. Just as today we perceive minerals, plants, and animals, and are aware of tones and colors, so primeval humanity was aware of the spiritual world as a concrete reality. In those days, when full waking consciousness of the outer, material world was dimmed in sleep or dream, there were really no human beings who would not have been connected with the dead who had been near them during life. In the waking state one could interact with the living; during sleep or dream, with the dead. Teaching about the immortality of the soul would have been as superfluous then as it would be today to set out to prove that plants exist. Just imagine what would happen now if anyone set out to prove that plants exist! Exactly the same attitude would have been adopted in primeval times if anyone had thought it necessary to prove the soul also lives after death.

Humanity gradually lost this faculty of living in communion with the spiritual world. Of course, there were always individuals who used every opportunity to develop "seership." But then it became increasingly difficult to develop this seership. How, then, did ancient peoples develop a particular gift of seership? If we study the philosophy of Plato, or what exists of that of Heraclitus, we must realize—and this applies especially to the still earlier Greek philosophies—that they are altogether different from later philosophies. . . .

When we read Plato, we feel his philosophy takes hold of the whole person. When we come to Aristotle, however, the feeling is that we are dealing with an academic, learned philosophy. To understand Plato requires more insight than modern philosophers usually have at their command. For this reason, there is a gulf between Plato and Aristotle. Aristotle is already a scholar in the modern sense. Plato is the last philosopher in the old Greek sense; he is a philosopher whose concepts are still imbued to some extent with *life*. As long as a philosophy of this kind exists, the link with the spiritual world is not broken, and indeed it continued for a long time, actually into the Middle Ages. The Middle Ages did not develop philosophy to further stages but simply took over Aristotelian philosophy; and up to a certain time this was all to the good. Platonic philosophy was taken over in the same way.

In those times when the aptitude for a certain kind of clairvoyance was still present, something important happened when people allowed philosophy to work upon them. Today, philosophy works only on the head, only on the thinking. The reason why so many people avoid philosophy is that they do not like thinking. They have no desire to study it. Ancient philosophy, when received into the human soul, was still able, because of its greater life-giving power, to quicken still existing gifts of seership. Platonic philosophy, indeed even Aristotelian philosophy, still had this effect. Being less abstract than the philosophies of modern times, they were still able to quicken faculties of seership inherent in the human soul. Thus those very faculties that were otherwise sinking below the surface were quickened to life in people who devoted themselves to philosophy. That is how seers came into existence. But because what had now to be learned about the physical world—and this also applies to philosophy—was increasingly important only for the physical plane, humanity became more and more alienated from the remnants of the old clairvoyance. Human beings could no longer penetrate to the inner depths of existence, and it was increasingly difficult to become a seer. Nor will this again be possible until the new methods indicated in the book *How to Know Higher Worlds* are accepted as feasible.[2]

I have said that a period of materialism reached its peak—one could also say, its deepest point—in the middle of the nineteenth century. Conditions will become more and more difficult. This is certain. Nevertheless, the threads of connection with earlier impulses in human evolution must not be broken.

[Here Steiner drew a diagram on the blackboard showing "seer-ship" in full flower, then dipping down below the horizon, reaching its nadir in the nineteenth century, then beginning to rise once again.]

In earlier epochs of humanity, seership was present in full flower. Then it declined, slowly vanishing until the lowest point was reached in the mid–nineteenth century. Following this, there was an ascent.

Understanding the spiritual world, however, is not the same thing as seership. Just as, in relation to the world, science is not the same thing as mere sensory perception, so clairvoyance itself is a different matter from understanding what is seen. In the earliest times, people were satisfied, for the most part, with *vision*. They did not reach the point of *thinking* to any great extent about what was seen, for their seership sufficed. Then thinking, reflection about the spiritual world, came to the fore.

In ancient times, humanity was satisfied with its visions. Thinking lay, as it were, in the subconscious regions of the soul. The ancient seers did not think, did not reflect. Everything came to them directly, through their vision. Thinking first began to affect seership about three or four thousand years before Christ. There was a golden age in the old Indian, Persian, and Egypto-Chaldean cultures. Then came ancient Greek culture, when a still youthful and fresh thinking was wedded with vision in the human soul. Thinking was not then the labored process it is in our day. Human beings moved between two poles. There were great, all-embracing notions, and there was vision. We can see this, although already in a weaker form, in the seers who founded the Samothracian Mysteries and gave us the monumental teaching of the four gods: Axieros, Axiokersos, Axiokersa, and Kad-millos.[3] In this great teaching originating on the island of Samothrace, lofty concepts were imparted to those who were initiated in the Mys-teries and were able to unite with these concepts the still surviving fruits of ancient seership. But then seership gradually sank below the threshold of consciousness and to call it up from the depths of the soul became more and more difficult. It was, of course, possible to retain some of the concepts, even to develop them further. Thus, a time finally came when there were initiates who were not necessarily seers—mark well, initiates who were not necessarily seers.

In different places, there were then assemblies of these initiates. They simply adopted those parts of what was preserved from ancient times that could be affirmed to have been revealed by ancient seers.

Or, where they could, they adopted what could be drawn forth from those still possessing the faculties of atavistic clairvoyance. Conviction came partly through historical traditions, partly through experiments. People convinced themselves that what their intellects *thought* was true. But as time went on the number of individuals in these assemblies who were still able to see into the spiritual world steadily diminished, while the number who had theories about the spiritual world and expressed them in symbols and the like steadily increased.

Then came the middle of the nineteenth century, when the materialistic tendencies reached their deepest point. Let us now consider the inevitable result of this. Naturally, there were those who knew that there is a spiritual world and also knew what is to be found in the spiritual world. But they had never seen it. Indeed, the most outstanding scholars of the nineteenth century were people who, although they had seen nothing of the spiritual world, knew that it exists and could reflect about it. With the help of certain methods and a symbolism that had been preserved in ancient tradition, they could even discover new truths. Nothing special, for example, is to be gained by looking at a drawing of a human being. But if a human being is drawn with a lion's head, or a bull's head, those who have learned how to interpret these things may glean a great deal. Such symbols were in frequent use. There were serious gatherings in which this language of symbols could be learned. I shall say no more about the matter than this, for the schools of initiation guarded these symbols very strictly, communicating them to no one who had not pledged to keep silent about them. However, to be a genuine *knower*, a person needed only to have mastered this symbolic language.

Thus the situation in the middle of the nineteenth century was such that humankind in general, especially civilized humankind, possessed the faculty of spiritual vision deep in the subconsciousness, yet had materialistic tendencies. However, at the same time, there were a great many people who knew that there was a spiritual world, who knew that we are surrounded by a spiritual world just as we are surrounded by air. These people then were burdened with a certain feeling of responsibility. They had no recourse to any actual faculties whereby the existence of a spiritual world could have been demonstrated, yet they were not willing to see the world outside succumbing altogether to materialism. So a difficult situation confronted those who were initiated. They were faced with the question, "Can we just continue to protect within our restricted circles the knowledge that has descended to us from ancient times and simply look on while the whole of humanity—with its culture and philosophy—sinks into materialism? Dare we just idly look on while this takes place?" Especially those who were truly earnest about these things dared not do so.

And so it came about that, in the middle of the nineteenth century the words "esotericist" and "exotericist," which were used by the initiates among themselves, acquired a meaning different from what it had previously been. The occultists divided into *exotericists* and *esotericists*. If, for purposes of analogy, expressions connected with modern parliaments are adopted—although naturally they are unsuitable here—the "exotericists" could be compared with *left-wing parties* and the "esotericists" with *right-wing parties*.

The esotericists were those who wished to continue to abide firmly by the principle of allowing nothing of what was sacred, traditional knowledge, nothing that might enable thinking people to gain insight into the symbolic language, to reach the public. The esotericists were, so to speak, the "Conservative Party" among the occultists.

The exotericists were and are those who wish to make public some part of the esoteric knowledge. Fundamentally, the exotericists were not different from the esotericists, except that the former were inclined to follow the prompting of their feeling of responsibility and make part of the esoteric knowledge public.

At that time there was widespread discussion of which the outside world knows nothing. It was particularly heated in the middle of the nineteenth century. Indeed the clashes and discussions between esotericists and exotericists were far more heated than the arguments between the Conservatives and Liberals in modern parliaments. The esotericists took the stand that only those who had pledged themselves to strictest silence and were willing to belong to some particular society should be told anything about the spiritual world or have any knowledge of it communicated to them. The exotericists said: "But if this principle is followed, people who do not join some such society or league will sink into materialism."

The exotericists then proposed a solution. I can tell you this: The way the exotericists proposed is the way we ourselves are taking. Their proposal was that a certain part of esoteric knowledge should be made public. Thus we too have worked through the medium of popular writings to lead people gradually to knowledge of the spiritual worlds.

However, in the middle of the nineteenth century things had not yet reached the point at which anyone would have ventured to admit this was their conviction. In such circles there is, of course, no voting, and to say the following is to speak in metaphor. Nevertheless it can be said that the esotericists won the day on the first "ballot," and the exotericists were obliged to submit. The esotericist party was not resisted, because of the good old precept of holding together. Not until more recent times has the point been reached when members of such occult associations are expelled or resign. Such things did not use to happen because people believed they had to hold together in brotherhood.

Thus, the exotericists could do nothing but submit. But their responsibility to the whole of humankind weighed upon them. They felt themselves, so to speak, to be guardians of evolution. This weighed upon them, with the result that the first ballot, if I may use this word again, was actually not adhered to, and—once again to use a word from ordinary parlance that must be taken metaphorically—a kind of "compromise" was reached. This led to the following.

It was said, and the esotericists also admitted this, "Humanity in general must come to realize that the world is not devoid of the spiritual. The world does not consist only of matter, nor is it subject only to purely material laws. Humanity must come to know that just as matter surrounds human beings, so also spirit surrounds them. Humanity must come to recognize that human beings are not just material, physical beings, but are beings of soul and spirit. The possibility of knowing this must be saved for humanity."

On this, agreement was reached — and that was the compromise.

But the esotericists of the nineteenth century were not prepared to surrender esoteric knowledge. Therefore, a new and different method of communication had to be considered. How this came into being is a complicated story. The esotericists said, "We do not wish the esoteric knowledge to be made public, but we realize that the materialism of the age must be faced."

In a certain way, the esotericists were justified. They based themselves on a well-founded principle. Indeed, when we see the kind of attitude that is adopted today toward esoteric knowledge we can understand and sympathize with those who said at that time that they would not hear of it being made public. We must realize, too, that history shows repeatedly that open communication of esoteric knowledge leads to calamity, and that those who get hold of such knowledge are themselves the cause of obstacles and hindrances in the way of its propagation. . . .

And so, in the middle of the nineteenth century this popularizing did not take place. An attempt was made, however, to deal with the materialistic tendencies of the age. It is difficult to express what has to be said, and I can only put it in words that were never actually uttered but nonetheless give a true picture. At that time the esotericists said: "What can be done about humanity? We may talk at length about the esoteric teaching but people will simply laugh at us and at you. At most you will win over a few credulous people, a few credulous women, but you will not win over those who cling to the strictly scientific attitude, and you will be forced to reckon with the tendencies of the age." The consequence was that endeavors were made to find a method by which attention could be drawn to the spiritual world. . . .

And so it came about that *mediumship* was deliberately brought on the scene. In a sense, the mediums were the agents of those who wished, by this means, to convince people of the existence of a spiritual world, because through mediums people could see with physical eyes what originates in the spiritual world. The mediums produced phenomena that could be demonstrated on the physical plane. Mediumship was a means of demonstrating to humanity that there is a spiritual world. The exotericists and the esotericists had united in supporting mediumship, in order to deal with the tendency of the times.

Think only of people such as Zollner, Wallace, du Prel, Crookes, Butlerow, Rochas, Oliver Lodge, Flammarion, Morselli, Schiaparelli, Ochorowicz, James, and others—how did they become convinced of the existence of a spiritual world? It was because they had witnessed manifestations from the spiritual world. But everything that can be done by the spiritual world and by initiates must, to begin with, be in the nature of experiments in the world of human beings. The maturity of humanity must always be tested. This support of mediumship, of spiritualism, was therefore also, in a certain sense, an experiment. All that the exotericists and esotericists who had agreed to the compromise could say was, "What will come of it remains to be seen."

What did, in fact, come of it?

Most of the mediums gave accounts of a world in which the dead are living. Just read the literature on the subject! For those who were initiated, the result was distressing in the utmost degree, the very worst it could have been. Two things could have happened. Mediums were used and made certain communications. They were able to relate what they communicated only to the ordinary environment—in whose material elements of course spirit is present. It was expected that the mediums would bring to light all kinds of hidden laws of nature, hidden laws of elemental nature. What actually happened, however, was inevitable.

The human being, as we know, consists of a physical body, an etheric body, an astral body, and the I. From the time of going to sleep to waking, therefore, the real person is in the I and astral body. At the same time, he or she is in the realm of the dead. The medium sitting there, however, is not an I and an astral body. I-consciousness and astral consciousness have been suppressed. As a result, the physical and etheric bodies become particularly active. In this condition the medium may come into contact with a hypnotist or an inspirer—that is to say, with some other human being. Another human being's I, or even the environment, can then have an effect upon the medium. It is impossible for mediums to enter the realm of the dead because the parts of their being that belong to that realm have been made inoperative. The mediums therefore made a great mistake when they gave accounts allegedly of the realm of the dead.

Thus it was obvious that this experiment had achieved nothing except to promulgate a great fallacy. One fine day, it had to be admitted that a path had been followed that was leading humanity into a fallacy, into purely Luciferic teachings bound up with purely Ahrimanic observations. A great fallacy from which nothing good could result had been spread abroad. This was realized as time went on.

You see now how an attempt was made with spiritualism to deal with the materialistic tendencies of the age and to bring home to human consciousness that there is a spiritual world around us. This path led to a fallacy, as we have heard—at least in the beginning. But you can see from this how necessary it is to take the other path, namely, actually to begin to make public part of the esoteric knowledge. This is the path that must be taken even if it brings one calamity after another. The very fact that we pursue spiritual science is, so to say, an acknowledgment of the need to carry into effect the principle of the exotericists in the middle of the nineteenth century. In fact, the aim of the spiritual science is nothing other than to carry this principle into effect, to carry it into effect honorably and sincerely. . . .

10

The Founding of
the Theosophical Society

Dornach, October 11, 1915

TODAY I WOULD LIKE to be allowed to include some personal references among matters of objective history. . . .

First, I want to speak about a particular experience connected with our movement. You know that we began by linking ourselves, outwardly only, with the Theosophical Society. We founded the so-called German Section of that society in the autumn of 1902 in Berlin. In 1904 prominent members of the Theosophical Society came to visit us in various towns in Germany. The episode that I want to start with occurred during one of these visits. In the spring of 1904, the first edition of my book *Theosophy* had just been published, and the periodical *Luzifer-Gnosis* was appearing. In it, I had published articles dealing with the problem of Atlantis and the character of the Atlantean epoch. These articles were afterward published as a separate volume entitled *Unsere atlantischen Vorfahren* (Our Atlantean Ancestors).[1] The articles contained a number of communications about the Atlantean world and the earlier so-called Lemurian epoch. A member highly respected in the Theosophical Society had read these articles dealing with Atlantis and asked me a question, which I want to mention as a noteworthy experience.

This member of the Theosophical Society, who had taken part in the proceedings when the Society was founded by Madame Blavatsky and therefore had participated fully in the activities of the Society, asked, *"How was this information about the world of Atlantis obtained?"*

This question was very significant because until that moment the member knew only the methods by which such information was usually obtained in the Theosophical Society—namely, by a certain kind of mediumistic investigation. Information published in the Theosophical Society at that time was based upon research connected in a certain way with mediumship. A person was put into a kind of mediumistic state. We cannot call it a trance; it was a mediumistic state. Then conditions were established that made it possible for that person, although not in the state of ordinary consciousness, to communicate certain information about matters beyond the reach of ordinary consciousness. That is how the communications were made at that time. This member of the Theosophical Society, who thought that information about prehistoric events could be gained only in this way, therefore inquired whom among us we could use as a medium for such investigations.

As I had naturally refused to adopt this method of research and had insisted from the outset upon strictly individual investigation, and as what I had discovered at that time was the result entirely of my own, personal research, the questioner did not understand me at all. He did not understand that it was quite a different matter from anything that had been done before in the Theosophical Society. The path I had appointed for myself, however, was this: to reject all earlier ways of investigation and, admittedly by means of supersensible perception, to investigate by making use only of what can be revealed to the one who is *himself* the investigator.

In accordance with the position I have to take in the spiritual movement, no other course is possible for me than to practice rigorously those methods of investigation appropriate for the modern world and for modern humanity. There is a very significant difference, you see, between the methods of investigation practiced in spiritual science and those that were practiced in the Theosophical Society. All communications received by that society from the spiritual world—including, for example, the ones given in Scott-Elliot's book on Atlantis—came entirely in the way described, because that alone was considered authoritative and objective.[2] The introduction of the spiritual scientific direction of our work was, from the very beginning, something entirely new in the Theosophical Society. It took account of modern scientific methods that must be elaborated and developed to make ascent to the spiritual realms possible.

This discussion, which took place in 1904, was significant. It showed how greatly spiritual scientific practice differed from what was being practiced by the rest of the Theosophical Society. It showed, too, that what we have in spiritual science was unknown in the Theosophical Society at that time, and that the Theosophical Society continued to work with the methods that had been adopted as a compromise between the extericists and the estericists. Such was the inevitable result of the developments I described yesterday. I said that seership gradually died away and that only a few isolated seers remained in whom mediumistic states could be induced and from whom some information might be obtained.

On this basis, "occult orders," as they were called, came into being. In these orders, there were many who had been initiated, but there were no seers. In the prevailing atmosphere of materialism, they had to cultivate and elaborate methods that had long been popular. Instruments for research had to be sought among persons in whom mediumistic faculties—that is to say, atavistic clairvoyance—could still be developed and produce results. In these circles there were also extensive teachings and also *symbols*. Those individuals, who wished to engage in actual research, however, were obliged to rely on the help of persons possessing atavistic clairvoyance. Such mediumistic methods were continued in the Theosophical Society, and the compromise of which I spoke yesterday really amounted to nothing other than that in the lodges and orders experiments were made whereby spiritual influences might be projected into the world. The desire was to demonstrate that influences from the spiritual world *actually influence* human beings.

Procedures adopted in esoteric schools had thus been brought into action. This attempt was a fiasco. It had been expected that the mediums would bring to light genuine spiritual laws prevailing in the surroundings. However, the only result was that nearly all the mediums fell into the error of supposing that everything emanated from the dead. They embellished this into communications alleged to have been made to them by the dead.

This led to a very definite consequence. Older members will be able to think back to the earliest period of the Theosophical Society and remember the literature produced under its aegis. If they do so, they will find that the astral world—the life immediately after death—was described by Mrs. Besant in books that merely reproduced what Blavatsky's *Secret Doctrine* contained or was to be read in books by Leadbeater.[3] *The Secret Doctrine* in fact was the origin of everything that was given out concerning human life between death and a new birth.

If you compare this with what is said in my book *Theosophy* about the soul world and the spirit world, you find considerable differences.[4]

This is precisely because in regard to these domains the methods of investigation were different. All the methods of research employed in the Theosophical Society, even including those used for investigating the life of the dead, originated from the procedures I have spoken of.

So, you see, what the Theosophical Society had to offer the world to begin with was in a certain respect a continuation of the attempt made previously by the occultists. In what other respect this was not the case we shall hear in a moment. Taken as a whole, however, it was a continuation of the attempt that, since the middle of the nineteenth century, had been the outcome of the compromise made between the exotericists and the esotericists, except that later on things were made rather more esoteric by the Theosophical Society. Whereas the previous attempt had been to present the mediums to the world, the members of the Theosophical Society preferred to work only in their inner circle and merely to give out the results. That was an important difference, for in this approach people were going back to a method of investigation established as a universal custom by the various orders before the middle of the nineteenth century. I mention this because I must stress that with the advent of our spiritual science an entirely new method, one that takes full account of the work and attitude of modern science, was introduced into the occult movement.

As I said, the compromise between the exotericists and the esotericists to convince the materialistic world through mediums of all types that a spiritual world exists was a fiasco. It was a fiasco because the mediums always spoke of a world that, under the existing conditions, simply could not be accessible to them, namely the world of the dead. The mediums spoke of inspirations claimed to have been received from a world in which the dead lived. The situation was that the attempt made by the exotericists and the esotericists had not achieved the result they had really desired.

How had such a state of affairs come about? What was the result of the remarkable attempt that had been made as a result of the compromise? The result was that initiates of a certain kind wrested power from the hands of those who had made the compromise. The initiates of the extreme left wing had taken possession of the proceedings. They acquired great influence, because what was obtained through the mediums did not spring from the realm of the dead at all, but from the realm of the living—from initiates who had put themselves either in distant or close rapport with the mediums. Because everything was done through these initiates and through the mediums, it was colored by the theories of those who wished to get the mediums under their control. Those among the exotericists and esotericists who had made the compromise wanted to convince people that there is indeed a spiritual world. That is what they wanted to impress. But when those who thought themselves capable of holding the guiding reins let them slip, the occultists of the extreme left wing took possession of them and endeavored through the mediums—if I may use this tautology—to communicate *their* theories and *their* views to the world.

For those who had made the compromise for the good of humanity, the position was disastrous, because they felt more and more strongly that false teachings about the supersensible were being brought into the world. This was what was happening as occultism was developing in the 1840s, 1850s, and even the 1860s.

As long as deliberation still continued in the circles of honest occultists, the situation was sinister. For the further the occultists inclined to the left, the less they were concerned to promote what alone is justifiable, namely the *universal human.* In occultism, people belong to the "left" when they try to achieve some ultimate end with the help of what they know of occult teaching. They belong to the "right" when they desire that end purely for its own sake. The middle party was in favor of making exoteric the esoteric knowledge needed to promote the interests of the universal human today. Those who belong to the extreme left are those who combine special aims of their own with what they promulgate as occult teaching. Individuals are on the left to the extent that they pursue special aims, lead people to the spiritual world, give them all kinds of demonstrations of it, and illicitly instill in them "promptings" that simply help to bring these special aims to fulfillment. The leading circle of modern initiates was faced with this situation. It was realized that control had fallen into the hands of people who were pursuing their own special aims. Such was the state of affairs confronting the esotericists and exotericists who had made the compromise referred to.

Then it was "heard" that an event of importance for the further continuation of spiritual development on the Earth must be at hand. The expression "heard" may not be quite exact, but absolutely exact words cannot be found because one is dependent on external language. Besides, communication among occultists is different from anything that external language is capable of describing.

I can describe this event only as follows. The individual orders in their research had preferred for a long time to make less use of female mediums. In the strict orders, where it was desired to take the right standpoint, on the other hand, no female mediums were ever used for obtaining revelations from the spiritual worlds.

Now the female organism is adapted by nature to preserve atavistic clairvoyance longer than the male organism. Whereas male mediums were becoming almost unknown, female mediums were still to be found, and a great number were used while the compromise still held. But now a personality who possessed mediumistic faculties in the very highest degree came into the occultists' field of observation.

This was Madame H. P. Blavatsky, a personality especially adapted by certain subconscious parts of her organism to draw a great deal, a very great deal, from the spiritual world. Consider what possibilities this opened up for the world! At one of the most crucial points in the development of occultism, a personality appeared who through the peculiar nature of her organism was able to draw many, many things from the spiritual world by means of her subconscious faculties.

Any occultists of that time, who were alert to the signs of the times, had to draw the following conclusion. Here, now, at just the right moment, a personality had appeared who by her peculiar organic constitution could produce the strongest evidence of the ancient, traditional teaching that existed among the occult orders only in the form of symbols. It was certainly true that here was a personality who simply because of her organic makeup afforded the possibility of demonstrating again many things that had long been known only through tradition. This was the fact confronting occultists just after the fiasco that had led to a veritable *impasse*. Let us be quite clear on the point: Blavatsky was regarded as a personality from whom, as from an electrically charged Leyden jar, the electric sparks—occult truths—could be produced. . . .

The right-wing occultists, who in conjunction with the middle party had agreed to the compromise, could well suppose that something very significant could come from this personality. At the same time, the left wing could also conclude with assurance that something extremely effective in the world could be achieved with the help of this personality! Thus a real battle was waged around her, on one side with the honest purpose of substantiating much of what the initiates knew; on the other side, for the sake of far-reaching, special aims.

I have often referred to the early periods in the life of H. P. Blavatsky, and have shown that, to begin with, attempts were made to get a great deal of knowledge from her. But in a comparatively short time the situation rapidly changed, owing to the fact that she soon came into the sphere of those who belonged, as it were, to the left. H. P. Blavatsky was very well aware of what she herself was able to see—for she was especially significant in that she was not simply a passive medium, but had a colossal memory for everything that revealed itself to her from the higher worlds. Nevertheless she was inevitably under the influence of certain personalities when she wanted to evoke manifestations from the spiritual world. And so she always referred to what ought really to have been left aside—she always referred to the "Mahatmas." They may be there in the background, but this is not a factor when it is a question of furthering the interests of humanity.

And so it was not long before H. P. Blavatsky was forced to face a decision. A hint came to her from a quarter belonging to the side of the left that she was a personality of key importance. She knew very well what it was that she saw, but she was not aware of how significant she was as a personality. This was first disclosed to her by the left wing. But she was fundamentally honest by nature and after this hint had been given her from a quarter of which, at the beginning, she could hardly have approved, because of her fundamental honesty, she tried on her side to reach a kind of compromise with an occult brotherhood in Europe. Something very fine might have resulted from this, because through her great gift of mediumship she would have been able to furnish confirmations of really phenomenal importance in connection with what was known to the initiates only from theories and symbolism. But she was not only thoroughly honest, she was also what is called in German a "Frechdachs"—a "cheeky creature." And she certainly was! She had in her nature a certain trait that is particularly common in those inclined to mediumship, namely, a lack of consistency in external behavior. Thus there were moments when she could be very audacious, and in one of these fits of audacity she imposed terms that could not be fulfilled on the occult brotherhood that had decided to make the experiment with her. But since she knew that a great deal could be achieved through her instrumentality, she decided to take up the matter with other brotherhoods. So she approached an American brotherhood. This American brotherhood was one in which the majority had always wavered between the right and the left, but at all events had the prospect of discovering things of tremendous significance concerning the spiritual worlds.

Now this was the period when other brothers of the left were showing intense interest in H. P. Blavatsky. Already at that time these left-wing brothers had their own special interests. At the moment I do not propose to speak about these interests; if it were necessary, I could do so at some future time. For the present it is enough to say they were brothers who had their special interests, which were above all of a strongly political character. They envisaged the possibility of achieving something of a political nature in America by means of persons who had first been given an occult preparation. The consequence was that at a moment when H. P. Blavatsky had already acquired an untold amount of occult knowledge through having worked with the American lodge, she had to be expelled from it, because it was discovered that there was something political in the background. So things couldn't continue.

The situation was now extremely difficult, tremendously difficult. For what had been undertaken in order to call the world's attention to the existence of a spiritual world had in a certain respect now to be withdrawn by the serious occultists because it had been a fiasco. It was necessary to show that no reliance could be placed on what was being presented by spiritualism, in spite of the fact that it had many adherents. For spiritualism had become only materialistic, was sheer dilettantism. The only scholarly persons who concerned themselves with it were those who wanted to get information in an external, materialistic way about a spiritual world.

H. P. Blavatsky, furthermore, had made it clear to the American lodge on her departure that she had no intention whatsoever of withholding what she knew from the world. And she knew a great deal, because she was able to remember afterwards what had been conveyed through her. What audacity she had!

Good advice is costly, as the saying goes. What was to be done?

Something now happened that I have referred to on various occasions, something called "occult imprisonment."[5] Madame Blavatsky was put into occult imprisonment. Through certain acts and machinations of a kind that can be performed only by certain brotherhoods who allow themselves to engage in illicit arts, certain brothers succeeded in compelling Madame Blavatsky to live for a time in a world in which all her occult knowledge was driven inward. Think of it in this way. The occult knowledge was in her aura. As the result of certain processes that were set in operation, everything in this aura was thrown back into her soul—for a long time! That is to say, all the occult knowledge she possessed was to be imprisoned; she was to be isolated as far as the outer world and her occultism were concerned.

This happened at the time when Madame Blavatsky might have become really dangerous through the spreading of teachings that are among the most interesting of all in the occult movements. But certain Indian occultists now came to know of the affair. These occultists for their part tended strongly toward the left. Their prime interest was to turn the occultism that could be given to the world through Madame Blavatsky in a direction where it could influence the world in line with their special aims. Through the efforts of these Indian occultists, who were versed in the appropriate practices, she was released from this imprisonment within her aura; she was free once again and could now use her spiritual faculties in the right way.

From this you can get an idea of what had taken place in this soul, and of what combination of factors all that came into the world through HPB was composed. But because certain Indian occultists had gained the merit of freeing her from her imprisonment, they had her in their power in a certain respect. And there was simply no possibility of preventing them from using her to send out into the world the part of occultism that suited their purposes. So something very remarkable was "arranged"—if I may use a clumsy word.

What was arranged may be put somewhat as follows. The Indian occultists wanted to assert their own special aims in opposition to those of the others. For this, they made use of Madame Blavatsky. She was given instructions to place herself under a certain influence, for in her case the mediumistic state always had to be induced from outside. This made it possible to bring all kinds of things into the world through her.

About this time, she came to be associated with a person who from the beginning had really no directly Theosophical interests, but did have a splendid talent for organization, namely, Colonel Olcott. I cannot say for certain, but I surmise that there had already been some kind of association at the time when Blavatsky belonged to the American lodge. Then, under the mask, as it were, of an earlier individuality, there appeared in the field of Blavatsky's spiritual vision a personality who was essentially the vehicle of what they wanted to launch into the world from India. Some of you may know that in his book *People from the Other World* Colonel Olcott has written a great deal about this personality who now appeared in Madame Blavatksy's field of vision behind the mask of an earlier individuality designated as Mahatma Kut-Humi. You know, perhaps, that Colonel Olcott has written a very great deal about this Mahatma Kut-Humi. Among other things he wrote that in 1874 this Mahatma Kut-Humi had declared which individuality was living in him. He indicated that this individuality was *John King* by name, a powerful sea pirate of the seventeenth century.[6] All this is to be found in Olcott's book *People from the Other World.*[7]

In the Mahatma Kut-Humi, therefore, we have to do with the spirit of a bold sea pirate of the seventeenth century who then, in the nineteenth century, was involved in significant manifestations made with the help of Madame Blavatsky and others. He brought teacups from some distance away, he let all kinds of records be produced from the coffin of Madame Blavatsky's father, and so forth. From Colonel Olcott's account, therefore, we must assume that these were deeds of the bold pirate of the seventeenth century.

Now Colonel Olcott speaks about this John King in a remarkable way. He suggests that perhaps we are dealing here not with the spirit of a pirate but with the creation of an order that, while depending for its results upon unseen agents, exists among physical men. According to this account, Kut-Humi might have been a member of an order engaged in practices such as I have described, whose results were to be communicated to the world through H. P. Blavatsky. But, of course, all this was bound up with all kinds of special interests, namely, that a specifically Indian teaching should be spread in the world.

This was approximately the situation in the 1870s. We therefore have evidence of very significant events that must be seen in a single framework when we are considering the whole course of events in the occult movement. It was this same John King who, by "precipitation," produced Sinnett's books, first *The Occult World* and then, especially, *Esoteric Buddhism.*[8]

Esoteric Buddhism came into my hands very shortly after publication, a few weeks in fact, and I could see from it that efforts were being made, especially from a certain quarter, to give an entirely materialistic form to the spiritual teachings. If you studied *Esoteric Buddhism* with the insight you have acquired in the course of time, you would be astonished at the materialistic forms in which facts are presented there. It is materialism in its very worst form. The spiritual world is presented in an entirely materialistic way. None who get hold of this book can shake themselves free from materialism. The subject is subtle but in Sinnett's book you cannot get away from materialism, however lofty the heights to which it purports to carry you. And so those who were Madame Blavatsky's spiritual "bread-givers"—forgive the materialistic analogy—not only had special aims connected with Indian interests, but they also made trenchant concessions to the materialistic spirit of the age. And the influence that Sinnett's book had upon very large numbers of people shows how correctly they had speculated. I have met scientists who were delighted with this book because everything fitted in with their stock-in-trade, and yet they were able to conceive of the existence of a spiritual world. The book satisfied all the demands of materialism and yet made it possible to meet the need for a spiritual world and to acknowledge its existence.

You know the further unfolding of these events. H. P. Blavatsky wrote *The Secret Doctrine* in the 1880s, and in 1891 she died. *The Secret Doctrine* is written in the same style as *Esoteric Buddhism,* except that it corrects certain gross errors that any occultist could at once have corrected. I have often spoken about the peculiar features of Blavatsky's book and need not go into the matter again now. Then, on the basis of what had come about in this way, the Theosophical Society was founded. Fundamentally speaking, it retained its Indian trend. Although no longer with the intensity that had prevailed under the influence of John King, the Indian trend persisted. What I have now described to you was, as it were, a new path that made great concessions to the materialism of the age, but was nevertheless intended to show humanity that a spiritual world as well as the outer, material world must be taken into account.

Many details should be added to what I have now said, but time is too short. I will now show you briefly how our spiritual scientific movement took its place in this already existing movement.

You know that we founded the German Section of the Theosophical Society in October 1902. In the winters of both 1900 and 1901 I had given lectures in Berlin that may be called "Theosophical," for they were held in the circle and at the invitation of the Berlin Theosophists. The first lectures ultimately became the book now called *Mystics after Modernism.*[9] These lectures were given to a circle of members of the Theosophical Society. I myself was not then a member.

Remember that at the beginning we were working with a teaching that was already widespread and had led numbers of people to turn their minds to the spiritual world. All over the world there were people who to a certain extent were ready and who wanted to know something about the spiritual world. They knew nothing of the things I have told you today, of course. But they had a genuine longing for the spiritual world. Therefore they joined the movement where this longing could be satisfied. In this movement, then, one could find people whose hearts were longing for knowledge of the spiritual world. . . .

It can truly be said, then, that there was a demand, even, as I could show, a public demand, that I speak about the aim and purpose of Theosophy. It was not a matter of arbitrary choice but, as the saying goes, a clear call of karma.

In the winter of 1900–1901, I gave the lectures on mysticism, and in that of 1901–1902 those dealing with the Greek and Egyptian Mysteries in rather greater detail. The lectures were subsequently printed in the book *Christianity as Mystical Fact* (which was published in the summer of 1902).[10]

The greater part of *Mystics after Modernism* was immediately translated into English, before I was a member of the Theosophical Society. I could tell you much more of importance, but time does not permit it now. One thing, however, I must add. . . .

So in 1901–1902, I gave the lectures that became *Christianity as Mystical Fact*. Frau Dr. Steiner attended those lectures. She had also heard the lecture I had given in the Theosophical Society during the winter of 1900 on Gustav Theodor Fechner. It was a special lecture, not forming part of the other series. Frau Dr. Steiner had therefore already been present at some of the lectures I gave during that time. It would be interesting to relate a few details here, but these may be omitted; they merely add a little color to the incident. If necessary, they can be told on another occasion.

After having been away for a time, Frau Dr. Steiner returned to Berlin from Russia in the autumn, and with an acquaintance of Countess Brockdorff was present at the second course of lectures given in the winter of 1901–1902. After one of the lectures on the Greek Mysteries, this acquaintance came up to talk to me. This lady subsequently became a more and more fanatical adherent of the Theosophical Society. Later, she was given a high position in the order founded to wait for the Second Coming of Christ.

At the time of which I am speaking, she came to me and, adopting the air of a really profound initiate of the Theosophical Society about to give evidence of her initiation, said, "You have spoken of Mysteries; but they are still in existence. There are still secret societies. Are you aware of that?" After another lecture on the same subject, she came to me again and said, "One sees that you still remember quite well what you were taught when you were in the Greek Mysteries!" This is something that, carried a little farther, borders on a chapter deserving the title of "mystical eccentricities"!

In the autumn of 1901, this lady organized a tea party. Frau Dr. Steiner always speaks of it as the "chrysanthemum tea" because there were so many chrysanthemums in the room. The invitation came from this acquaintance of Countess Brockdorff and I often thought that she wanted—well, I don't quite know what it was! The day chosen for the founding of the Theosophical Society was one of special importance for this lady. She may have wanted to enlist me as a coworker on her own lines, for she put out feelers and was often very persistent—but nothing of any account came of it. I should like, however, to relate a conversation between Frau Dr. Steiner and me that took place in the autumn of 1901 on the occasion of that "chrysanthemum tea." She asked me whether it was not urgently necessary to call to life a spiritual scientific movement in Europe.

In the course of the conversation I said in unambiguous terms: "Certainly it is necessary to call such a movement to life. But I will ally myself only with a movement that is connected exclusively with *Western* occultism and cultivates its development." And I also said that such a movement must link to Plato, to Goethe, and so forth. I indicated the whole program that was then actually carried out.

In this program there was no place for unhealthy activities, but naturally a few people with such tendencies came; they were people who were influenced by the movement of which I have spoken. But from the conversation quoted at the beginning of this lecture that I had with a member of the English Theosophical Society, you will see that a complete rejection of everything in the nature of mediumship and atavism was implicit in this program.

The path we have been following for long years was adopted with full consciousness. Although elements of mediumistic and atavistic clairvoyance have not been absent, there has been no deviation from this path, and it has led to our present position.

I had, of course, to rely on finding people within the Theosophical movement who desired and were able to recognize thoroughly healthy methods of work. The invariable procedure of those who did not desire a movement in which a healthy and strict sense of scientific responsibility prevails has been to misrepresent the aim we have been pursuing. This they have done to suit their own ends. The very history of our movement affords abundant evidence that there has been no drawing back from penetrating into the highest spiritual worlds. On the other hand, what cannot be attained by a healthy method for entering the spiritual worlds has been strictly rejected. Those who recognize this and who follow the history of the movement do not need to take it as a mere assurance, for it is evident from the whole nature of the work that has been going on for years. We have been able to go very, very much further in genuine investigation of the spiritual world than has ever been possible for the Theosophical Society. But we take the sure, not the unsure, paths. This may be said candidly and freely.

I have always refused to have anything to do with forms of antiquated occultism, with any brotherhoods or communities of that kind in the domain of esotericism. And it was only under the guarantee of complete independence that I worked for a time in a certain connection with the Theosophical Society and its esoteric procedures, but never in the direction toward which it was heading. Already by the year 1907 everything really esoteric had completely vanished from the Theosophical Society, and later happenings are sufficiently well known to you.

It has also happened that occult brotherhoods made proposals to me of one kind or another. A certain highly respected occult brotherhood suggested to me that I should participate in the spreading of a kind of occultism calling itself "Rosicrucian," but I left the proposal unanswered, although it came from a much-respected occult movement. I say this in order to show that we ourselves are following an independent path, suited to the needs of the present age, and that we inevitably regard unhealthy elements as being undesirable in the extreme.

11

The Significance of the Eighth Sphere

Dornach, October 17, 1915

I WANT TO ADD some things today and thus fill out these lectures about the development of spiritual life in the nineteenth century. . . .

We will take as our starting point the fact that the nineteenth century was the epoch when materialism as a worldview arose in the natural course of progress. As you know, the middle of that century was the time when the whole human race was, as it were, to be put to the test by materialism. Materialism stood on the horizon like a temptress, and humanity fell in love with it. It may truly be said that in the nineteenth century humanity was enamored of materialism.

And yet, we have seen how greatly materialism deserves praise. As a method, materialism made possible the great achievements of natural science. If the faculties of soul necessary for materialistic observation of the world had not been developed, the natural sciences, with all their technical, economic, and social consequences, would not have been possible. Two factors combined to make this happen. On the one hand, human evolution had to progress to the point where materialistic interpretations were inevitable if the study of nature was to be carried to a further stage. Honest thinkers had to arrive at materialism if they adopted certain methods of investigation established by natural science. After all, materialism was good as a method for investigating and observing the secrets of the material world.

That was one aspect. The other was that the hearts and souls of human beings were so attuned as to make them love materialism. Everything tended toward it. All the factors combined to put human beings to the test, as it were, through a materialistic view of the world.

I have already told you that among the occultists who, so to speak, had the responsibility of seeing that humanity would not completely sink into materialism, an attempt was made with mediumship, and I showed that mediumship led to aberrations. I have already indicated one of the most significant of these aberrations. It was remarkable that mediums everywhere professed to be able to give information, revelations, from the realm of the dead, the realm where people live after death. Besides all I have already told you, the most remarkable thing was that the communications that were coming through mediums— allegedly from the realm of the dead—everywhere disclosed a strongly tendentious character. If you examine all these proclamations made by the mediums, you find that they invariably have a strongly tendentious character, especially where the life of the soul after death is concerned.

In important circles where mediums were used, declarations were made that were the cause of great consternation to the old esotericists, who did not wish certain occult truths to be made public. I can indicate the reason for their consternation in the following way.

In order to be quite clear about the matter, please read the lecture course I gave in Vienna in 1914, entitled *The Inner Nature of Man and Life between Death and a New Birth.*[1] The lectures contain very important facts that emerge from approaching the realm of the dead in the right way by putting oneself into the condition in which they are able to speak to one.

But in very many circles where mediums were used, revelations of a quite different kind were made. If you peruse the mass of literature compiled from the communications of different mediums, you will discover—especially when these mediums were guided by the souls of living persons—that everything has a strongly tendentious character. Descriptions of the life after death were given that, if you compare them with what was said in the Vienna lectures, are entirely false. You will perceive, too, the tendency in the different mediums to allow nothing concerning repeated earthly lives to emerge. Wherever the mediums alleged that the dead had spoken to them, they described the life after death in such a way that the conclusion was: there can be no repeated earthly lives! In the development of mediumship there was the tendency to make false assertions about precisely the most important aspects of the life between death and a new birth—especially to make assertions precluding the fact of reincarnation. It was desired to speak to this effect through mediums. That is to say, certain people who exploited this tendency in pursuance of their special aims desired that revelations indicating there are no repeated earthly lives should be proclaimed through the mediums. The desire, therefore, was to use the mediums to oppose the teaching of repeated Earth lives.

That was a very striking fact, a fact that caused the right-wing occultists the greatest consternation of all, for they themselves had been a party to the use of mediumship and what it produced—and this was being made to serve tendentious interests instead of the unbiased truth.

All these things were possible because the leaning toward materialism was so strong in people. Now what is said in the Vienna lectures about life between death and a new birth is irreconcilable with any form of materialism as a view of the world. But people can be materialists in their thinking and give credence to what different mediums have said about life after death. For to do so is really only a kind of concealed materialism that is ashamed of being materialistic and therefore has recourse to mediums in order to glean something about the spiritual world. Materialism was therefore a factor to be reckoned with, and those who did reckon with it fared the best.

In addition to all this, there was something else. Even among those who knew something about the spiritual worlds great confusion had arisen in the course of the nineteenth century with regard to something about which, if a spiritual movement is to make any real progress, it is absolutely essential to be clear. The confusion was due to the fact that Ahriman and Lucifer were continually being intermixed. People were no longer able to distinguish between them. A principle of evil and the representative of the evil—they understood that. But they saw no need for any sharper distinction. Even Goethe could not distinguish Ahriman—whom he called Mephistopheles—from Lucifer. In Goethe's work they are indistinguishable, for Mephistopheles is a mixture, a cross between Ahriman and Lucifer. In the nineteenth century, people had no faculty for making a distinction between the representatives of the two spiritual streams, Ahriman and Lucifer. I can only make certain statements on this subject today, but later on I shall be able to elaborate them and then confirmation will be possible.

Now, when it is a matter of having clarity about the spiritual world, a great deal depends upon being able to distinguish between Ahriman and Lucifer. That is why a strict distinction between the figures of Ahriman and Lucifer will be made in the representations in our building in Dornach. Lack of clear distinction between these two Powers leads to a particular kind of confusion in spiritual understanding. If Ahriman and Lucifer are intermixed as they are in Goethe's figure of Mephistopheles, the danger is that Ahriman will constantly appear in the form of Lucifer. There is no knowing whether one has to do with Ahriman himself or with Lucifer in the form of Ahriman. Ahriman wishes to convey untruths by way of the materialistic view of the world. . . .

Materialism cannot be surmounted without far-reaching thinking. But when Ahriman and Lucifer are intermixed, people accept the Ahrimanic picture of the world that is presented to them because Lucifer comes to the aid of Ahriman. As a consequence, a kind of longing arises in people to weave certain fallacies in the guise of truths into humanity's conception of the world.

A remarkable trend thus developed, namely, to harbor fallacies that could flourish only in the age of materialism—one might say, the age of Ahrimanic deception—because Lucifer was helping from within. Ahriman insinuates himself into the concepts formed of outer phenomena and deceives us about them. We would see through these wiles, however, if Lucifer did not incite us to lend force to certain materialistic facts in our view of the world.

Such was the situation in which people lived in the nineteenth century, and those who wished to could take advantage of it. A person able to see through such matters might set out to strengthen some tendency with a bias toward the left. This would not have been such a simple matter if people had not been in a position where they could so easily be misled as a result of the intermixture of Ahriman and Lucifer.

This made it happen that certain entirely materialistic natures had just enough of the Luciferic element in them not to believe in materialism, but to attempt to find in materialism itself a spiritual conception of the world. Just think of it, the nineteenth century could produce a type of person whose head produced thoroughly materialistic thinking but whose heart longed for the spiritual! When that happens, a person will try to find the spiritual in materiality itself and will seek to give to the spiritual a materialistic form.

Now if behind a personality of this type there happens to stand an individual who sees to the root of such matters, the latter has a very easy game to play. For, if it is in the interests of this individual, he or she can induce such a person to mislead others into envisaging the spiritual in a material form. Procedures that are calculated to trick those others could then take effect. These measures succeed best when they are carried out at just the right place, when truths are imparted and the door is opened for people to the things they long for. Thus, certain spiritual truths could be brought to humankind and a one-sided bias could be oriented in a certain direction. On the one hand, a number of truths—with a materialistic coloring, but truths for all that—were communicated. On the other, at a certain place, something was introduced that would quite inevitably lead to fallacy but could not easily be detected.

This was what happened in the case of Sinnett's book *Esoteric Buddhism*. Sinnett wrote it, but behind Sinnett was the one he calls his "inspirer," whom we later know under the mask of a Mahatma individuality. Sinnett was a journalist. He was therefore steeped in the materialistic tendencies of the century. Here, then, was a personality whose brain tended entirely to materialism, but one in whom the longing for a spiritual world was also present. Sinnett therefore had every aptitude for seeking the spiritual world in a materialistic form. Thus it was easy for the Mahatma individuality, in whose interest it was to make use of materialism in this way for special aims of his own, to develop an ostensibly spiritual teaching with an eminently materialistic coloring in Sinnett's *Esoteric Buddhism*.

Now you may say, "But Sinnett's book surely does not contain materialistic teaching!" The fact that this is not perceived—there you have the gist of the whole matter! Everything is embellished and disguised and can be understood only when one knows the antecedents I have just spoken of.

Of course, the teaching about the different parts of the human being, the doctrine of karma and reincarnation, are truths. But materialism has been woven into all these truths. In Sinnett's *Esoteric Buddhism* a genuinely spiritual outlook is combined with an eminently materialistic tendency. This combination was not easy to detect because there was scarcely anyone who could discern that something entirely materialistic had insinuated itself into a spiritual teaching—something that was materialistic not merely in the intellectual sense, but materialistic as opposed to a spiritual view of the world.

Here I refer to what is said in *Esoteric Buddhism* about the "Eighth Sphere."[2]

Here, then, are teachings containing a great deal that is correct and into which an utterly materialistic and misleading statement about the Eighth Sphere has been woven. This culminates in the assertion made in *Esoteric Buddhism* that the Eighth Sphere is the *Moon*. Owing to its journalistic qualities and the good style, the book was a tremendous draw and captivated many hearts. Consequently these readers imbibed, not the true teaching concerning the Eighth Sphere, but the strange assertion made by Sinnett that the Moon is the Eighth Sphere.

So there was Sinnett's *Esoteric Buddhism*. The book was written at the time when Blavatsky, after all the happenings of which I have told you, had already been driven into the one-sided sphere of influence of those Indian occultists who belonged to the left and had special aims of their own. Hence teachings relating to human nature and to reincarnation and karma are given in *Esoteric Buddhism*. It is therefore written in opposition to those who wanted the knowledge of reincarnation to be allowed to disappear. This will also show you how vehemently the conflict was being waged.

Blavatsky had been connected with American spiritualists who wanted to let the teaching of reincarnation disappear. Mediumship was a means to this end and that method was adopted. As Blavatsky revolted, she was expelled and came more and more under the sway of the Indian occultists. She was driven into their hands. This led to a conflict between American and Indian views in the sphere of occultism. On one side there was the strong tendency to let the teaching of reincarnation vanish from the scene, and on the other the urge to bring this teaching into the world, but in a form that took advantage of the materialistic leanings of the nineteenth century.

This was a possibility if the teaching about the Eighth Sphere was presented as Sinnett presented it in *Esoteric Buddhism*. There are a number of other facts of perhaps sufficient importance to be at least indicated. I do not want to shock you by what I am saying but to explain the spiritual principle our own standpoint is based upon.

Two difficulties had arisen as a result of the way in which the teaching about the Eighth Sphere had been presented in Sinnett's book. Blavatsky had created one of the difficulties herself. She knew that what Sinnett had written on this subject was false, but she also knew that she was in the hands of those who desired that the false teaching should be inculcated into humanity. Therefore she tried in a certain way—as you can read in *The Secret Doctrine*—to correct this conception of the Eighth Sphere and matters relevant to it. But she did this in such a way as to cause confusion. Hence there is a certain discrepancy between Sinnett's *Esoteric Buddhism* and Blavatsky's *Secret Doctrine*. Blavatsky corrected it in a way that actually reinforced the bias of the left-wing Indian occultists. She tried by very peculiar means, as we shall presently see, to let more of the truth come to light in order to overshadow the error. She was therefore obliged, in turn, to create a counterweight, for from the standpoint of the Indian occultists it would have been very dangerous to allow the truth to be revealed in this way.

She set out to create this counterweight—we shall gradually understand it—by pursuing a definite course. She came nearer to the truth about the Eighth Sphere than Sinnett had done, but she created the counterweight by venting in *The Secret Doctrine* a volley of abuse on the subjects of Judaism and Christianity, interwoven with certain teaching about the nature of Jehovah. In this way, what she had put right on one side she tried to balance out on the other, so that too much harm would not be done to the stream of Indian occultism. She knew that such truths do not remain theory or without effect as do other theories relating to the physical plane. Theories like those we are speaking of penetrate into the life of soul and color perceptions and feelings. Indeed, they were calculated to turn souls in a certain direction. The whole affair is an inextricable jumble of fallacies.

Madame Blavatsky herself did not, of course, know that the driving forces behind both tendencies were directed toward a special aim. This special aim was to foster this particular kind of error instead of the truth. In general, the aim was to foster errors of a type that would be advantageous to the materialism of the nineteenth century: errors that could be possible only at the high tide of materialism. There you have one side of the situation.

On the other side, Sinnett's *Esoteric Buddhism,* and in a certain respect Blavatsky's *Secret Doctrine* too, made a great impression, especially upon those who were really intent upon seeking the spiritual world. And that again naturally alarmed those who had cause to be alarmed at the possibility that an occult movement with such an Oriental trend should appear.

Now a number of senseless polemics have been leveled against Blavatsky, against Sinnett, against the Theosophical movement, and so forth. But among the different attacks made upon the Theosophical movement in the course of time, there have been some emanating from well-informed but biased quarters. The tendency of Anglican spiritual life was that as little as possible of Oriental teaching, as little as possible of any teaching concerning repeated earthly lives, should be allowed to come to the knowledge of the public.

There is no doubt that among those who, from the standpoint that here lay a danger to Christianity in Europe, set themselves in opposition to the Oriental teachings were people who may be called "Christian esotericists." The Christian esotericists connected with the High Church party in England set themselves in opposition with this in mind. From this side, then, there came declarations calculated both to stem the current of Oriental thought proceeding from Blavatsky and Sinnett, and to foster in the outside world esotericism of a kind intended to conceal the teaching of repeated earthly lives. To amalgamate a certain trend of thought with the form of Christianity customary in Europe—such was the aim of this group. It desired that the teaching of repeated earthly lives—which it was essential to make known—should be left out of account. And a method similar to that used in the case of Sinnett was put into operation.

I must emphasize once again that those who made the corresponding preparations were probably not fully aware that they were tools of the individuality who stood behind them. Just as Sinnett knew nothing of the real tendency of those who stood behind him, neither did those who were connected with the High Church party know much of what lay behind the whole affair. But they realized that what they were doing could not fail to make a great impression upon the occultists, and that determined them to support the direction of those who were intent upon eliminating the teaching of repeated lives.

After these preliminary indications, let us turn to consider the particular fallacy contained in Sinnett's book. We find there the teaching that the Eighth Sphere makes itself manifest above all in the Moon, that the Moon with its influences and effects upon humanity is, in fact, the Eighth Sphere. Expressed in this form, this is a fallacy.

Here is the essential point. If we started from Sinnett's assumption in investigating the Moon's influences, we would be trapped in a grave error arising from materialistic thinking and not easily fathomed.

What, then, was necessary if the truth were to be fostered? It was necessary to point out the true state of things in regard to the Moon as opposed to the erroneous presentation in Sinnett's *Esoteric Buddhism*.

Read chapter 4 dealing with this subject in the book *An Outline of Esoteric Science*.[3] It was my purpose there to describe how the Moon left the Earth. I attached particular importance to the fact that the exit of the Moon should be described with the utmost clarity. It was essential to indicate the truth here as opposed to the fallacy. Thus in order to counter the Indian influence it was necessary to describe in all clarity the function of the Moon in the evolution of the Earth. That was one of the things that had to be done in my book.

The other thing that was necessary will be clear to you if you think of the people of whom I have just spoken. These were people who were also under a certain leadership and who did not wish the teaching of repeated earthly lives to be spread among humanity as a truth because they considered that it would alter the form of Christianity customary in Europe and America. They went to work in a particular way, a way that is clearly discernable if we picture how these occultists set about refuting Sinnett's *Esoteric Buddhism*. The occultists connected with the High Church party took upon themselves the task of refuting Sinnett's *Esoteric Buddhism* and Blavatsky's *Secret Doctrine*.

In point of fact a great deal of good was done in regard to Sinnett's statement about the Eighth Sphere, for the falsity of the indications about the Eighth Sphere and the Moon was emphasized very poignantly from that side. But at the same time this was combined with another teaching. It was stated from that quarter that humanity is not connected with the Moon in the way described by Sinnett, but in a different way. True, this different way was not specifically described, but it could be perceived that these people had realized something about the process of the Moon's departure from the Earth as I presented it in *Esoteric Science*. But now they laid great stress on the following. They said: The Earth—and above all, humanity—was never connected with the other planets of the solar system . . . therefore humanity could never have lived on Mercury, Venus, Mars, or Jupiter. From that side, therefore, it was sharply emphasized that there is no connection between the human being and the planets of the solar system. But this is the best way to instill yet another fallacy into the world, and to spread the greatest possible obscurity over the teaching of reincarnation. The other fallacy, Sinnett's fallacy, actually furthers the teaching of reincarnation in a sense, but in a materialistic form. The fallacy asserting that during earthly evolution human beings have never had any connection with Mercury, Venus, Mars, Jupiter, and so forth was not actually spread abroad by those who gave it publicity, but by those who stood behind them. It was they who worked upon human souls in such a way that these souls could never seriously believe in reincarnation. What, therefore, was strongly emphasized from this quarter was that human beings had never been connected with any planet other than the Earth nor ever had anything to do with the other planets of the solar system.

If we think about a human being as he/she is between birth and death, we can envisage that, in relation to evolution, the human being stands under the aegis of the Spirits of Form. This too is set forth in *Esoteric Science.* But if we then think of life from death to the next birth, another essential fact must be taken into consideration. The spheres of activity of these Spirits of Form fall as it were into *seven* categories, only one of which is allotted to Jehovah—the one concerned primarily with life between birth and death. The six other categories of the Spirits of Form guide life between death and a new birth.

We can discover this, however, only if we investigate life between death and a new birth. Just as Jehovah has to do with the Earth and actually made the sacrifice of going to the Moon in order to neutralize from there certain things in earthly evolution, so the other Spirits of Form likewise have to do with the other planets. But this fact must be hidden, concealed, if you want the conception of repeated earthly lives to be withheld from human beings. Moreover the concealment must be really effective; it must be brought about in such a way that people do not become alive to the secret I have just spoken of. For if they are diverted from a true view of life between death and a new birth, their attention will be drawn to life between birth and death. And they will allow mediums to talk them into believing that life after death is simply a continuation of the life on Earth.

In this domain a tremendous amount of scheming goes on. Occultists who undertake anything of this nature naturally know, if they belong to the left, which direction to turn thoughts to bring feelings into line and thus divert attention from certain secrets and ensure that these do not come to light.

That is what actually happened, and you can read about it in the relevant literature. You will often find the statement that humanity has nothing to do with the other planets of our solar system.

This implies, of course, that humanity has nothing to do with the Guiding Spirits of these planets of our solar system. This was emphasized to make sure people would never evolve concepts that would lead them to realize the credibility of the teaching of reincarnation.

The other task was to present the truth as opposed to the fallacy. If you read *Esoteric Science* you will again find emphasis laid upon the fact that human beings must leave the Earth so that part of their lives will be spent on other planets. *Esoteric Science* deals in detail on the one hand with humanity's relation to the Moon, and on the other with its relation to the planets.

What these people set out to achieve can be indicated briefly by saying that they too made use of the materialistic outlook of the time. For if you present things as I have done in *Esoteric Science,* you will show what has to be accomplished in earthly evolution through its connection with the planets. *For the other planets, too, belong to the evolution of the Earth.* To the materialist, the planets move around in space as mere clods of matter. Therefore, when describing their functions in the spiritual evolution of humanity, I had to go back to their spiritual realities, to the Spirits of the planets.

You see from this how the spiritual movement was wedged as it were between two set purposes, one intent upon distorting the truth concerning the Moon, the other upon distorting the truth concerning the planets. Such was the situation at the end of the nineteenth century. H. P. Blavatsky and Sinnett were to distort the truth about the Moon; the others set out to distort the truth about the connection of the planets with the evolution of the Earth. Do not imagine that it is an easy position to be wedged between two such currents; for here we have to do with occultism, and where occultism is involved a stronger force is necessary for grasping its truths than for grasping the ordinary truths of the physical plane. Furthermore, there a far stronger force of deception—which it is essential to see through—is also at work.

It is not easy to be in such a position, because of the strong force required to counter it. On the one side, the truth about the Moon is veiled by the distortion, and, on the other, the truth about the planets. One was wedged between two fallacies committed in the interests of materialism. First, it was a matter of reckoning with the materialism emanating from the Oriental side, which was responsible for promoting the fallacy about the Moon in order to introduce the Oriental teaching of reincarnation. The teaching of the fact of reincarnation was of course correct, but we shall soon see what a strong concession had been made to materialism in *Esoteric Buddhism.*

On the other side there was the desire that a certain form of Catholic esotericism should be protected from the assault of the Indian influence. There, more than ever, the tendency was at work to allow all spiritual reality connected with the evolution of the planetary system as a whole to be submerged in materialism. The mission of spiritual science was wedged between these two currents. This was the situation which one was confronted with. Everywhere there were strong forces at work, intent upon making the one or the other influence effective.

Now I have to show you in what respect this distorted teaching about the Moon is a very special concession to materialism, and how the way it was then corrected by H. P. Blavatsky actually made matters even worse. It did so because, on the one side, with a great talent for occultism—which Sinnett did not possess—Blavatsky amended his statements, but on the other side she made use of particular methods whereby the error could be preserved with even greater certainty.

The first essential is to discern how far Sinnett's teaching about the Eighth Sphere is a fallacy. Here you must keep firmly in mind the teaching regarding the whole process of the evolution of the Earth, namely, the teaching that the planet Earth passed through the Old Saturn, Old Sun, and Old Moon periods of evolution before entering its present stage. You must remind yourselves that the composition of the Old Moon was essentially different from that of the Earth. The mineral kingdom was added for the first time during the Earth period, and what constitutes the material world of the physical plane is entirely impregnated with the mineral element. All that you perceive in the plant, animal, and human kingdoms is the mineral element that has been impregnated into them. Your body is "mineralized" through and through. What is not mineral—the Moon nature, the Sun nature—is only *occultly* present there. We see only the mineral, the earthly. This must be firmly borne in mind if, starting from what humanity now actually is on the Earth, we are to find the answer to the question, What is it in us that is the heritage of the Old Moon?

The Old Moon human is present within human beings as we now are, but in a form that must be pictured as containing nothing mineral whatever. If you envisage the earthly human such that you see only the mineral constituents, you must picture the Moon human within. But there is nothing mineral in this Moon human; hence this Moon human cannot be seen with physical eyes but only with spiritual sight. A Moon form underlies certain members of the physical human, is commingled within them, but this can be perceived only with the eye of clairvoyance. Needless to say, what is there within was present on the Old Moon. But just remember how it was seen on the Old Moon. It was seen through imaginative cognition—in surging, undulating pictures. These are still present today, but to behold them, atavistic clairvoyance was then necessary. The Old Moon humans could be perceived only by atavistic clairvoyance, which in that era was the normal faculty of vision. Consequently everything connected with this Old Moon evolution can also be seen only in imaginations, with ancient visionary clairvoyance. It must never be thought that the Old Moon human could be formed out of the mineral Earth; this Moon human was the product of the Old Moon as it might be seen in imaginative clairvoyance. And so in connection with the Old Moon we must picture to ourselves that the whole environment was visible to the imaginative clairvoyance of the Moon humans—just as our own environment, with plants, animals, rivers, mountains, is visible to our physical eyes.

We know that the forces contained in the Old Moon inevitably appear again in the Earth's evolutionary process but that earthly evolution would have been doomed to perish, as I have shown in *Esoteric Science,* if these Moon forces had not subsequently left. They could not have maintained their existence within the earthly forces.

Remember that the whole planet Earth had to receive the mineral kingdom into itself, to be mineralized, as it were. While the Moon formed part of the Earth, the Moon forces were still within the Earth. But these forces had to be expelled; hence the Moon itself was obliged to separate from the Earth, because it could not have existed in the mineralized Earth, and human beings would not have been able to evolve as they have actually evolved. I have spoken of all this in *Esoteric Science.* But now recall exactly what I have told you today—that this Moon can be perceived only through imaginative clairvoyance. If, therefore, you picture how humans developed as earthly humanity, with a constitution organized for perception with physical senses, you will understand that such human beings could never have beheld the departure of the Moon. The departure of the Moon and also its position out there in the cosmos could only have been apprehended clairvoyantly. Human beings were so organized that the whole process of the departure of the Moon could have been seen only with clairvoyant sight. Therefore, the influences then proceeding from the Moon could only have been those of the Old Moon—that is to say, influences that worked in such a way upon human beings that, among other things, imaginative clairvoyance would have been evoked in them.

Try to imagine the situation in that ancient time! "Human beings" were to come into being, souls to come down from the planets, and so forth. But the Moon would have continued to work such that the forces in the descending human being would have been the same as were present in the Old Moon that preceded the Earth. Nobody except one endowed with visionary clairvoyance could have seen this Moon.

Then, as a material phenomenon accompanying this process of the departure of the Moon forces, something else came about.

I have already told you how Jahve, or Jehovah, is related to the Moon. What happened was that through the connection of Jahve with the Moon, the Moon was also made material, mineralized, but with a much denser materiality than that of the Earth. Therefore what can be seen today as the physical Moon, which can be assumed to contain a mineral element, is to be traced back to the deed of Jahve whereby certain elements were added to the Old Moon.

Thereby, however, the Old Moon forces were crippled and now work in a quite different way. Had the Moon remained unmineralized, its forces would have worked in such a way that its rays would always have evoked the old atavistic clairvoyance, and the effects of the Moon upon the will would have made humans somnambulists in the most marked form. This was neutralized through the mineralization of the Moon. The old forces can now no longer develop in such a way.

This is a truth of tremendous importance, for now you will realize that the Moon had to be mineralized so that it might not work in the old way. Thus, when speaking of the Moon as a recapitulation of the Old Moon, we must speak of a celestial body that is not visible with physical eyes. This body is a concern of the spiritual world, albeit only the subconscious spiritual world that is perceptible to visionary clairvoyance. We must therefore speak of something *spiritual* if we are speaking of the recapitulation of the Old Moon; what is mineral in the present Moon has been added to the spiritual and does not belong to the Moon when the Moon is referred to in the old sense.

How was the materialism of the nineteenth century to be grappled with? Its adherents would certainly not believe that behind the material Moon lies the very important remainder of the old, nonmineralized Moon; they would never believe such a thing. So a concession was made to materialism by speaking only of the physical, materialized Moon. Hence when Sinnett spoke of the Moon, he left out the spirit. In *Esoteric Buddhism* he merely says that the materiality of the Moon is far denser than that of the Earth. That is so, indeed must be so, but that the occult reality I have indicated lies behind it—that fact he omits altogether. He therefore made the concession in that he speaks only of the materiality of the Moon. But the spirituality behind the Moon does not come into consideration; it does not belong essentially to the Earth but is connected much more closely with the Old Moon than with the Earth. This fact was completely veiled, and the consequence was of tremendous import; for Sinnett had thereby brought a true fact—that the Moon has something to do with the Eighth Sphere—into an utterly false light and distorted it with great subtlety.

He omits all mention of the spiritual aspect of the Eighth Sphere. He does not say that the Eighth Sphere, whose representative is alleged to be the Moon, is what lies *behind* the Moon. He calls what was actually placed there to neutralize, to counter the effects of the Eighth Sphere, the Eighth Sphere itself. As we have heard, the materiality of the Moon is there in order to neutralize the Eighth Sphere, to render it ineffectual.

People do not realize what the effect of the Eighth Sphere would be if materiality were taken away from the Moon. The whole nature of the human soul would have become quite different on the Earth, and that this has not happened is due to the fact that materiality of a greater density was incorporated into the Moon. What actually makes the Eighth Sphere ineffectual, namely its materiality, Sinnett calls the Eighth Sphere, and what is actually the Eighth Sphere, namely the Old Moon forces, he obscures. A trick frequently used in occultism is to say something that is true fundamentally but to put it in such a way that it is absolutely false—forgive the paradox! It is false to say that the material Moon is the Eighth Sphere, because actually it is the neutralizer of the Eighth Sphere. But it is quite correct that the "Moon" is the Eighth Sphere, because the Eighth Sphere is centered in the Moon, is actually present up there.

And now we have reached the point where we can say more specifically than has hitherto been possible what the Eighth Sphere is in reality. This is a matter most intimately connected with the spiritual aspect of evolution in the nineteenth century.

12

More on the Eighth Sphere

Dornach, October 18, 1915

IT IS VERY DIFFICULT indeed to speak about the so-called "Eighth Sphere," which was referred to openly for the first time by Sinnett. One cannot say that he gave "information" about it, for what he said was wrong. You can certainly realize, then, why it is difficult to speak about this subject. I have often emphasized that our language has been coined for the outer, material world. Perhaps that is why the Eighth Sphere was regarded as a secret matter until Sinnett mentioned it.

Consequently there are not many words that can be used for characterizing the Eighth Sphere. The fact that all mention was avoided for so long will also enable you to understand what is involved when one speaks of it. You will therefore have to take the aphoristic remarks I shall make today as a kind of introductory exposition, given with the object of throwing out certain indications, which to begin with can contribute only a little to the subject. It is to be hoped, however, that there will be opportunities for saying more at some later time.

For the moment, based on what I said in my last lecture I shall try to characterize what is called the "Eighth Sphere." I shall do so in order that we may have a foundation for describing the development of the spiritual movement in the nineteenth century and at the beginning of the twentieth century.

From what I said yesterday, you will have understood that the Eighth Sphere cannot be anything that belongs to the material world. Thus the greatest fallacy in Sinnett's statement is that the physical Moon is directly connected with the Eighth Sphere. Yesterday, I tried to make it understandable that the actual foundation of the error is that this pointed to something material and physical.

From this you will be able to conjecture, even if not to understand fully, that what is called the Eighth Sphere can have nothing directly to do with anything within the material world. That is to say, what can be perceived by our senses and thought out based on sensory perception plays no part in the Eighth Sphere. So it will be useless to look for the Eighth Sphere anywhere in the material world.

You now have a basis on which we may begin to approach a conception of the Eighth Sphere. I have said that the Eighth Sphere has something to do with the residue left from the Old Moon and its evolution. So much you can gather from the studies we have pursued in the course of time. I tried to make it clear yesterday that on the Old Moon the natural mode of perception of human beings was visionary and imaginative in character, so that any substantiality to be discerned in the Eighth Sphere must be found with this kind of vision. That is to say, it must be presumed at the outset that the Eighth Sphere is found by way of visionary imaginations.

How did the expression "Eighth Sphere" come to be used?

You know that human evolution takes its course through the seven spheres of Saturn, Sun, Moon, Earth, Jupiter, Venus, and Vulcan. We will conceive that besides these seven spheres there is still something else that lies outside these and yet is in some way related to the Earth. Here, then, we have a sphere, visible only to visionary-imaginative clairvoyance, which stands as an *Eighth* Sphere over and above the seven that make up the domain of the ordered and regular evolution of humankind. All such sketches are, of course, purely schematic. It is only for the sake of the diagram that spheres must be drawn separately that, in fact, can be observed only each *within* the others. You will certainly have realized from our studies that as long as human beings are in the material world, make observations through the senses, and think with the intellect, they are standing in the Fourth Sphere, the Earth Sphere. If they develop their faculties of soul sufficiently to be able to see the Third or Moon Sphere, they fly far, but not of course in the spatial sense. Observing from the Moon Sphere, they do not observe from another place, but—physically or spatially speaking—from the same place. The seven spheres therefore ought in reality to be drawn within one another.

These seven spheres, in fact, are successive stages and states of evolution. Fundamentally, then, such a diagram has no other value than if one were to say that human beings develop from birth to the seventh year in a first stage, from the seventh to the fourteenth year in a second stage, and so on. The being who has developed from the first to the seventh year cannot be thought of as separate from the being who is developing from the seventh until the fourteenth year. In the same way it is incorrect to think of the seven successive spheres or stages of the Earth's evolution as separate from each other.

This will give you an inkling that the Eighth Sphere is to be observed within the Earth Sphere. It cannot properly be drawn either above or below. To depict reality it would have to be sketched into the Earth Sphere. I have often given a crude example to express what is meant here: just as the physical air is around us, so is the spiritual around us; we have to look for the spiritual within what is actually physical in our environment. Hence, just as the spiritual is round about us, so too the Eighth Sphere must be around us in our environment. We must look for it there. This means we must develop an organ enabling us to perceive the Eighth Sphere, just as we have developed our physical senses to enable us to perceive the material Earth. We could then experience the Eighth Sphere quite consciously; but unconsciously we are always within it—just as we are always within the air, even if we are not aware of it. If we have developed an organ for experiencing the Eighth Sphere, we are conscious of it around us. So if the Eighth Sphere is to be described, it must obviously be described as a realm in which we are living all the time.

Now, as I said, all that I can do in these introductory studies is to give some general information—the rest will emerge as we proceed.

First of all, you can understand that what is around us as the Eighth Sphere is accessible to imaginative-visionary clairvoyance. To develop imaginative clairvoyance without perceiving something of the Eighth Sphere is impossible. The reason it is so difficult to speak of matters such as the Eighth Sphere is because so very few people possess really clear and discriminative clairvoyance. In the Eighth Sphere we have to do with imaginations, and what constitutes the essential nature of Earth evolution—that is to say, the Fourth Sphere—is *not* present in the Eighth Sphere. The essential nature of the Fourth Sphere is constituted, as I indicated yesterday, by the mineral impregnation of this world-body. That we are able to live on the Earth is due to the fact that this Fourth Sphere has been mineralized: we live in a mineralized environment. Perceived through the physical senses, this can be coordinated by the intellect. But we must recognize that the mineral element is totally absent from the Eighth Sphere.

When we eliminate the mineral element in thought, all that remains is a later stage of the Old Moon evolution, for whence could anything else originate? But evolution proceeds; something that is perceptible through imaginative-visionary clairvoyance but could be nothing else than a residue of the Old Moon would not be the Eighth Sphere. All that could be said would be that the Third Sphere had left something behind.

To have some inkling of the facts relating to the Eighth Sphere, we must also keep the following in mind. In the course of its regular evolution, the Third Sphere became the Fourth Sphere; that is to say, a transition of the third elemental kingdom—for that is what we must call it—to the mineral kingdom took place. The mineral element was added. Otherwise we should have to conceive of the Old Moon as a sum total of substantiality, imaginatively perceptible! It must therefore be assumed that the regular progression from the Old Moon to the Earth, from the Third Sphere to the Fourth Sphere, consists in what was formerly only imaginatively perceptible becoming materially perceptible, that is, becoming mineralized. To begin with, the Old Moon element, as the Eighth Sphere, remains, but due to a particular happening this element undergoes a change. What took place so that the Fourth Sphere might be able to arise from the Third is clearly described in *Esoteric Science*. I show there how the activities of the Spirits of Form, who guide the whole process of the transformation, are added to those of the Spirits of Movement. We may therefore say that the Fourth Sphere arises out of the Third because the Spirits of Form add their activities to those of the Spirits of Movement.

If the Spirits of Form had achieved everything that their own nature desired and moreover was able to achieve, when the mission of Sphere Three was fulfilled in the cosmos, Sphere Four would have arisen quite naturally from Sphere Three. That is obvious. But we know that Luciferic and Ahrimanic spirits are at work. They hold back for themselves something of the Old Moon substantiality. They wrest it away, as it were, from the Spirits of Form. The fact that Lucifer and Ahriman do so is indicative of their essential nature. Thus as Sphere Three is advancing to a further stage, something is wrested from the Spirits of Form by Lucifer and Ahriman. And into this part that is wrested away, Lucifer and Ahriman penetrate instead of the Spirits of Form. The activities of Lucifer and Ahriman are added to those of the Spirits of Movement and, as a result, Eight arises out of Three: the Eighth Sphere out of the Third Sphere.

Something else must be there then, not merely the Old Moon. This "something else" that comes into being as Sphere Four is constituted by the fact that mineral substantiality, as it comes into being, is wrested away at the moment of the birth of the Fourth Sphere. Thus when the mineral comes into existence out of the imaginative substantiality, it is snatched by Lucifer and Ahriman and made into imaginations. Instead of an Earth arising from the remaining Old Moon substantiality, a cosmic body takes shape whose birth is due to the fact that the substantiality wrested from the Earth is made into what has come over from the Old Moon.

Now recall how I have described the conditions pertaining to the Old Moon in *Esoteric Science.* In the Old Moon there was as yet nothing mineral. Had mineral substance been present, that world-body would have been Earth, not Moon. Sphere Four comes into being through the birth of the mineral element. In that Lucifer and Ahriman approach, snatch mineral substantiality out of Sphere Four, and infuse it into Sphere Three, the Old Moon is recapitulated, but now with materiality that belongs properly to the Earth.

Mark this well: instead of pure imaginations being there, the imaginations are identified by the infusion of a mineral element that has been wrested from the Earth. Identified imaginations are thus created. We are therefore drawn into a world of identified imaginations that are not lunar in character because materiality belonging to the Earth has identified them. They are ghosts, specters—that is to say, behind our world there is a world of specters created by Lucifer and Ahriman.

Let me express it schematically. On the Old Moon certain pictures were present. These should have passed over to the Earth as something everywhere perceptible. But Lucifer and Ahriman retained them for themselves. Lucifer and Ahriman wrested from the Earth certain of its constituents and made them into imaginations, so that these Earth substances became not earthly formations, but Moon formations.

Into our Fourth Sphere, therefore, there has been instilled a sphere that is really a Moon Sphere, but is filled with earthly substantiality and is *therefore a bogus creation* in the universe. To the seven spheres, an eighth, created in opposition to the progressive Spirits, has been added. The necessary consequence of this is that the Spirits of Form must do battle on the Earth for every morsel of substantiality capable of mineralization, lest it should be wrested from them by Lucifer and Ahriman and carried into the Eighth Sphere.

In truth, therefore, our Earth—the Fourth Sphere—is simply not what it appears outwardly to be. Were it really to consist of atoms, all these atoms would still be impregnated by formations belonging to the Eighth Sphere, which are perceptible only to visionary clairvoyance. These formations are present everywhere; so too are the specter-like contents of the Eighth Sphere. These can therefore be perceived just as actual specters are perceived. All earthly being and existence are involved here. Lucifer and Ahriman strive unceasingly to draw from the Earth's substances whatever they can snatch, in order to form their Eighth Sphere, which then, when it is sufficiently advanced, will be detached from the Earth and go its own way in the cosmos together with Lucifer and Ahriman. Needless to say, the Earth would then pass over to Jupiter as a mere torso. As you know, as human beings we have an established place in the whole of the evolution of the Earth, because we are mineralized through and through. We are permeated by the mineralizing process that is itself drawn into this battle, so that morsels of this substance can be continually wrested from it. Therefore we ourselves are involved in the battle. Lucifer and Ahriman battle against the Spirits of Form, with the aim of wresting mineral substance from us everywhere.

But the strength of the process varies in the different regions of our organism. We are diversely constituted. Some organs are more perfect than others. Our most perfect organ is our organ of thinking, the brain and the skull. There the battle is the most violent, precisely because this human head, this human brain, is fashioned as it is. In fact, it is so fashioned because it is at this place in our body that Lucifer and Ahriman have been the most successful in wresting mineral substance from us. Physical substance is more spiritualized there than anywhere else. The formation of our skull is due to the fact that there the most has been wrested from us. Hence it is precisely through the head that we can emancipate ourselves from our organism to the greatest extent. We can soar upwards in thoughts, we can distinguish between the good and the evil. And for that very reason, Lucifer and Ahriman have there been the most successful in wresting away substantiality. They have been able to wrest away the greatest amount of mineralized substantiality in the so-called noblest organ. This alchemy—by which mineral substance is sent over into the Eighth Sphere—takes place all the time behind the scenes of our existence.

If everything were to run smoothly for Lucifer and Ahriman—if they were able to wrest from everywhere as much as they wrest from the organ of the head—then earthly evolution would soon reach a point where Lucifer and Ahriman could succeed in destroying our Earth. Thereby they would lead the evolution of all the worlds into the Eighth Sphere. And the whole evolution of the Earth would take a different course. Thus Lucifer tries to unfold his greatest strength where we are the most vulnerable, namely, in our heads.

The stronghold that is easiest for Lucifer to capture is the human head and everything else similar in the distribution of the mineral element. These can be drawn out in the same way, are equally exposed to the danger of being dispatched into the Eighth Sphere. No less a prospect looms as a consequence of this intention of Lucifer and Ahriman than that the whole evolution of humanity may be allowed to disappear into the Eighth Sphere, so that this evolution would take a different course.

That, you see, was the intention of Lucifer and Ahriman from the beginning of earthly evolution—to let the whole of this evolution disappear into the Eighth Sphere. It was therefore necessary that a counterweight be created by those Spirits who belong to the Hierarchy of the Spirits of Form. The outer counterweight they created consists in this. They inserted something into the "space," as it were, of the Eighth Sphere that works against this Eighth Sphere. To present this correctly, we must understand the Earth (and the Moon) to be surrounded by the Eighth Sphere. The Eighth Sphere belongs to our physical Earth in the sense indicated.

We are surrounded everywhere by the imaginations into which Lucifer and Ahriman intend that mineral materiality shall be drawn continually. There lies the reason for the sacrifice made by Jahve — the precipitation of substance far denser than other mineralized substance. Jahve established this as Moon, as the counteracting agent. It was substance of extreme density. Sinnett described this density as substance of a far denser physical-mineral character than exists anywhere on Earth. Hence Lucifer and Ahriman cannot dissolve it away into their world of imaginations.

And so this Moon circles around as a material globe, solid, dense, and indestructible. If you read carefully enough you will find that even the descriptions of the Moon given by physicists tally with this. Everything that was available on the Earth was drawn out and placed there so that there would be enough physical matter incapable of being wrested away. When we look at the Moon, we see a substance far more intensely mineralized, far denser physically, than exists anywhere on

Earth. Jahve or Jehovah, then, must be regarded as the being who, even in the physical domain, has ensured that Lucifer and Ahriman cannot draw all materiality away. And then, at the right time, equal care will be taken by the same Spirit that the Moon will reenter the Earth when the Earth is strong enough to receive it, when the danger is averted by the development that has meanwhile taken place.

This applies to the external physical-mineral domain. But in the human domain too it was necessary that a counterweight be created to the intention aimed at the human head. Just as in the outside world materiality had to be identified that Lucifer and Ahriman cannot dissolve by their alchemy, so in the human being something had to be set over against the organ that can most easily be attacked by Lucifer and Ahriman. Jahve had therefore to take care, just as he had done for the mineral domain, that not everything can succumb to the attacks of Lucifer and Ahriman.

Care had to be taken that not everything proceeding from the head could become the prey of Lucifer and Ahriman. Care had to be taken that not everything would depend upon the activity of the head and the outward senses. If this had not been done, Lucifer and Ahriman would have been victors. It was necessary that a counterweight be created in the domain of earthly life, that there be in the human being something entirely independent of the head. And this was achieved through the work of the good Spirits of Form, who implanted the principle of *Love* into the principle of heredity on Earth.

That is to say, there is now operative in the human race something that is independent of the head, that passes from generation to generation and has its deepest foundations in the physical nature of humankind.

What is connected with propagation and with heredity and is independent of us in the sense that we cannot penetrate it with our thinking is the gift of the Moon in the celestial firmament and proceeds from the principle of Love permeating the process of propagation and heredity. Hence the violent battle that persists through history, the battle waged by Lucifer and Ahriman against everything that comes from this domain. Lucifer and Ahriman want to force on us the exclusive sovereignty of the head, and they launch their attacks by way of the head against everything that is purely natural affinity. For whatever is hereditary substance on the Earth cannot be wrested away by them. What the Moon is in the heavens, heredity is on the Earth below. Everything that is grounded in heredity, everything that is not charged with thought, that is connected intrinsically with physical nature—that is the Jahve principle. The Jahve principle unfolds its greatest activity where nature is working *as* nature; it is there that Jahve has outpoured in greatest measure the Love that is his natural attribute, in order to create a counterweight to the lovelessness, the mere wisdom, of Lucifer and Ahriman.

It would be necessary to go very thoroughly into matters recently presented from quite different points of view to show how in the Moon and in the process of human heredity the Spirits of Form have created barricades against Lucifer and Ahriman. If you think more deeply about these matters, you will find something of immense importance here.

Now, to reach at least some measure of understanding, the subject must also be approached from a rather different standpoint. If you remember what is said in *Esoteric Science* about the evolution of humankind through the Old Saturn, Old Sun, and Old Moon stages of the evolution of the Earth, you will realize that in these stages there can be no question of *freedom*. In those other stages human beings were enclosed in a web of *necessity*. In order that they might be ripe for freedom, mineral nature had to be incorporated. They had to become beings permeated with the mineral element. Hence human beings can be educated for freedom only within the earthly material world.

This by itself indicates the tremendous significance of the earthly material world. What humanity must acquire—freedom of will—can be acquired only during earthly evolution. In the Jupiter, Venus, and Vulcan stages we will need this freedom of will. Thus, when we consider the question of freedom, we are in a realm of great importance; for we know that Earth is the begetter of freedom precisely because it is Earth that impregnates us with the physical-mineral element.

From this you will understand that what stems from free will must be kept within the *realm of Earth*. It is impossible to apply anything that stems from the principle of freedom to Spheres Three, Two, and One. But the endeavor of Lucifer and Ahriman is to drag the free will, and whatever stems from it, into the Eighth Sphere. This means we are perpetually exposed to the danger of having our free will wrested from us and dragged by Lucifer and Ahriman into the Eighth Sphere.

This happens if the element of free will is transformed, for example, into visionary clairvoyance. When this happens, a person is already in the Eighth Sphere. This is a matter occultists are so reluctant to speak of, because it is an awful, terrible truth. The moment the free will is transformed into visionary clairvoyance, what unfolds in the human being becomes the booty of Lucifer and Ahriman. It is immediately captured by them and thereby spirited away from the Earth. You can see from this how the specters of the Eighth Sphere are created through the shackling of free will. Lucifer and Ahriman are engaged perpetually in shackling our free will and in conjuring all sorts of things before us in order to tear away what we make out of these things and let it disappear in the Eighth Sphere.

When clairvoyance in all kinds of different forms develops in naive, credulous, superstitious people, it is often the case that their free will has been sacrificed. Then Lucifer instantly seizes hold of it, and whereas these people imagine they have had an experience of immortality, the truth is that in their visions they see a part, or a product, of their souls being wrested away and prepared for the Eighth Sphere.

You can imagine from this how deep was the concern of those who, having compromised by agreeing that by way of mediumship all kinds of truths relating to the spiritual world should be given to the public, then found the mediums believing that the dead were speaking to them. But the occultists knew that what takes place between mediums and the living is that the stream of free will is passing into the Eighth Sphere. Instead of a link being formed with the eternal, the mediums were testifying precisely to what was continually disappearing into the Eighth Sphere.

From this you will realize that Lucifer and Ahriman have an avid desire to bring as much as possible into the Eighth Sphere. Although Goethe mixed Lucifer and Ahriman together, he has nevertheless correctly described how a soul is wrested away from the clutches of Mephistopheles-Ahriman! It would be the richest prize for Lucifer and Ahriman if they could ever succeed in capturing a whole soul for themselves; for thereby such a soul would disappear into the Eighth Sphere and be lost from Earth evolution. The greatest victory for Lucifer and Ahriman would be if one day they could claim that countless numbers of the dead had passed into their sphere. That would be their greatest victory.

Moreover they have a way of achieving it. Lucifer and Ahriman could think somewhat as follows: Human beings long to know something about life between death and a new birth. If, therefore, we tell them that they are learning something from the dead, they will be satisfied and will direct their feelings toward the realm from which announcements are made to them as coming from the dead. If therefore we desire that human hearts and minds shall be guided toward the Eighth Sphere, let us say to them: we are telling you something that comes from the dead. We shall capture souls by alleging that the dead are in our domain.

This devilish plan—for here we have indeed to do with the devil—was put into effect by Lucifer and Ahriman when it had occurred to occultists to endeavor to accomplish something through mediumship. Lucifer and Ahriman inspired the mediums, through whom they arranged the whole business, so that people might be guided to the realm whence the dead were alleged to be speaking. Lucifer and Ahriman could then lay hold of their souls. The occultists were alarmed when they saw the course things were taking, and they took counsel among themselves about how to steer away from it. Even those who belonged to the left wing realized what was happening. They wanted to do something different!

Then an opportunity presented itself. A remarkable personality, namely H. P. Blavatsky, appeared. Now, after the plan had been seen through and the occultists on Earth no longer lent their hands to it, Lucifer and Ahriman were obliged to pursue their aim a different way.

Materialism had come upon the scene in the natural course of earthly evolution. Therefore, in order to reckon with the mineralized process of evolution, it was necessary that the attention of human beings should be focused entirely on material things. That is materialism pure and simple! The occultists who had special aims of their own said, Well and good, we will rely upon materialism. If, however, we take materialism in its purely earthly form, people will inevitably discover one day through their thinking that atoms do not exist—so that will not be very fertile soil. But human thinking can certainly be perverted if materialism is made *occult*. The best way of doing this is to present the sphere to be created as a counterweight to the Eighth Sphere as the Eighth Sphere itself! If people can be led to believe that the materiality created as a counterweight to the Eighth Sphere is the Eighth Sphere itself, then that will outstrip every conceivable earthly materialism!

Earthly materialism was indeed outstripped in the assertion made by Sinnett. Materialism is there imported into the realm of occultism;

occultism there becomes materialism. Sooner or later people would have been bound to discover this.

H. P. Blavatsky, who had deep insight into this phase of the Earth's evolution, divined something of what was happening. She did so after she had seen through the tricks of that strange individuality of whom I spoke in the last lecture. She concluded that what was happening could not go on as it was. She said that it had to be changed! But she said that under the influence of the Indian occultists who belonged to the left wing. She realized that things must change but that something not easily detectable must be created. In order to create something herself that would outstrip Sinnett's assertion, she acceded to the proposals of the Indian occultists who were inspiring her. These occultists, being adherents of the left path, had no other aim than the promotion of their own special interests—Indian interests. They had in mind to establish all over the Earth a system of wisdom from which Christ, and Jahve too, were excluded. Therefore something whereby Christ and Jahve were eliminated would have to be interpolated.

The following method was then adopted. It was said: Lucifer is in truth the great benefactor of humankind. (Of Ahriman there was no mention; so little was known of him that one name was used for both.) Lucifer brings to humanity all that they have gained through the head—science, art, in short all progress. He is the true Spirit of Light; it is to him that humanity must adhere. And Jahve—what has he done, in reality? He has established the principle of physical heredity! He is a Moon God who has introduced elements pertaining to the Moon. Hence the statement in *The Secret Doctrine* that people should not adhere to Jahve, for he is only the Lord of materiality, of all the lower, earthly impulses; the true benefactor of humankind is Lucifer. This shimmers through the whole of *The Secret Doctrine* and moreover is clearly stated there. So for occult reasons H. P. Blavatsky was prepared in such a way as to become a hater of Christ and Jahve. For in the occult domain such an utterance signifies exactly the same as Sinnett's statement that the Moon is the Eighth Sphere.

It is through knowledge alone that an approach can be made to these things. Truly, through knowledge alone. Therefore when we began the periodical *Luzifer-Gnosis,* the first article was necessarily on the subject of Lucifer, in order that he should be rightly understood, in order that it should be realized that inasmuch as he brings about head activity, he is a benefactor of humankind. But the counterweight must also be there. *Love* must be there as the counterweight. This was stated in the very first article of the periodical, because at that point it was essential to intervene.

As you see, things were complicated. Fundamentally, it was desired to achieve through H. P. Blavatsky that human beings should be misled into believing in the Eighth Sphere. They could most easily be misled into this belief by something false being presented to them as the Eighth Sphere. Naturally, people were led to the spiritual world, for Blavatsky's *Secret Doctrine* has this great merit, that through it minds were directed to the spiritual world. But the path followed was in pursuance of special interests, not the interests of the evolution of humanity in general. All these things must be kept strictly in mind if we are to be quite clear about which is the healthy path. We must not accept empty words without verification if we desire to have genuine occultism; we must resolve to see things clearly. Particularly at the present point in our development it has been necessary for me to give certain indications about these things, indications that can be supplemented at some other time by matters of even greater significance.

I had to give these indications because if you keep them rightly in your minds you will see how our ship has been steered from the beginning of our movement. It has been steered in such a way that account has been taken of all the false paths that can be pursued and of all those things that were a menace to the spiritual development of humanity.

Indications of a path into the spiritual world must not be given blindly. Above all, they must not be given as the result of rapturous fanaticism. That is why the exhortation has again and again had to be made among you, my dear friends, that it is urgently necessary not to allow yourselves to be duped by what leads to the Eighth Sphere. I have said repeatedly that more caution should be exercised in the domain of visionary clairvoyance, that validity should be ascribed only to clairvoyance that, in leading into the higher worlds, excludes Lucifer and Ahriman. Then it will be seen that everything capable of bringing the soul into connection with the Eighth Sphere must be rejected. . . .

13

Some Background to the Role of Madame Blavatsky

Berlin, March 28, 1916

I WANT TO SPEAK today of a deep historical impulse. As you know, spiritual forces, spiritual intentions, spiritual goals stand behind everything that happens in the universe. Spiritual science, for its part, helps us to see the spiritual processes that stand behind historical occurrences. Indeed, to understand history, we must not only know the material, historical facts, but be able to complete them by knowing the sort of facts I am going to present to you today.

I will start by talking about a personality you all know, namely Madame Blavatsky. You all know that Madame Blavatsky was a particularly psychic person in a time when materialism was at the high point in outer life, and that she stood in a very special relationship to the spiritual movement of the second half of the nineteenth century. She was not a personality that one can designate in the ordinary sense as a medium, but she had, in the deepest sense, very pronounced psychic abilities. She was a psychic personality. If you want to understand this you must realize the milieu from which she emerged. She came out of Russia. Now, in the Russian milieu, the spiritual and physical work together in a way that, for us, is not normal, but abnormal. To understand this, we must consider the special folk characteristics of the Russians and how they differ from those of Central and Western Europeans.

The Central and Western Europeans are in a certain sense the continuation and in another sense a new creative configuration of the culture that proceeded out of the so-called Greco-Latin cultural epoch, the fourth post-Atlantean period. What had lived in the Greco-Latin cultural period continued especially in Central and Western Europe, because there physical bodies developed so that they could become instruments for thinking, feeling, and willing. What can be brought together through thinking, feeling, and willing through the instrument of the physical body emerged primarily in Western and Central Europe.

However, the situation is different with the Slavic peoples in Eastern Europe and in particular with the Russians. One can say that the way in which the physical body is mechanized as it is in Western and Central Europe cannot occur with the Russians so long as this people retains its national quality. You cannot understand the Russians with Western European science. You can only understand them when you know that an *etheric* body exists. The precise characteristic of the Russian people consists in the fact that the most important activity of life does not enter into the physical body as it does in Western and Central Europe, but rather into the etheric body. Therefore, it does not permeate the physical body as much. Among the Russian people, the etheric body has a greater significance than it has for Western and Central Europeans (and above all for Americans). A strong I cannot be developed within the Russian people—the folk, not the ruling classes—in the same sense that it can among Western and Central Europeans. The I is always veiled over by a kind of dreaminess. It has something of a dreamy nature in it. This is because the I, as it now lives in the fifth post-Atlantean period, is conditioned by a special development of the physical body. The Russian people are not yet far enough advanced for the direct building of the I as such. What lives and weaves in the etheric body should not imprint itself into the physical body as it does among the Russians. This means that what the Russian people are destined to bring to human evolution cannot at the present time, generally speaking, come to external manifestation.

Helena Petrovna Blavatsky grew out of the Russian people, out of the Russian Folk Soul. From this it follows that in her case, as far as cognition—cognitive activity—is concerned, the etheric body is much more powerful than the physical. Hence, generally speaking, in Blavatsky, we have a personality who can experience much of her etheric body. This is naturally quite different from what one can experience by thinking and cognition with the aid of the brain. Because Blavatsky grew out of the Russian folk, she was able to experience an immense amount in her etheric body. Connected with this, however, is also the fact that she lacked certain qualities Western Europeans must have if they are to receive revelations from the spiritual worlds— she lacked the possibility of thinking *logically*. If Western Europeans are to obtain proper revelations from the spiritual world, they must have this capacity. But Madame Blavatsky lacked precisely the capacity to logically group together her knowledge. On the other hand, precisely what permeated her etheric body, her etheric cognitive ability, helped her to receive significant revelations.

In other words, precisely at the time when humankind was at the height of materialism, a personality stemming from Eastern Europe was present who still had a "dose" of Central Europe in her stream of heredity, her bloodstream. For Madame Blavatsky still had within her, although it was overpowered by the Eastern European element, that which among Central Europeans leads to a logical nature and, above all, to acts of will—neither of which as a general rule the Russians, as a people, usually have.

But what actually happened?

First, you know that we have books written by Blavatsky in English: *English books*. When we put these two extreme poles (Russian and English) together, we may say that what arose from her roots in her *Russian* nature (which came out of her etheric body) was taken hold of by the "being" of the *English*. Thus, it appears that her books are worked out in English. However, the most important thing is what lies between her Russian nature and her English "being." To understand this, one must understand that through this English or British "being" a certain kind of occult science penetrates extensively into Western Europe. As far as one can speak of English history, this was always the case. Throughout the whole evolution of its spiritual culture, Central Europe never had the slightest idea of how a kind of occult working always came from Britain and spread over Western Europe, Southern Europe, and so on.

To know how things stand, then, one must at least begin to understand this "British"—or British-tinged—occultism. This occultism is absolutely present. What people know of as all sorts of high grades of Scottish Freemasonry and so on is actually only the external side of this occultism—the side shown to the world. However, comprehensive and working occult schools actually stand behind this external side. These are schools that have taken up the ancient occult traditions and the ancient occult stream to a much higher degree than is the case among similar groups in Central Europe. In Central Europe, however, we strive more and more to allow knowledge of the spiritual world to rise up out of our own spirituality. In the British tradition, they have preferred to lean on what has been traditionally handed down from the more ancient occult schools. In fact, going back to the beginning of the seventeenth century, we find particularly in England, Scotland, and Ireland (less in Ireland, but all over Scotland) such occult societies. In these societies they continued to propagate ancient occult knowledge, while transforming it in a certain way.

To find the reason for this transformation, you must know that the fourth post-Atlantean (Greco-Latin) cultural epoch lasted until the beginning of the fifteenth century. The task of this epoch was to penetrate in a purely human spiritual way what was present as revelation in earlier epochs. Then came the fifth epoch, ours. This began with the beginning of the fifteenth century. Humanity was supposed to focus more upon the outer, physical world. Human beings were not supposed to work out new concepts. All the concepts that we have today derive from the Greco-Latin epoch. No really new concepts have been developed since the fifteenth century. What we have are only ancient concepts applied in a new way to physical processes. Darwinism did not introduce a single new concept of evolution; it only applied older concepts to certain processes. Thus, not one single new concept has arisen. This period was supposed to direct its gaze on the outer physical plane, for which the British were especially prepared. They were especially adapted for this task because of the characteristics that developed in the British Isles.

Now, at the beginning of the fifteenth century a danger arose. A kind of confusion threatened to arise. The purely outer, physical striving of the British, which was their task, threatened to become confused by a more spiritual striving that was fructified by knowledge arising from ancient times. This danger occurred when English dominion crossed the channel into France. It was averted and a real separation was effected from the spiritual world through the appearance of Joan of Arc who, precisely from the spiritual world itself, was called to create order at the beginning of the fifteenth century. As I have said before, the whole outer evolution of Western Europe hangs on this appearance of Joan of Arc.

At the time of Joan, then, a complete separation was made between the natures of the French and the British. British being originally arose from the invasion of the Angles and Saxons, who had their occult sagas of Hengist and Horsa.[1] Now, at the time of Joan of Arc, this Anglo-Saxon layer was ruled by the Norman-Roman element and formed a lower caste. The particular British being that is now superior only gained the ascendancy since the seventeenth century when the French element was still working, and the Anglo-Saxons were the lower layers and the French spirit was the aristocratic spirit. This French spirit despised everything coming from the Angles and Saxons.

For example, in the tenth, eleventh, and twelfth centuries, there was a common expression used as a curse by the aristocracy who still lived in France: "God damn me if I become English." This curse was often heard. If you wished to be well regarded you were not supposed to become English. However, all of this changed after the separation brought about through Joan of Arc. The English aspect then began to develop.

There are many different processes involved here and it would take too long to describe them completely, but deep spiritual forces were at work behind the Wars of the (Red and White) Roses. The important thing to note is that at the beginning of the seventeenth century, a certain soul incarnated in the British Isles who did not work outwardly in a very significant way, but worked nevertheless in a most stimulating way. This person incarnated in a British body in whom there was more French and Scottish blood and very little British blood. From this soul there actually came what gave the impulse in Britain not only for external spiritual life but also for *occult life*. Of course, there were also other factors, intermediate processes that also formed this occult spiritual life of the British. But to describe these would cause us to go too far off our theme.

I have told you that this British spiritual life was a continuation of the occult streams of the fourth post-Atlantean epoch. The British knew an immense amount precisely because physical bodies had the most significance. In British occult life, they knew the significance of the physical body. They made the etheric body least active, and regarded the physical body as an instrument of all spiritual life. Because of this, in these occult schools one could not experience very much from the spiritual world. However, the ancient traditions were preserved. The occult schools preserved what had been handed down of what ancient clairvoyance observed, and then they sought to permeate this with concepts. Thus an occult science arose that really worked only with the experiences passed on from what had been seen by clairvoyance in the previous post-Atlantean periods. In these schools, they penetrated what originated in clairvoyance with purely physical concepts derived from thinking with the physical body. In this way an actual occult science arose that covered all domains of life.

It is particularly interesting to realize that in this chapter of occult science, facts about the destiny of the European peoples were actually taught in these British occult schools. This was a very important part of those occult schools. I will now try to characterize what was taught about the destiny of the European peoples.[2]

They said the following. There was a fourth post-Atlantean period—they had this from tradition. This fourth post-Atlantean period was filled with spiritual life. It created our conceptual world, how we perceive the social organization. This fourth post-Atlantean epoch unfolded in Southern Europe on the Greek and Italian peninsulas and radiated out from there. During this time, the people of Central and Western Europe were in their infancy. I am telling you what was taught in these schools. The Central and Western Europeans were infants in spiritual life, infants in relation to what radiated out from Greece and Italy. Gradually, however, as they moved toward and through the Renaissance and the Reformation, the Central and Western Europeans worked themselves up out of their infancy. They became more and more mature. When I say Reformation, I do not mean the German Reformation but the English Reformation under James I.

The Central and Western Europeans were now able to separate themselves. And a quite definite dogma arose within the British occult schools, a dogma that was very strongly held. This was the dogma that just as the Greco-Latin people were the leading people of the fourth post-Atlantean epoch, so now Anglo-Saxon culture would take the lead in the fifth post-Atlantean period. This was stressed repeatedly. Anglo-Saxon culture was to reign spiritually through the fifth post-Atlantean period. The teaching concerning human evolution and development embodied this dogma of the superiority of the Anglo-Saxon people as the leaders of the fifth post-Atlantean period. Today, it is the East European peoples who are in the same condition in which the Central and Western Europeans were at the time of the Greco-Latin epoch. The Slavic people in Eastern Europe are now in their infancy. And the British occult schools realize that these Slavic peoples must develop out of their infancy, just as the Central and Western Europeans did. And just as the Greco-Romans were spiritually the wet nurse for Western and Central Europe, so (it is taught) must the Anglo-Saxon peoples be the wet nurse for the Eastern European peoples and lead them over to their mature spiritual period. They also taught that just as the Germanic peoples differentiated themselves into the Gothic and other tribes in the course of European history, so do the Slavic peoples also have to differentiate themselves. Therefore, the British occult schools described how present forces point to certain future configurations.

For example, they taught that in Russia itself there were a number of different communities. These could be grouped geographically, spatially, just as once different peoples were grouped in Central and Western Europe. But the people grouped together in Russia were, so to speak, artificially held together by a state bond. A people like the Poles were held together by their religion and, in spite of their attempts to become independent, the Poles (according to the British) had to be inserted into the "being" of Russia. In these schools, it was believed that whatever was Polish—Polish "being"—was to be shoved into Russian "being." Moreover, they said that in the lower valley of the Danube single Slavic peoples existed in isolated kingdoms.

These schools further said the following. Independent Slavic folk states are forming. However, these will only last until the next great European war, which is going to bring everything into disorder. The independence of the Slavic states, therefore, will last only a while. In the future, the East European peoples who are now in their infant state will therefore be constituted differently. This was the teaching that was given. It was not just theory but was practiced in these occult schools. Therefore, many people tried to influence outer reality so that it conformed to this dogma. People do not realize what enormous attempts these occult brothers in the British Isles, who had other groups in Western Europe and Italy, made. They knew what one person must do, what another must do, and how to work in life in order to achieve their aims. For example, there was an English statesman who became friendly with a certain statesman from a small state on the Danube that was part of Austria. They established a friendly arrangement, arranging things so that, for example, on the one side they became friends, while at the same time they put forth all sorts of criticism about this same small state. This is significant. You methodically develop friendship on the one hand to win a certain people over, and on the other you begin to reveal the shadow side of this same people and attack them. This is a devilish thing, an Ahrimanic trick you can use. One member of such a brotherhood would write a book that would cause a terrible movement, and another would write a book to develop friendship. That is how they work in between the lines. All this was done so that the British could become the ruling culture.

Let us now consider how the personality of Blavatsky works in this occult brotherhood situation. These occult brothers have become aware of her. These Ahrimanic occultists know very well when there is a person who is organized as H. P. Blavatsky was organized. All sorts of evolutionary forces happen.

Here, then, we have Madame Blavatsky, in whom the etheric body is active in a special way, and they wanted to use her so that certain spiritual truths could emerge that would be favorable to their dogma of the superiority of the Anglo-Saxon people. Therefore in the 1860s and the beginning of the 1870s the tendency arose among these occult brothers of the West to use Madame Blavatsky to place spiritual truths before the world of which one can say the following. Here is a person (HPB) whose ideas do not come out of an ordinary human brain, but rather out of an etheric body. Furthermore, elements of the future may be predicted from such an etheric body—a future that holds a foundation for the sixth post-Atlantean period. And, since the sixth post-Atlantean period has not yet arrived, they can then make certain preparations in the fifth. In the case of Blavatsky, who was not an ordinary medium, they could influence her mediumistic forces so that she would say what the British brotherhoods wanted. They themselves could not come before the world and say Britain shall be the rulers, but they could say, Look here, here is a person, whom we are not influencing in any way, who brings something quite new out of her own etheric body, new knowledge. The goal was that this new knowledge should be placed in the service of the Anglo-Saxon brotherhoods. These brotherhoods related to HPB as if they were a sort of wet nurse and she were the infant. Their intention was to put into the world a new kind of occult science that would be appropriate to their own special aims.

They would have succeeded in their intentions if Blavatsky had been a pure Russian. However, as I mentioned, she had a certain dose of Central Europe in her. She had an independent nature and very soon became aware of what lived in her etheric body. She did not want to go along with what these occult brotherhoods wanted. They wanted to develop her as a higher medium. She resisted. She developed many things in a good way. Then she entered a high order in Paris. This Parisian order, however, was dependent on the British occult streams that tried to prepare her so that what they wanted would come out of her soul. But, as I said, she had much of the Germanic element in her and insisted on certain conditions that were impossible to fulfill. As a consequence, she was excluded from this order. In the meantime, she assimilated many deep secrets present in these orders. Indeed, she began to acquire a very special taste for the whole role. She wanted to play the leading occult role herself; she wanted to direct the thing herself. Then she entered an American order where they told her many secrets given only to those in high grades. This American order had a very definite intention, and in time she received into her consciousness a great deal of knowledge. Therefore a whole new situation was created. Here was a personality who knew much of the occult knowledge the secret orders had preserved and protected. It was a situation that had never occurred before. In America she tried again to establish certain conditions the American order could not agree to, because if they had done so terrible confusion would have come about.

Therefore, through very dubious means, they put her in what is called *occult imprisonment*. One does this through ceremonial magic in which the soul you are imprisoning can have ideas that go to a certain sphere and then are reflected back. The person can see everything that happens in them but cannot share it with the external world. A person's spiritual life works only within itself; it is therefore an occult imprisonment. The particular ceremonial magic leading to occult imprisonment was done to try to render H. P. Blavatsky harmless.

In 1879 there was an association of occultists of various lands, and it was decided that an occult imprisonment was to be placed over Madame Blavatsky. Thereafter she lived for a number of years in real occult imprisonment. It then so happened that Indian occultists freed her from this occult imprisonment. Thus the time when Blavatsky falls under Indian influence now began.

All that I have told you up to now, however, is only a kind of prehistory of Madame Blavatsky.

We now come to the development that everyone knows about. All of the difficulties and problems that Blavatsky had are connected with this prehistory. Certain Indian occultists, who strove to save themselves from the British, applied certain means to release her from her occult imprisonment. This was actually done with the consent of those who had put her into the imprisonment. Consequently, what streamed into her soul was connected only with Indian occultism. All of this happened because of the British brotherhoods, who completely rejected what was appropriate for Central Europe. These brotherhoods tried to use Madame Blavatsky for their political objectives. But in Paris and America she objected. Her own Russianness objected to making the Russians dependent upon Western Europe and America. When she was in Paris, she made a special demand that could not be met because it would have necessitated a political transformation in France. In America, she herself did not put forth the demand. She allied herself with Colonel Olcott, who was interested in all sorts of political machinations. These people originally wanted to guide her into a certain channel. They failed because she was released from this channel and went into a different channel, where the Mahatma, the Master, was not who Blavatsky thought he was.

You can see in the well-known novel of George Sand how in occult societies and particular movements in Western Europe, people have a hidden role and are not externally visible. I mentioned all these things in the public lecture on Friday, all the occult streams that produce conspirators resulting in the assassination of Jura, also the murder of Franz Ferdinand.[3] Here you have the whole source of the conspiracy of which the outside world knows very little. It begins in London, spins over into the rest of Europe, then goes into Southern Europe, the Balkans, and finally to St. Petersburg. There, it plays into the whole circle. I tell you all this because one must know that much of what is happening is produced by causes one knows nothing about.

Our Society has a special task of freeing itself from the influence of these Western European brotherhoods. For example, remember how I was attacked in 1909, how I was accused of wanting to become president of the whole Theosophical Society, of wanting to go to India in order to influence certain political activities. On the one side you have the Berlin-Baghdad Railway and on the other side Anthroposophy. I was trying to work for the Pan-Germanic tendency, to separate India from England. In 1909 in Budapest, Mrs. Besant's intention was to make Krishnamurti the bearer of the Christ. I was to have been the reincarnated St. John the Evangelist—to get my recognition. I would not go along with that sort of thing. Many other Theosophists, too, were against all this. In fact, the International Society of Honest People was formed. It included really noble people like Mr. Keightly, whom Mrs. Besant used earlier to correct the mistakes in her books. This International Society asked me to become its president. In 1909 I told Mrs. Besant that I did not want to connect myself with any other occult movements. I wished to connect myself only with what is at work in German culture in Europe. At that time I asked her what she thought about the great movement of German occultism that had appeared at the end of the eighteenth and the beginning of the nineteenth century. This is what she said: "Ah, what appeared in Germany was an unsuccessful attempt in occultism that took other forms, and because that failed, England must now take the situation in hand and occultism must be brought to Europe from England." Now you can see how the situation stands. I tell you all these things because as students of esoteric wisdom you need to know them. . . .

14

Occult Brotherhoods

Berlin, April 4, 1916

... WHAT WE MEAN by the designation "occult brotherhoods" is very complex. However, this complex entity rests upon a foundation that educates people in a certain direction. It unites them in a kind of ritual, whereby certain symbols are transmitted. People are united, as it were, in a kind of ritual containing certain symbols. Today, many people take the significance of the ceremonies and symbolic matters connected with occult brotherhoods very lightheartedly. They tend to dismiss them as a laughing matter. However, some people—Goethe, for example—attach a great deal of importance to the fact that something special quite definitely exists in such ceremonial situations. Goethe knew this very well and often expressed it in different ways. He was grateful in fact that he did not go through a normal school system, but received his education only later through his connection with certain orders.

Since the beginning of the fifteenth century, we have lived in the fifth post-Atlantean period. This was preceded by the fourth post-Atlantean period, which started in 747 B.C.E. and ended in 1413 C.E. During this period, people were so organized that the etheric body was much more receptive than it has been since the fifteenth century. Earlier, the etheric body could see much more of what was around it.

Now, when the etheric body perceives, it sees the elementary or elemental world. This is the world of elemental beings in plants, animals, and minerals. People in the previous epochs were still able to speak of these—of the cobbies and gnomes to be seen in the mountains and approached in certain mines. When ordinary people hear about this today, they think the people of earlier times were just being poetical. But it was not poetical to the people of those centuries; they still knew something about the presence of an elementary world behind the physical world. You can see from historical documents that people in past ages possessed a different sort of perception.

For example, there is a painting in the Hamburg Museum depicting the first chapter of Genesis: the Fall into Sin, the Expulsion from the Garden of Eden. Now, we know from our studies that the tempter was Lucifer. Lucifer is not a being that can be seen with our present-day physical eyes; Lucifer can be seen only with the awakened etheric body, with awakened clairvoyance. Seen clairvoyantly, in fact, Lucifer is a particular being who was left behind during the Moon phase of evolution. Human beings already possessed the physical body during Moon evolution, but it was not physically visible. It was only etherically visible. As far as our head is concerned, what we have today is a reflection of what was already present on the Moon. But the rest of our body, which is attached to the head, was not attached to the head then as it is today. It was attached in the form of a spinal column descending from the head. Furthermore, *it was serpent-like in form*. To represent Lucifer as he was, therefore, one should represent him with a human head with a spinal column attached to it in serpent form. And this is exactly how the painter Master Bertram pictured Lucifer in his Hamburg painting. At the time of Master Bertram, then, human beings still had a perception of the elementary world.[1]

The symbols that form the foundation for certain occult brotherhoods also arose, perceived in a living way, in the fourth post-Atlantean period. Goethe realized that this type of symbolism could still be made fruitful for outer life. In *Wilhelm Meister* you can read how education was conceived so that human beings grew up with a certain type of symbolism.[2] Goethe wanted people to learn about the four types of reverence that human beings can experience through symbols. First, there is the reverence for the spiritual world; second, the reverence for the physical world; third, the reverence for other people; and fourth, the reverence that can develop from the three reverences—namely the reverence for oneself.

How did Goethe want people to develop this reverence of the spiritual? He wanted to teach them certain *gestures*—crossed arms over the breast with the gaze turned upward. Practicing this position, people can acquire a reverence for the ways the spiritual world can influence human life. Goethe combined this gesture with acquiring the feeling of reverence for what is above. This is significant because when human beings really experience reverence for the spirit, they can do nothing other than express this feeling. If they put their physical hands together behind their backs, then their etheric hands cross in front. If they direct a physical glance downward, then their etheric eyes turn upward. The natural gesture for the etheric eyes is to turn up and for the etheric hands to cross in front. This is something that the etheric body actually does when reverence for the spiritual is present.

In the fourth post-Atlantean epoch, people still knew this because they were still able to perceive the movement of their etheric bodies. Goethe knew that this was the way to grow into spiritual life. He knew, too, that if you wished to develop reverence for the earthly, bodily aspect, there was an appropriate gesture for that. And likewise he knew that to develop the third aspect—reverence for other people— the gesture required was outstretched hands, the gaze directed left and right. He knew that this gesture expressed reverence for other reverential souls and that one might thereafter acquire reverence for one's own soul. Goethe's knowledge of these gestures is correct. It is not something arbitrary, but is connected with the spiritual nature of human beings—which, generally speaking, has been lost since the fourteenth century.

Now, before the fourteenth century, one could lead people to gestures of this kind and also more complicated gestures. The gestures had only to be accompanied by something that would easily awaken an inner life. In our own fifth post-Atlantean period, the situation is such that quite specific instructions like those that Goethe knew must accompany the gestures. In *Wilhelm Meister*, in fact, Goethe gives such corresponding instructions. However, in the secret brotherhoods, the complicated language of gestures involving extensive use of sign, grip, and word is unaccompanied by such instructions. Therefore, in these groups, since the fourteenth and fifteenth centuries, the realities in these gestures could no longer be brought to people.

In other words, this process of transmission by gestures—which belonged in that form to the fourth post-Atlantean era—continued into the fifth by means of the brotherhoods.

In the three grades, among other symbolic things, the Masons have the grip and the word. But from the beginning these were used by souls who were organized differently from those of the earlier periods. Such people could no longer connect anything real with the sign, grip, and word, because they could not rise to what corresponded to these in the etheric body. The gestures were merely an external aspect as far as the soul was concerned. Previously, in the age of the intellectual soul (during the fourth post-Atlantean period), there was a possibility of such gestures having a real substantial content. However, when the consciousness soul began to develop, at the beginning of the fifth period, human consciousness began to center upon the physical brain and the sensitivity of the etheric body receded.

The consequences are interesting. The occult brotherhoods continue these practices into the fifth post-Atlantean period. They take in people and familiarize them with certain corresponding symbols. People learn certain signs by bringing their bodies into certain positions. They learn certain grips ("handshakes") by taking hold of someone's hand in an unusual way. They learn to say certain words that imply a certain activity of the etheric body, and so on. I mention only the elementary aspects.

From the fifteenth century, then, people have learned sign, grip, and word. But human beings are now so organized that their center of activity is the consciousness soul. Sign, grip, and word do not work into this consciousness. The gestures remain external signs. But do not think that when sign, grip, and word are transmitted to people they do not act upon their etheric bodies. They do. Performing sign, grip, and word, a person does take in what was once united with sign, grip, and word.

You instruct a number of people in sign, grip, and word. Through that you bring something into their *unconscious* that they cannot have in their consciousness. But this appeal to the unconscious is inappropriate for our present evolutionary stage. This requires that one teach by intellect what can be understood by the intellect. You must bring what you teach to the intellect. This actually is the way of spiritual science. First, you must stand within the spiritual scientific movement in some way; then, after a certain time, you can be led to receive sign, grip, and word. In this way you are prepared to see something that you know about, something that one can at least understand. However, as a general rule, this is not done in these occult brotherhoods. People enter the first grade in these occult brotherhoods without being prepared with spiritual science or any other occultism. Sign, grip, word, and many other things are transmitted to them. In this way, they can be worked upon unconsciously.

The consequence of this is that such people can be adapted to become tools for all sorts of plans. When you can work over the etheric body in such a way that a person does not understand what is going on, you eliminate those forces that would otherwise be present in a person's understanding. Thus, these brotherhoods can become tools for those who want to execute their own plans. The brotherhoods can be used to further certain political goals, or to set up a dogma such as Krishnamurti Alcyon being the physical incarnation of Christ Jesus. Those who are prepared in this way become instruments to carry this sort of thing out into the world. But those, for instance, who have studied my books *Theosophy* or *Outline of Esoteric Science* and understood them can never be damaged by any transmission of symbols.

In Britain, for instance, no sort of explanation or instruction is given preceding the symbolic aspect. This lack is widespread there. When I speak of explanation I do not mean something like, "This symbol means this and that symbol means that." You can give all sorts of nonsense that way. Instruction must be so arranged that the mysteries can be revealed from the study of the whole process of earthly and human development. The symbolism must be allowed to arise out of that.

A great deal of damage occurred in France, for instance, through the occult writings of Éliphas Lévi, whose books *Dogma and Ritual of Higher Magic* and *Key to Higher Magic* surely contain great truths but also terrible errors.[3] But these books are not organized in such a way that they can be followed with the intellect as may be done with our spiritual science. They have to be read symbolically. Just read Éliphas Lévi. You can read him without danger because you have been prepared. Read *Dogma and Ritual of Higher Magic* and you will see how the whole methodology of symbolism is different. In fact, if you instruct people with symbols as is done in this book, then you prepare them so that you can use them in any way you see fit. Actually, after Éliphas Lévi the situation worsened through Dr. Encausse, Papus, who had a terrible influence on the Court of St. Petersburg, where he played a fateful political role.[4] Now, however paradoxical it seems, because there are terrible things there, the task is not to refute Papus, because there is also a great deal that is correct in him. What is dangerous is the way in which these truths are given to people. What you find in Papus's books penetrates into weak souls and puts their intellects to sleep. The result is that you can then use them any way you wish. At the present moment, such people indeed have a certain influence. . . .

There are many things we must know. We must know that every occult brotherhood builds itself up on the basis of three grades. In the first grade, when symbolism is used correctly, souls advance to the point that they experience the fact that there is knowledge that can be acquired independently of ordinary physical knowledge. (When I say correctly, I obviously mean appropriate to our fifth post-Atlantean period.) In the first grade, then, you must be able to acquire a certain body of such knowledge that is independent of the physical. For this everyone in this first grade ought today to know something of what is contained in my *Outline of Esoteric Science*. For the second grade, everyone should know — have inner living knowledge — of what is in my book *How to Know Higher Worlds*. Then the person in the third grade, who receives the significant symbols of sign, grip, and word, will really know what it means to live outside the body. This is the way the whole procedure should be carried out. . . .

I would like to point out that it is especially significant when pure symbolism is employed in a community that has not arrived at complete maturity—for that is how terrible conditions occur. Under the Empress Catherine of Russia, the followers of Paul and others who tried to transplant certain secret brotherhoods into Russia from the West were also the bearers of a certain kind of "Voltairism," or Enlightenment thinking. That has had a greater influence than you would believe upon the whole spiritual development of Russia since then. Naturally such influences group themselves in various directions. For example, these influences work in literature through novels and in politics through political writings. However, those influences become very significant for the subsequent development through certain channels that are always present. In fact, everything significant in the spiritual life of Russia up to Tolstoi leads, in the main, back to the implanting of certain occult brotherhoods in Russia from Western Europe.

In the occult brotherhoods, then, you have the foundation, established through these three initial grades. However, there are people who advance to the so-called higher grades. With regard to these higher grades, we enter a domain subject to a great deal of vanity, because there are brotherhoods in which the people can be brought to the 90th degree or higher. Just imagine what it means to carry such a high order within you! The idea of the 33rd degree, however, results from a mistake springing from complete ignorance of the so-called Scottish high grades, which are based upon three grades that follow in the way I just described. Thus you have the three grades which have their deep significance. Thirty others follow after these three grades! If you are already in the third grade and you are able to achieve the experience of living outside your body, then just imagine where you will have advanced when you are able to go through thirty more grades. This all rests, however, upon a grotesque ignorance, because people do not know that things are not read in occult science in the decimal system. When you write the 33rd degree, in reality that signifies, according to the system of numbering applicable there, that 33 really means $3 \times 3 = 9$. This played a great role with Blavatsky. In her *Secret Doctrine*, you will find a long debate about the number 777. There are people who have fantasized all sorts of things about what this number 777 means. However, it actually is $7 \times 7 = 49$, $49 \times 7 = 343$, $7 \times 7 \times 7 = 343$. That is what it really means. Because the people could not read 33 correctly, they read it as a 33 instead of reading it as 9.

Let us forget all these vanities and continue. First you have the three grades as a foundation. Then there are six more after the first three degrees. Once you have passed through these six additional degrees, you have experienced something of great significance. However, in our present age, these additional six degrees cannot be completely fulfilled. It cannot be done. They cannot be completely fulfilled because human beings in our fifth post-Atlantean period are not advanced enough to experience all that can actually be experienced — that will come later, gradually.

Since 1413 we have been in the fifth post-Atlantean period. This period will last 2,160 years and will end in the year 3573. Hence we are really at the beginning of our period, and in its course a great deal will happen through the development of spiritual science. All this, however, can only reveal itself gradually, step by step. Today, I can impart only its great lines. We can learn many details, but a great deal will come only when it has strengthened itself on the resistances; and these resistances will become greater and greater.

Today we live in a relatively idealistic spiritual age compared with what will come in the future. We are living at the end of the second post-Christian millennium; it will not be long until we reach the year 2000, when humanity will experience something of a special nature. Things are preparing themselves very gradually right now in a twofold manner. Two poles are emerging that are going to meet as time goes on, one pole from the East and another from the West. In the East, there will be a gradual evolution to the point that another kind of thinking will hold sway. Whenever a child is born, it will be asked, "What can come from this child? In this child, we have a hidden spiritual being who wants to develop." People will want to solve the riddle of this child and, to begin with, will unite in a kind of cult dealing with the growing up of the child. This is what is being prepared in the East. Naturally, this mood will pass over into Europe and as a consequence an immense reverence will develop for what might called "genius." There will be a seeking for genius. This will come from the East, but will affect only a smaller portion of humankind. The larger part of humankind will be influenced from the West, from America, and this process will move along an entirely different line of development.

We might say that the present time is doing very well, compared with what will come in the future as Western development blossoms more and more. Very shortly, when one will have written the year 2000, a kind of prohibition against all thinking—not a direct prohibition, but a sort of law intended to suppress all individual thinking—will come from America. A start has already been made in this direction of suppressing individual thinking. We are already seeing a purely materialistic thinking in which there is no need to work on the soul but only to conduct external experiments in which the human being is treated like a machine.

I hope you will not misunderstand me. In this domain we on the so-called spiritual side sin a great deal. For example, someone will come to me and say, "I have sought all kinds of medical treatment and I was not healed, so I went to a healer who treated quite spiritually." When I ask this person what the healer said the answer is, "There are evil spirits in my body and I must pray them out of myself." I ask if this helped, and I am told, "No, I became worse and worse." Just imagine the situation. But do not just imagine that this person said something wrong. She was quite right to say that there were spiritual beings in her that were the cause of what happened. But the very fact that the healer said something correct damaged the person.

Think of it this way. A scamp destroys a machine. He is the cause of the machine no longer running. How can I bring this machine back into proper working order? According to the method of your spiritual healer, I must get hold of this scamp and give him a thorough thrashing so that he will run away and then everything should be in order. Obviously the spiritual healer told you that as soon as the evil spirits have gone away your machine will be in order. However, the machine is not now in order just because the scamp was thrashed and has run away. Now I must work on repairing the machine. And so it is with the person who was sick. Of course, the spiritual healer was able to drive the evil spirits out, but the damage had been done, and now the body must be healed. You can see that so much has been sinned against from this side, precisely because today people have lost the ability to think. For example, we have machines today that add and subtract. Everything is convenient. Now, in the future, there will be no law passed that says you must not think. What will happen is that things will be invented whose effect will be to exclude all individual thinking. This is the other pole to which we are heading. It is being prepared in the West.

We must develop a certain counterweight against this tendency in world evolution. In fact, Anthroposophical spiritual science is this counterweight. But what do we have? We have these brotherhoods in which people entering in the first grade are given symbols. Then they are promoted to the second grade, then the third, where they actually learn the symbolic language, but without learning anything spiritual. And if you were to ask these people if they are satisfied with the fact that they have learned ceremonies, hand grips, certain signs, and certain symbolic activities that occur in the temple room, they will say: "Ah, we are very happy with that. We do not need to do any more thinking. Each person may interpret it as they wish."...

15

Madame Blavatsky's Occult Imprisonment

Dornach, December 26, 1916

. . . From what I have said you will have seen that the painful events of our day are connected with impulses at work in more recent human karma, namely, the karma of our whole fifth post-Atlantean period. Those who want to go more deeply into these matters will have to link outer events with what is happening more inwardly. But this can be understood only in the context of human evolution as seen by spiritual science.

To begin with, we must take at face value certain facts that I have pointed out a number of times. I have frequently said that in the middle of the nineteenth century an attempt was made to draw the attention of modern humanity to the fact that, in addition to forces and powers recognized by natural science, other forces of a spiritual kind exist in the universe.

In other words, the attempt was to show that just as we perceive what is visible around us with our eyes, indeed, with all our senses, so there are also spiritual impulses around us, which people who know about such things, can bring to bear on social life—impulses that cannot be seen with the eye but are known to a more spiritual science.

We know what path this more spiritual science took, so I need not go over it again.

Around the middle of the nineteenth century, then, it was the concern of a certain center to draw people's attention to the existence, as it were, of a spiritual environment. This had been forgotten during the age of materialism. You also know that such things have to be tackled with caution because a certain degree of maturity is necessary in those who assimilate such knowledge. Of course, not everyone who comes across this knowledge or is affected by it can be mature. This is in accordance with the laws of our time that underlie public life. Part of what must be done at such a time requires the testing of whether the knowledge may yet be revealed publicly.

In the middle of the nineteenth century two paths were possible to make this knowledge public. One, even then, would have been what we could describe by mentioning our Anthroposophical spiritual science, namely, to make comprehensible to human thinking what spiritual knowledge reveals about our spiritual environment. It is a fact that this could have been attempted at that time, but this path was not chosen. The reason was, in part, that those who possessed this esoteric knowledge were prejudiced because of traditions descending from ancient times against making such things public. These people felt that certain knowledge guarded by the secret brotherhoods—for it was still guarded at that time—should be kept within the circle of these brotherhoods. We have since seen that, so long as matters are conducted in the proper way, it is perfectly acceptable today to reveal certain things. Naturally, it is unavoidable that some malicious opponents should appear, and always will appear, in circles in which such knowledge is made known. Such people are adherents for a time because it suits their passions and their egoism, but then they become opponents under all sorts of guises and make trouble. Also when spiritual knowledge is made known in a community, this can easily lead to arguments, quarrelling, and disputes, of which, however, not too much notice can be taken, since otherwise no spiritual knowledge would ever be made known. But, apart from these things, no harm is done if the matter is handled in the right way.

But at that time this was not believed. Ancient prejudice won the day. It was agreed to take another path. But, as I have often said, this failed. It was decided to use the path of mediumistic revelation to make people recognize the spiritual world in the same way they recognize the physical world. Suitable individuals were trained to be mediums.[1] What they then revealed through their lowered consciousness was supposed to make people recognize the existence of certain spiritual impulses in their environment. This was a materialistic way of revealing the spiritual world to people. It corresponded to some extent to the conditions of the fifth post-Atlantean period, in so far as this is materialistic in character.

This way of handling things began, as you know, in America in the middle of the nineteenth century. But it soon became obvious that the whole thing was a mistake. It had been expected that the mediums would reveal the existence of certain elemental and nature spirits in the environment. Instead, they all started to refer to revelations from the kingdom of the dead. So the goal that had been set was not reached. I have often explained that the living can only reach the dead with an attitude that does not depend on lowering consciousness. You all know these things. At that time this was also known and that is why, when the mediums began to speak of revelations from the dead, it was realized that the whole thing was a mistake. This had not been expected. It had been hoped that the mediums would reveal how the nature spirits work, how one human being affects another, what forces are at play in the social organism, and so on. It had been hoped that people would start to recognize what forces might be used by those who understand such things, so that people would no longer be dependent solely on one another in the way they are when only their sense perceptions come into play, but would be able to work through the total human personality. This was one thing that went wrong.

The other was that, in keeping with humanity's materialistic inclinations, it soon became obvious what would have begun to happen if the mediumistic movement had spread in the way it threatened to do. Mediums would have been used to accomplish aims that ought to be accomplished only under the influence of natural, sense-bound reasoning. For some individuals it would have been highly desirable to employ a medium who could impart the means of discovering the knowledge that such people covet. I have told you how many letters I get from people who write, "I have a lottery ticket"; or, "I want to buy a lottery ticket; I need the money for an entirely selfless purpose. Could you not tell me which number will be drawn?" Obviously, if mediums had been fully trained in the techniques of mediumship, the resulting mischief with this kind of thing would have been infinite, quite apart from everything else. People would have started to go to mediums to find a suitable bride or bridegroom, and so on.

Thus it came about that, in the very quarter that had launched the movement in order to test whether people were ready to take in spiritual knowledge, efforts were now made to suppress the whole affair. What had been feared in bygone times, when the abilities of the fourth post-Atlantean period still worked in people, had indeed now come to pass. In those days witches were burned, simply because those people who were called witches were really no more than mediums, and because their connections with the spiritual world—though of a materialistic nature—might cause knowledge to be revealed that would have been very awkward for certain people. For instance it might have been very awkward for certain brotherhoods if, before being burned at the stake, a witch had revealed what lay behind them. For it is true that when consciousness is lowered there can be a kind of telephone connection with the spiritual world, and that by this route all sorts of secrets can come out. Those who burned the witches did so for a very good reason: It could have been very awkward for them if the witches had revealed anything to the world, whether in a good or a bad sense, but especially in a bad sense.

So the attempt to test the cultural maturity of humankind by means of mediums had gone awry. This was realized even by those who, led astray by the old rules of silence and by the materialistic tendencies of the nineteenth century, had set this attempt in train. You know, of course, that the activities of mediums have not been entirely curtailed, that they still exist, even today. But the art of training mediums to a level at which their revelations could become significant has, so to speak, been withdrawn. By this withdrawal, the capabilities of mediums have been rendered more or less harmless. In recent decades, as you know, the pronouncements of mediums have come to amount to little more than sentimental twaddle. The only surprising thing is that people still set so much store by them. But the door to the spiritual world had been opened to some degree, and, moreover, this had been done in a manner which was untimely and a mistake.

The birth and work of Madame Blavatsky came during this period. You might think that the birth of one person is insignificant, but this would be a judgment based on illusion. The important thing is that this whole undertaking had to be discussed among the brotherhoods. Much was discussed and brought into the open within the brotherhoods. But the nineteenth century was no longer like earlier centuries when many methods had existed for keeping secret those things that had to be kept secret. Thus, at a certain moment, it happened that a member of one of the secret brotherhoods, who intended to use what he learned within these brotherhoods in a one-sided way, approached Madame Blavatsky. Apart from her other capacities, HPB was an extremely gifted medium, and this person induced her to act as a connecting link for machinations that were no longer as honest as the earlier ones.[2] The first, as we have seen, were honest but mistaken. Up to this point the attempt to test people's receptivity had been perfectly honest, though mistaken. Now, however, came the treachery of a member of an American secret brotherhood. His purpose was to make one-sided use of what he knew, with the help of someone with psychic gifts, like Madame Blavatsky. Let us first look at what actually took place.

When she heard what the member of the brotherhood had to say, Madame Blavatksy naturally reacted inwardly to his words because she was psychic. She understood a great deal more about the matter than the one who was giving her the information. The ancient knowledge formulated in the traditional way lit up in her soul a significant understanding, which she could hardly have achieved solely with her own resources. Inner experiences were stimulated in her soul by the ancient formulations, stemming from the days of atavistic clairvoyance, that were preserved in the secret brotherhoods, often without much understanding for their meaning on the part of the members. These inner experiences led in her to the birth of a large body of knowledge. She knew, of course, that this knowledge must be significant for present human evolution, and also that by taking the appropriate path the knowledge could be utilized in a particular way.

But Madame Blavatsky, being the person she was, could not be expected to use such lofty spiritual knowledge solely for the good of humankind as a whole. She hit upon the idea of pursuing certain aims that were within her understanding because she had come to this point in the manner I have described. So now she demanded to be admitted to a certain occult brotherhood in Paris. Through this brotherhood she would start to work. Ordinarily she would have been accepted in the normal way, apart from the fact that it was not normal to admit a woman; this rule would have been waived in this case because it was known that she was an important individuality. However, it would not have served her purpose to be admitted merely as an ordinary member, so she laid down certain conditions. If these conditions had been accepted, many subsequent events would have been very different but, at the same time, this secret brotherhood would have pronounced its own death sentence—that is, it would have condemned itself to total ineffectiveness. So it refused to admit her.

She then turned to America, where she was indeed admitted to a secret brotherhood. In consequence, she of course acquired extremely significant insights into the intentions of such secret brotherhoods: not those striving for the good of humankind as a whole, disregarding any conflicting wishes, but those whose purposes are one-sided and serve certain groups only. But it was not in Madame Blavatsky's nature to work in the way these brotherhoods wished. So it came about that, under the influence of what was termed an attack on the Constitution of North America, she was excluded from this brotherhood.

So now she was excluded. But of course she was not a person who would be likely to take this lying down. Instead, she began to threaten the American brotherhood with the consequences of excluding her in this way, now that she knew so much. The American brotherhood now found itself sitting under the sword of Damocles, for if, as a result of having been a member, Blavatsky had told the world what she knew, this would have spelled its death sentence. The consequence was that American and European occultists joined forces to inflict on Blavataky a condition known as occult imprisonment. Through certain machinations a sphere of imaginations is called forth in a soul that brings about a dimming of what that soul previously knew, thus making it virtually ineffective. It is a procedure that honest occultists never apply, and even dishonest ones only very rarely, but it was applied on that occasion in order to save the life, that is the effectiveness, of that secret brotherhood.

For years Madame Blavatsky existed in this occult imprisonment, until certain Indian occultists started to take an interest in her because they wanted to work against that American brotherhood. As you can see, we keep coming up against occult streams that want to work one-sidedly. Thus Blavatsky entered this Indian current, with which you are familiar. The Indian brotherhood was very interested indeed in proceeding against the American brotherhood, not because they saw that they were not serving humanity as a whole, but because they in turn had their own one-sided, patriotically Indian viewpoint. By various machinations the Indian and the American occultists reached a kind of agreement. The Americans promised not to interfere in what the Indians wanted to do with Madame Blavatsky, and the Indians engaged to remain silent on what had gone before.

You can see just how complicated these things really are when you add to all this the fact, which I have also told you about, that a hidden individual, a Mahatma behind a mask, had been instituted in place of Blavatsky's original teacher and guide. This figure stood in the service of a European power and had the task of utilizing whatever Blavatsky could do in the service of that particular European power. One way of discovering what all this is really about might be to ask what would have happened if one or the other of these projects had been realized.

Time is too short to tell you everything today, but let us pick out a few aspects. We can always come back to these things again soon.

Suppose Blavatsky had succeeded in gaining admission to the occult lodge in Paris. If this had happened, she would not have come under the influence of that individual who was honored as a Mahatma in the Theosophical Society—although he was no such thing—and the life of the occult lodge in Paris would have been extinguished. A great deal that this same Paris lodge may be seen to stand behind would not have happened, or perhaps it would have happened in the service of a different, one-sided influence. Many things would have taken a different course. For the intention was also to exterminate this Paris lodge with the help of the psychic personality of Blavatsky. If it had been exterminated, there would have been nothing behind all those people who have contributed to history, more or less like marionettes. . . .

Later on, certain matters were hushed up, obscured, by the fact that Madame Blavatsky was prevented by her occult imprisonment from publicizing the impulses of that American lodge and giving them her own slant, which she would doubtless otherwise have done. Once all these things had run their course, the only one to benefit from Blavatsky was the Indian brotherhood. There is considerable significance for the present time in the fact that a certain sum of occult knowledge has entered the world one-sidedly, with an Indian coloring. This knowledge has entered the world; it now exists. . . .

Those who reckon with such things always count on long stretches of time. They prepare things and leave them to develop. These are not individuals, but brotherhoods in which successor takes over from predecessor, carrying on in a similar direction with what has been started.

On the basis of the two examples I have given you of occult lodges, you can see that much depended on the actual impulses not being made public. I do not wish to be misunderstood, and I therefore stated expressly that the first attempt I described to you was founded on a certain degree of honesty. But it is extremely difficult for people to be entirely objective about humanity as a whole. There is little inclination for this nowadays. People are so easily led astray by the group instinct that they are not objective about humanity as a whole, but pay homage to one group or another, enjoying the feeling of "belonging."

But this is something that is no longer really relevant to the point we have reached in human evolution. The requirement of the present moment is that we should, at least to some degree, feel ourselves to be individuals and extricate ourselves, at least inwardly, from group things, so that we belong to humanity as human *individuals*. Even though, at present, we are shown so grotesquely how impossible this is for some people, it is nevertheless a requirement of our time. . . .

Now if Blavatsky had been able to speak out at that time, certain secrets would have been revealed, secrets I have mentioned as belonging to certain secret brotherhoods and connected with the striving of a widespread network of groups. I said to you earlier that definite laws underlie the rise and evolution of peoples, of nations. These laws are usually unknown in the external, physical world. This is right and proper, for in the first place they ought to be recognized solely by those who desire to receive them with clean hands. What underlies the terrible trials humanity is undergoing and will undergo in the future is the interference in a one-sided way by certain modern brotherhoods with the spiritual forces that pulse through human evolution in the region in which, for instance, nations, peoples, come into being. Evolution progresses in accordance with definite laws; it is regular and comes about through certain forces. But human beings interfere, in some part unconsciously, though if they are members of secret brotherhoods, they do so consciously.

To be able to judge these things you need to acquire a wider horizon. I showed you the forces of which Blavataky became the plaything, in order to point out how such a plaything can be tossed about, from West to East, from America to India. This is because forces are at work that are managed by human beings for certain ends, by utilizing the passions and feelings of nationality, which have, however, in their turn first been manufactured. This is most important. It is important to develop an eye for the way in which a person, because of the type of passions in her, in her blood, can be put in a certain position and be brought under the sway of certain influences. Equally, those who do this must know that certain things can be achieved, depending on the position in which the person is placed. Many attempts fail. But account is taken of long periods of time and of many possibilities. Above all, account is taken of how little inclination people have to pay attention to the wider—even the widest—contexts. . . .

Part Four

From Theosophy to Anthroposophy

16

Homeless Souls

Dornach, June 10, 1923

THE REFLECTIONS we are beginning today are meant to encourage all those who have found their way to Anthroposophy to think about their current position. . . .

There are those who found this path through an inner necessity of the soul or heart. Others, perhaps, found it through the search for knowledge. There are many, however, who entered the Anthroposophical movement for more or less mundane reasons. Through a deepening of the soul they have subsequently perhaps encountered more within it than they at first anticipated. But there is something that all those who end up in the Anthroposophical movement have in common: they are initially driven by their inner destiny, their karma, to leave the ordinary highway of civilization on which the majority of humankind at present progresses, to search for their own path.

Let us think for a moment about the conditions in which most people now grow up. They are born to parents who are French or German, Catholic or Protestant or Jewish, or who belong to some other faith, and may hold a variety of beliefs. But parents have the almost unquestioned assumption, which remains unspoken and sometimes unthought, that their children will grow up like themselves. These kinds of feelings naturally engender a social ambience, indeed social pressures, which more or less consciously push children into the kind of life that has been mapped out by these more or less clearly defined beliefs. The life of a child then follows its natural course of education and schooling. And during this time parents once again have all kinds of beliefs that exert a decisive influence on their children's lives—the belief, for instance, that my son will, as a matter of course, enter the secure employment of the civil service, or inherit the parental business, or that my daughter will marry the man next door. It simply lies in the nature of social circumstances that people are governed by impulses arising in this way. They have no choice in the matter because that is the effect of the beliefs governing life. It may not always be obvious to parents, but schooling and all the other circumstances of childhood and youth imprison us and determine our position in life. The institutions of state and religion make the adult.

If the majority of people were asked to explain how they got where they are today, they would not be able to do so, because there would be something unbearable about having to think deeply about such matters. This unbearable element tends to be driven underground into subconscious or unconscious areas of our soul life. At best, if it behaves in a particularly recalcitrant manner down there in those unknown provinces of the soul, then a psychiatrist will dredge it up. But mostly one's own personality, the Self, is simply not strong enough to assert itself against what one has grown into in this way.

Occasionally people have the urge to rebel when their situation as a trainee or student, or even after graduation, unexpectedly dawns on them. You might, if you are a man, clench your fist in your pocket, or, if you are a woman, create a scene at home because of such disappointed life expectations. These are reactions against what people are forced to become. We also frequently seek to anesthetize ourselves by concentrating on the pleasant things in life. We go to dances and follow this with sleeping in. We fill up time in one way or another. Or some might join a thoroughly patriotic party because their professional position demands that they belong to something that will reflect their values. . . . This is roughly how people who move in the mainstream of life grow into their existence.

Those who find it difficult to accept this end up on many possible and impossible byways. Anthroposophy is precisely one of these paths on which human beings are seeking to realize themselves. They come to Anthroposophy because they want to live with a more conscious understanding of themselves. They want to experience something that, to some extent at least, is under their control. Anthroposophists are for the most part people who do not walk along the main highways of life. If we investigate further why that should be, we find that this is linked with the spiritual world.

Human beings, after a life on Earth, relive the course of that life in the spiritual world after death. There they enter a region where they become increasingly assimilated into the spiritual world, where their lives consist of working together with the beings of the higher Hierarchies, where all their acts are related to this world of substantive spirit.

But a time arrives when they begin to turn their attention to Earth again. For a long time in advance of their birth, human beings unite on a soul level with the generations at the end of which stand the parents who will give birth to them—not only as far back as their great-great-grandparents, but much further back in the line of preceding generations. The majority of souls nowadays look down, as it were, to Earth from the spiritual world and display a lively interest in what is happening to their ancestors. Such souls move in the mainstream of contemporary life.

In contrast, there are a number of souls, particularly at present, whose interest is concentrated less on worldly happenings as they approach a new life on Earth than on the question of how they can develop maturity in the spiritual world. Their interest lies in the spiritual world right up to the moment before they find their way to Earth. As a consequence, when they incarnate they arrive with a consciousness that has its origins in spiritual impulses. With their spiritual ambitions they outgrow their environment. They are predestined and prepared to go their own way.

Thus the souls who descend from pre-earthly to earthly existence can be divided into two groups. One group, to which the majority of people today still belong, comprises those souls who can make themselves remarkably at home on Earth. They feel thoroughly comfortable in their warm nest, which so fascinated them long before they came down to Earth, even if this does occasionally appear unpleasant (of course, that is only appearance, or maya).

Other souls, who may appear to pass patiently through childhood, are less able to make themselves at home. They are homeless souls, and grow beyond the warmth of the nest much more than they grow into it. This latter group includes those souls who are subsequently attracted to the Anthroposophical movement. It is therefore clearly predetermined in a certain sense whether or not an individual is led to Anthroposophy.

The things that are being sought by these souls on the byways of life, away from the major highways, manifest themselves in many ways. If the others did not find it so agreeable to take the well-trodden paths and did not put such obstacles in the way of homeless souls, the numbers of the latter would be much more obvious to their contemporaries. But it is widely apparent today how many souls have a hint of such homelessness about them.

The tendency to such homelessness could be anticipated. There is the rapidly growing evidence of a longing for an attitude to life that was not laid out in advance. There is a longing for the spirit in the chaos of contemporary spiritual life. In sketching an outline of this gradual development, you can find in it, if you reflect a little, something of what I would like to describe as the Anthroposophical origins of each one of you.

By way of introduction today I will do no more than pick out in outline some characteristic features. Consider the last decades of the nineteenth century. We could take any number of fields, but let us take a very characteristic one, the cult of Richard Wagner. It is certainly true that much of this cult consisted of a cultural flirtation with new ideas, sensationalism, and so on. All kinds of people gathered in Bayreuth. One could see people who thought of the long journey to Bayreuth as a kind of modern pilgrimage. But even among these bohemian types there were those who were also homeless souls.

The essential effect of Wagnerism, not just as a musical element but also as a cultural phenomenon, was to offer people something that went beyond all the usual offerings of a materialistic age. This gave people a feeling that here there was a gateway to a more spiritual world, a world that was different from their normal environment. What went on in Bayreuth led to a great longing for more profound spiritual aspirations.

It was, of course, difficult at first to understand Richard Wagner's characters and dramatic compositions. But many people felt that they were created from a source very different from the crude materialism of the time. And the homeless souls who were driven in this particular direction were prompted into all kinds of dark, instinctive intuitions through what I might call the suggestive power of Wagnerian drama, and specifically through the way of life it introduced into our culture. Indeed, it is true to say that subsequent interpretations by Theosophists of *Hamlet* or other works of art are very strongly reminiscent of certain essays written by Hans von Wolzogen, who was not a Theosophist but a trained Wagnerian, in the *Bayreuther Blatter.*[1]

One may say, then, that Wagnerism was the reason why many people, possessed of a homeless soul, became acquainted with a way of looking at the world that led away from crude materialism toward something spiritual. All those who became part of such a current not because of a superficial flirtation with the idea, but because of an inner compulsion of the soul, wanted to develop their experience of a spiritual world because they felt this kind of inner longing. They were no longer concerned with the evidence underpinning the materialistic worldview. That was true irrespective of their position in life, whether they were lawyers or artists, cabinet ministers, officials, parliamentarians, or even scientists.

As I said, such homeless souls can be found everywhere. But Wagnerism provides a particularly characteristic example of the presence of very many such souls.

In the late 1880s in Vienna I encountered several of those people whose first spiritual taste had been the Wagnerian experience.[2] This was a group consisting entirely of such homeless souls. People no longer really appreciate the way that homelessness was visible for anyone to see even then, because many of the things that then required a great deal of inner courage have become commonplace today.

For example, I do not believe that many people today could imagine the following. I was sitting once in a circle of such homeless souls. All kinds of things had already been discussed. One person started to speak about Dostoyevsky's Raskolnikov.[3] He spoke in such a way that the group felt as if it had been struck by lightning. A new world opened up. It was like suddenly finding oneself on a new planet. That is how these souls felt. . . .

Having passed through their Wagnerian metamorphosis, these homeless souls were also involved in a second process of change. For example, in this group were three good acquaintances, intimate friends even, of H. P. Blavatsky. They were keen Theosophists in the way that Theosophists were when Blavatsky was still alive.[4] But a peculiar quality adhered to Theosophists at that time, the period following the appearance of Blavatsky's *Isis Unveiled* and *The Secret Doctrine.* They all had a desire to be extremely esoteric. They had nothing but contempt for their normal life, including, of course, their work. Exoteric life, however, was not something that could be avoided. That was accepted. But everything else was esoteric. In this setting you spoke only to fellow initiates, only within a small group. And those who were not considered worthy of talking to about such things were seen as people with whom one spoke only about the ordinary things in life. It was with the former that you discussed esoteric matters. They were people who, although they might be engineers from the moment they stepped into practical life, would avidly read a book like

Sinnett's *Esoteric Buddhism*. These people possessed a certain urge—partly still as a result of their Wagnerian past—to explain all legends and myths from an esoteric perspective.

As more and more of these homeless souls began to appear at the end of the nineteenth century, one could begin to see how the most interesting among them were not those who studied the writings of Sinnett and Blavatsky with at most a nine-tenths honest mind, but those who did not wish to read for themselves because they still had great inhibitions about such things. They listened with gaping mouths when those who had been reading expounded on these things. It was most interesting to observe how these listeners, who were sometimes more honest than the narrators, grasped these ideas with their homeless souls as essential spiritual nourishment. To listen was for them spiritual nourishment which, despite the relative dishonesty with which it was being presented to them, they were able to transform into something more honest through the greater honesty of their souls. One could see in them the yearning to hear something completely different from what was offered in the ordinary mainstream of civilization. How they devoured what they heard! It was most interesting to observe how on the one hand the tentacles of mainstream life kept drawing people in, and how on the other they would appear at one of the meeting places (often a coffeehouse) and listen with great yearning. The point is that the honest souls, the ones who had been subject to the vagaries of life, were there too.

How souls unwilling to admit to their homelessness were unable to find their bearings was particularly evident toward the latter part of the nineteenth century. A person might, for instance, listen with profound interest to an explanation of the physical, etheric, and astral bodies, *kama manas, manas, buddhi,* and so on. At the same time he was obliged to write the article his newspaper expected, including all the usual goodies. It really became clear how difficult it was for some to leave the mainstream of life. For there were several among them who behaved as if they wanted to slink away, and would prefer that no one knew where they had gone when they wished to attend what was most important and interesting to them in life. It was indeed interesting how spiritual life, spiritual activity, the yearning for a spiritual world began particularly to establish itself in European civilization.

Now you have to remember that circumstances in the late 1880s were really much more difficult than today. Even if it was less harmful, it was nevertheless more difficult then to admit to the existence of a spiritual world, because the physical world of the senses with all its magnificent laws had been proven of course! There was no way of getting round that! All the proofs were there in the physics laboratories and the hospitals; all the evidence declared in favor of a world for which there was proof. But the world that could be proven was unsatisfactory for many homeless souls. It was useless to their inner souls, to such an extent that many crept away from it. And at the same time that this great contemporary culture was on offer to them by the sack—no, by the ton, in giant quantities—they took what nips they could from what has to be seen as the flow of the spiritual world into modern civilization. It was not at all easy to speak about the spiritual world; a suitable point of entry had to be found.

Let me again introduce a personal note. I had to find a suitable opportunity on which to build. One could not simply crash in on our civilization with the spiritual world. In the late 1880s, I linked what I had to say about the spiritual world, about its more intimate aspects, with Goethe's *Fairy Tale of the Green Snake and the Beautiful Lily.*[5] Using something that had been created by no less a figure than Goethe, when it was as obvious as it is in the *Fairy Tale* that spiritual impulses had flowed into it, was a suitable basis. I certainly could not use what was then being peddled as Theosophy, what had been garnered from Blavatsky, from Sinnett's *Esoteric Buddhism,* and from similar books by a group of people who were undeniably hardworking. For someone who wanted to preserve his scientifically schooled thinking in the spiritual world this was simply impossible.

Neither was it easy in another respect. Why? Well, Sinnett's *Esoteric Buddhism* was soon recognized as the work of a spiritual dilettante, a compendium of old, badly understood esoteric bits and pieces. But it was less easy to find access to a phenomenon of the period such as Blavatsky's *Secret Doctrine.* For this work did at least reveal in many places that much of its content had its origins in real, powerful impulses from the spiritual world. The book expressed a large number of ancient truths gained through atavistic clairvoyance in distant ages of humankind. People thus encountered in the outside world, not from within themselves, something that could be described as an uncovering of a tremendous wealth of wisdom that humanity had once possessed as something exceptionally illuminating. This was interspersed with unbelievable passages which never ceased to amaze, because the book is a sloppy and dilettantish piece of work as regards any sort of methodology, and includes superstitious nonsense and much more. In short, Blavatsky's *Secret Doctrine* is a peculiar book: great truths side by side with terrible rubbish. One might almost say that it sums up very well the spiritual phenomena to which those who developed into the homeless souls of the modern age were subjected.

In the following period in Weimar I was, of course, occupied intensively with other things,[6] although even then there were numerous opportunities to observe such searching souls. . . . And subsequently when I went to Berlin, destiny once again introduced me to a group of homeless souls. In fact, I became involved to such an extent that this group asked me to hold lectures, which have now been published in my *Mystics after Modernism.*[7] They were people who found their way into the Theosophical Society at a somewhat later date than my Viennese acquaintances. Only a few of them studied Blavatsky's *Secret Doctrine,* but they were well versed in what Blavatsky's successor, Annie Besant, proclaimed as the Theosophical ideas of the time.

So I found myself once again in a similar situation to the one in Vienna in the late 1880s, in which it was possible to observe such homeless souls. And Anthroposophy at first grew up, one might say, together with, not in, but together with, homeless souls who had initially sought a new home in Theosophy. . . .

17

The Unveiling of Spiritual Truths

Dornach, June 11, 1923

WHEN WE DISCUSS the history and position of Anthroposophy in relation to the Anthroposophical Society, any such reflections have to take into account two questions. First, why was it necessary to link the Anthroposophical movement to the Theosophical movement in the way they were connected? And second, why is it that malicious opponents still equate the Anthroposophical Society with the Theosophical Society? The answers to these questions will only become clear from a historical perspective. Yesterday, I said that when we talk about the Anthroposophical Society, the first thing of relevance is that of the people who feel the need to pursue their path through an Anthroposophical movement. I tried to describe the sense in which the souls who come into contact with Anthroposophy in order to satisfy their spiritual yearning are homeless souls in a certain respect. There were more of them about than is normally suspected, because there were many people who in one way or another tried by various means to develop their more profound human qualities.

Quite apart from the reaction to modern materialism, which subsequently led to various forms of spiritualism, many souls sought to fulfill certain inner needs by reading the work of people like Ralph Waldo Trine[1] and similar writers. They tried, one might say, to compensate for something missing in their nature. They sought something they wanted to feel and experience inwardly, but could not find on the well-trodden paths of modern civilization. They could find it neither in the popular literature and art of a secular age, nor in the traditional religious faiths. . . .

Those who were engaged in this search included human beings who joined the various branches of the Theosophical Society. And if we ask whether there was something that distinguished those who joined the Theosophical Society from others, the answer has to be yes. There was what I might call a special sort of endeavor present. We know from the way the Theosophical Society developed that it was not unreasonable to assume that the thing people were looking for at the start of our century as Anthroposophy was most likely to be understood within the circles then united by Theosophy. . . .

I would therefore like to draw a sketch of what the Theosophical Society, which found its most potent expression in the English Theosophical Society, represented at the time. Indeed, the latter was then joined by what emerged immediately as Anthroposophy.

If we look at the character of the English Theosophical Society as expressed in its members, we have to look into their souls in order to understand their thinking. After all, their consciousness was expressed in the way they went about things. They assembled. They held meetings, lectures, and discussions. They also met and talked a great deal in smaller groups: at general meetings, for instance, there was always time to have a meal together, or a cup of tea, and so on. People even found time to change clothes in the intervals. It was really what might be described as a reflection of the kind of social behavior one might find in daily life. It was particularly noticeable that there were highly conflicting forces at play in the consciousness of those people.

To anyone who was not a dyed-in-the-wool Theosophist it was evident that those people sought to have two conceptions of every person. The first one was the direct impression on meeting someone. But the other was the conception that everyone else had of each individual. This was based on very generalized ideas about the nature of human beings, about universal human love, about being advanced (as they called it) or not, about the seriousness of a person's inclinations in order to prove worthy of receiving the doctrines of Theosophy, and so on. These were pretty theoretical considerations. And everyone thought that something of all this had to be present in people walking around in flesh and blood. The naive impressions of individuals were not really alive in the members, but each one had an image of all the others that was based on theoretical ideas about human beings and human behavior.

In fact, no one saw anyone else as that person really was, but rather as a kind of specter. And thus it was necessary on meeting Mr. Smith, for example, and forming a naive impression of him, to form a spectral idea of him by visualizing what someone else thought of Mr. Smith. Thus it was necessary to have two images of each person. However, most of the members dispensed with the image of the real person and merely absorbed the image of the specter, so that in reality members always perceived one another in spectral form. The consciousness of the members was filled with specters. An interest in psychology was necessary to understand this.

Real interest required a certain generosity and lack of preconception. It was, after all, very interesting to be involved in what existed there as a kind of spectral society. Its leaders were perceived in a very peculiar manner. Reference might be made to a leading individual, let us call him X. During the night his astral form went from house to house (only members' houses, of course), as an invisible helper. All kinds of things emanated from him. The spectral ideas about leading individuals were in part extraordinarily beautiful. Often, it was a considerable contrast to meet these leading personalities in the flesh. But the general ethos then ensured that as far as possible only the spectral conception was allowed to exist and the real conception was not permitted to intrude.

A certain view of things, a doctrine, was definitely required for this. Since not everyone was clairvoyant, although there were many people at the time who at least pretended to be, certain theories were necessary to give form to these specters. These theories had something exceedingly archaic about them. It was hard to avoid the impression that these spectral human constructs were assembled according to old, rehashed theories. In many cases it was easy to find the ancient writings that provided the source material. Thus, on top of their ghostly nature these human specters were not of the present time. They were from earlier incarnations; they gave the impression of having clambered out of Egyptian, Persian, or Ancient Indian graves. In a certain sense any feeling of the here and now had been lost.

These ancient doctrines were difficult to understand, even when clothed in relatively modern terminology. The etheric body was borrowed from medieval concepts, as was perhaps the astral body. But then we move on to *manas, kama manas,* and suchlike, which everybody talked about, but no one really understood. How could they, when they approached them with very modern, materialistic ideas? These teachings were meant to be seen in a cosmic context; they contained cosmic concepts and ideas that made it easy to feel that souls were talking in a language not of centuries, but of millennia past.

This process spread far and wide. Books were written in such an idiom. But there was another side to all this. It had its beautiful aspect, because despite the superficial use of words, despite the lack of understanding, something did rub off on people. One might almost say that, even if it did not enter their souls, an extraordinary amount adhered to the outer garment of their souls. They went about not exactly with an awareness of the etheric body or *kama manas,* but they had an awareness that they were enveloped in layers of coats: one of them the etheric body, another *kama manas,* and so on. They were proud of these coats, of this dressing of the soul, and that provided a strong element of cohesion among them.

This was something that forged the Theosophical Society into a single entity in an exceptionally intense manner. It created a tremendous communal spirit in which every single person felt himself or herself to be a representative of the Theosophical Society. Beyond each individual member, the Society itself had what might be described as an awareness of itself. This identity was so strong that even when the absurdities of its leaders eventually came to light in a rather bizarre manner, the members held together with an iron grip because they felt it was akin to treachery if people did not stick together. This was so even when the Society's leaders had committed grave mistakes.

Anyone who has gained an insight into the struggles that later went on among certain members of the Theosophical Society long after the Anthroposophical Society had separated itself, when people realized repeatedly the terrible things their leaders were doing but failed to see that as a sufficient reason to leave—anyone who saw the struggle will have developed a certain respect for this self-awareness of the Society as a whole.

And that leads us to ask whether the conditions surrounding the birth of the Anthroposophical Society might not allow a similar self-awareness to develop.

From the beginning the Anthroposophical Society had to manage without the often very questionable means by which the Theosophical Society established its strong cohesion and self-awareness. The Anthroposophical Society had to be guided by the ideal that wisdom can only be found in truth.[2] This is something that has remained little more than an ideal. In this area in particular the Anthroposophical Society leaves a lot to be desired, having barely begun to address the development of a communal spirit, an identity of its own.

The Anthroposophical Society is a collection of people who strive very hard as individual human beings. But as a society it hardly exists, precisely because this feeling of a common bond is not there, as only the smallest number of members of the Anthroposophical Society feel themselves to be representatives of the Society. They all feel that they are individuals, and forget altogether that there is supposed to be an Anthroposophical Society as well.

Having characterized the people attracted to Anthroposophy, what has been the response of Anthroposophy to their endeavors? Anyone with sufficient interest can find the principles of Anthroposophy in my *Philosophy of Freedom*.[3] I wish to emphasize that this refers with inner logic to a spiritual realm that is, for example, the source of our moral impulses. The existence of a spiritual realm takes concrete form when human beings develop the awareness that their innermost being is not connected to the sensory world but to the spiritual world. These are the two basic points made in *The Philosophy of Freedom*: first, that there is a spiritual realm and, second, that the innermost part of a person's being is connected to this spiritual realm.

Inevitably the question arose of whether it is possible to make public in this way what was to be revealed to contemporary humanity as a kind of message about the spiritual world. After all, one could not simply stand up and talk into the void. . . . One must create a link with something that already exists in contemporary civilization. And basically there were few opportunities like that around, even at the turn of the century. At that time people's search led them to the Theosophical Society, and they, finally, were the ones to whom one could talk about such things.

But a feeling of responsibility toward the people we were addressing was not enough; a feeling of responsibility toward the spiritual world was also required, and in particular toward the form in which it appeared at that time.

Here I might draw attention to the way that what was to become Anthroposophy gradually emerged from those endeavors which I did not yet publicly call Anthroposophy.

In the 1880s I could see, above all, a kind of mirage. . . . If one opened oneself to the worldviews of that time, one was liable to encounter something very peculiar. Consider Central Europe. The philosophy of idealism from the first half of the nineteenth century presented a world-shattering philosophy whose aim was to provide a complete metaphysical conception of the world. In the 1880s there were echoes of, let us say, Fichte's, Hegel's, and Solger's philosophies, which meant as much to some of their adherents as Anthroposophy can ever mean to people today.[4] But these philosophies were basically a sum of abstract concepts.

Take a look, for instance, at the first of the three parts of Hegel's *Encyclopedia of Philosophy* and you will find a series of concepts which are developed one from the other: the concepts of being, not-being, becoming and existence, ending with the idea of purpose.[5] It consists only of abstract thoughts and ideas. And yet this abstraction is what Hegel describes as God before the creation of the world. So if one asks what God was before the Creation, the answer lies in a system of abstract concepts and abstract ideas.

Now when I was young, a Herbartian philosopher called Robert Zimmermann lived in Vienna.[6] He said we should no longer be permitted to think in the Hegelian mode, or in that of Solger or similar philosophers. According to Zimmermann these men thought as if they themselves were God. That was almost as if someone from the Theosophical Society had spoken, for a leading member of the Theosophical Society, Franz Hartmann,[7] said in all his lectures something to the effect that you had to become aware of the God within yourself, and when that God began to speak you were speaking Theosophy. But Hegel, when in Zimmermann's view he allowed the God within himself to speak, said: Being, negation of being, becoming, existence; and then the world was first of all logically put in a state of turbulence, whereupon it flipped over into its otherness, and nature was there.

Robert Zimmermann, however, said that we must not allow the God in human beings to speak, for that leads to a theocentric perspective. Such a view is not possible unless one behaves rather like Icarus. And you know what happened to him: you slip up somewhere in the cosmos and take a fall! You have to remain firmly grounded in the human perspective. And thus Robert Zimmermann wrote his *Anthroposophy* to counter the theosophy of Hegel, Schelling, Solger, and others, whom he also treats as theosophists in his *History of Aesthetics*. It was from the title of this book, *Anthroposophy,* that I later took the name. I found it exceedingly interesting then as a phenomenon of the time. The trouble is, it consists of the most horribly abstract concepts.

You see, human beings want a philosophical framework that will satisfy their inner selves, that will give them the ability to say that they are connected with a divine-spiritual realm, that they possess something eternal. Zimmermann was seeking an answer to the question,

When human beings go beyond mere sensory existence, when they become truly aware of their spiritual nature, what can they know? They know logical ideas. According to Zimmermann, if it is not God who is thinking in human beings, but human beings themselves, then five logical ideas emerge. First, there is logical necessity; second, the equivalence of concepts; third, the combination of concepts; fourth, the differentiation of concepts; and fifth, the law of contradiction, that something can only be itself or something else. That is the sum total of the things which human beings can know when they draw on their soul and spirit.

If this anthroposophy were the only thing available, the unavoidable conclusion would be that everything connected with the various religions, with religious practice and so on, is a thing of the past, Christianity is a thing of the past, because these are things that require a historical basis. When people think only of what they can know as *anthropoi*, independent of sensory impressions, of worldly history, it is the following. They know that they are subject to logical necessity, to the equivalence of concepts, the combination of concepts, differentiation, and the law of contradiction. That, whatever name it is given, is all there is.

It can then be supplemented by aesthetic ideas, five ideas again, including perfection, consonance and harmony, conflict and reconciliation. Next, five ethical ideas form the basis for human action: ethical perfection, benevolence, justice, antagonism, and resolution of antagonism. As you can see, that has all been put in an exceedingly abstract form. But it is preceded by the title *Anthroposophy: An Outline.* The dedication shows clearly that this was intended to be a major project.

You can see that it was very remarkable, in the way that a mirage is remarkable. Zimmermann transformed theosophy into anthroposophy, as he understood the word. But I do not believe that if I had lectured on his kind of anthroposophy we would ever have had an Anthroposophical movement. The name, however, was very well chosen. And I took on the name when, for fundamental reasons that will become clear in the course of these lectures, I had to start dealing with particular subjects, starting with the spiritual fact that is a certainty for everyone with access to the spiritual world, namely the fact of repeated earthly lives.

But if I wanted to deal with such things with a degree of spiritual responsibility, they had to be put in a context. It is no exaggeration to say that it was not easy at the turn of the century to put the idea of repeated lives on Earth into a context that would have been understood. But there were points where such a link could be established. And before going any further I want to tell you how I myself sought to make use of such points of contact.

Topinard[8] wrote a very interesting synopsis of anthropological facts, leading to the conclusion, acceptable of course to everyone who subscribed to modern thinking at that time, that all animal species had evolved one from the other. Topinard quotes his facts and, after presenting twenty-two points, writes that the twenty-third point is what he claims to be the transformation of animal species. But then we face the problem of the human being. He does not provide an answer to this. So what happens there?

Now, by taking the biological theory of evolution seriously, it is possible to build on such an author. If we continue, and add point twenty-three, we must conclude that animal species always repeat themselves at a higher level. But in the human being we progress to the individual. When the individual begins to be repeated we have reincarnation. As you can see, I tried to make use of what was available to me, and in that form attempted to make something understandable that is, in any case, present before the soul as a spiritual fact. But in order to provide a point of access for people in general, something had to be used that was already in existence but that did not come to an end with a full stop, but with a dash. I simply continued beyond the dash where natural science left off. I delivered that lecture to the group that I mentioned yesterday.[9] It was not well received because it was not felt necessary to reflect on the issues raised by the sciences, and of course it seemed superfluous to that group that the things in which they believed should, in any case, need to be supported by evidence.

The second thing is that at the beginning of the century I delivered a course of lectures entitled *From Buddha to Christ* to a group that called itself Die Kommenden.[10] In these lectures I tried to depict the line of development from Buddha to Christ. I sought to present Christ as the culmination of what had existed previously. The lecture cycle concluded with an interpretation of St. John's Gospel that starts with the raising of Lazarus. Thus the Lazarus issue, as represented in my *Christianity as Mystical Fact*, forms the conclusion of the lectures *From Buddha to Christ*.[11]

This coincided roughly with the lectures published in my book *Mystics After Modernism*[12] and the task of addressing Theosophists on matters that I both needed and wanted to speak about. That occurred at the same time as the endeavor to establish a German Section of the Theosophical Society. Even before I had become a member, or indeed shown the slightest inclination to become a member, I was called upon to become the General Secretary of this German Section of the Theosophical Society.

At the inauguration of the German Section I delivered a cycle of lectures which were attended by, I think, only two or three Theosophists, and otherwise by members of the circle to which I had addressed the lectures *From Buddha to Christ*.[13] To give the lecture cycle its full title: *Anthroposophy or the Evolution of Humanity as exemplified by world conceptions from ancient Oriental times to the present*. I gave this lecture cycle at the same time as the German Section of the Theosophical Society was being established. I even left the meeting, and while everyone else was continuing their discussion and talking about Theosophy I was delivering my lecture cycle on Anthroposophy.

One of the Theosophists, who later became a good Anthroposophist, said to me afterward that what I had said did not accord at all with what Mrs. Besant was saying and what Blavatsky was saying. I replied that this is how it was. In other words, someone with a good knowledge of all the dogmas of Theosophy had discovered correctly that something was wrong. Even at that time it was possible to say that it was wrong, that something else applied.

I now want to put to you another apparently completely unconnected fact that I referred to yesterday. Consider Blavatsky's books *Isis Unveiled* and *The Secret Doctrine*. There really was no reason to be terribly enthusiastic about the kind of people who took what was written in these books as holy dogma. But one could see Blavatsky herself as an exceedingly interesting phenomenon, if only from a deeper psychological point of view. Why? Well, there is a tremendous difference between the two books. This difference will become most clearly apparent if I tell you how those who know such things judged them.

Traditions have been preserved which have their origins in the most ancient Mysteries and which were then safeguarded by a number of so-called secret societies. Certain secret societies also bestowed degrees on their members, who advanced from the first degree to the second and the third, and so on. As they did so they were told certain things based on those traditions. At the lower degrees people did not understand this knowledge but accepted it as holy dogma. In fact they did not understand it at the higher degrees either, but the members of the lower degrees firmly believed that the members of the higher degrees understood everything.

Nevertheless, a pure form of knowledge had been preserved. A great deal was known if we simply take the texts. You need do no more than pick up things that have been printed, and revitalize this with what you know from Anthroposophy—for you cannot revitalize it in any other way—and you will see that these traditions contain great, ancient, and majestic knowledge. Sometimes the words sound completely wrong, but everyone who has any insight is aware that they have their origin in ancient wisdom. But the real distinguishing mark of the activity in these secret societies was that people had a general feeling that there were human beings in earlier times who were initiates. . . .

Then Blavatsky's *Isis Unveiled* appeared. The people who were particularly shocked by its publication were those who held traditional knowledge through their attainment of lower or higher degrees in the secret societies. They usually justified their reaction by saying that the time was not yet ripe to make available through publication the things that were being kept hidden in the secret societies. It was, furthermore, their honest opinion. But there were a number of people who had another reason. And this reason can really be understood only if I draw your attention to another set of facts.

In the fifth post-Atlantean epoch, specifically in the nineteenth century, all knowledge was transformed into abstract concepts and ideas. In Central Europe one of those who began with such abstract ideas was the philosopher Schelling. Schelling was among those who taught these ideas at a time when they could still enthuse others because they contained inner human emotional force. A few years later he no longer found any satisfaction in this mode of thought and began to immerse himself in mysticism, specifically in Jakob Boehme, allowing himself to be influenced by Boehme's thinking and extracting from it something which immediately took on a more real quality. But what Schelling said was no longer really understood, for no one could make sense of what he wrote. In the 1820s, following a lengthy reclusive period, Schelling began to speak in a curious manner. There is a small booklet by him called *Die Weltalter*.[14] You may feel that it is still rather nebulous and abstract, but a curious feeling remains. Why is it that Schelling does not advance to the stage where he can talk about what was later discussed on an Anthroposophical basis as the truths about Atlantis, for instance, but only reaches the point at which he almost, rather clumsily, hints at them? It is quite interesting.

In 1841 he was appointed to teach at the University of Berlin. That is when Schelling began to lecture on his *Philosophy of Revelation.*[15] Even that is still terribly abstract. He talks about three potentialities, A1, A2, A3. But he follows this line until he achieves some kind of grasp of the old Mysteries. He achieves in fact some kind of grasp of Christianity. Nevertheless, his is not really the appropriate way to come to terms with the ideas that he briefly puts forward. Schelling was never properly understood, but that is not really surprising because his method was a dubious one. All the same, there was something in the general awareness of the time. We can take the above as evidence for this. People like Schelling were led to conclude that a spiritual world needed to be investigated.

This feeling took a different form in England. It is exceedingly interesting to read the writings of Lawrence Oliphant.[16] Of course Oliphant presents his conclusions about the primeval periods of human development on Earth in quite a different way, because the English approach is quite distinct from the German one; it is much more physical, down-to-earth, material. The two approaches are in a certain sense, taking into account differing national characteristics, parallel phenomena: Schelling in the early part of the nineteenth century with his idealism, Oliphant with his realism, both of them displaying a strong drive to understand the world that is revealed by the spirit. These two men grew into the culture of their time; they did not stop until they had taken the philosophical ideas of their time about human beings, the cosmos, and so on to their ultimate conclusion.

Now, you know from my Anthroposophical explanations that human beings develop in early life in a way that makes physical development concomitant with soul development. That ceases later on. As I told you, the Greeks continued to develop into their thirties in a way that involved real parallel development of the physical and the spiritual. With Schelling and Oliphant something different happened from what happens with the average person of today. One may work on a concept and develop it further, but Schelling and Oliphant went beyond this, and as they grew older their souls suddenly became filled with the vitality of their previous lives on Earth; they began to remember ancient things from their earlier incarnations. Distant memories, unclear memories, arose in a natural way. Suddenly that struck people like a flash. Both Oliphant and Schelling were suddenly seen in a different light.

Both establish themselves and begin by becoming ordinary philosophers, each in his own country. Then in their later years they begin to recall knowledge they have known in earlier lives on Earth, only now it is like a misty memory. At this point Schelling and Oliphant begin to speak about the spiritual world. Even if these are unclear memories they are, nevertheless, something to be feared by those who have only been through the old style, traditional development of the societies, to the extent that they might spread and gain the upper hand. These people lived in terrible fear that human beings could be born with the facility to remember what they had experienced in the past and speak about it. Furthermore, it also called into question all their principles of secrecy. Here we are, they thought, making members of the first, second, third grades, and so on swear holy oaths of secrecy, but what remains of our secrecy if human beings are now being born who can recall personally what we have preserved and kept under lock and key?

Then *Isis Unveiled* appeared! The notable thing about it was that it brought openly onto the book market a whole lot of things that were being kept hidden in secret societies. The great problem the societies had to come to terms with was how Blavatsky obtained the knowledge that they had kept locked away and for which people had sworn holy oaths. It was those who were particularly shocked by this who paid a great deal of attention to *Isis Unveiled*.

Then *The Secret Doctrine* appeared. That only made things worse. *The Secret Doctrine* presented a whole category of knowledge that was the preserve of the highest grades in the secret societies. Those who were shocked by the first book, and even more so by the second one, used all kinds of expressions to describe them both, because Blavatsky as a phenomenon had a terribly unsettling effect, particularly on the so-called initiates. *Isis Unveiled* was less frightening because Blavatsky was a chaotic personality who continually interspersed material that contained deep wisdom with all kinds of stuff and nonsense. So the frightened, so-called initiates could still say about *Isis Unveiled* that what was true in it was not new and what was new was not true! The disagreeable fact for them was that things had been revealed—after all, the book was called *Isis Unveiled.* They reassured themselves by saying that the event was an infringement of their rights.

But when *The Secret Doctrine* appeared, containing a whole lot of material that even the highest grades did not know, they could no longer say that what was true was not new and what was new was not true. For it contained a large body of knowledge that had not been preserved by tradition. . . .

18

The Opposition to Spiritual
Revelations

Dornach, June 12, 1923

. . . BLAVATSKY'S WORKS have very little to do with Anthroposophy. I do not, however, want simply to describe the history of the Anthroposophical movement, but also to characterize its aspects that relate to the Society. That requires the kind of background I have given you.

If we want to be critical, it is of course quite easy to dismiss everything that can be said about Blavatsky by pointing to the questionable nature of some episodes in her life.

I could give you any number of examples. I could tell you how, within the Society that took its cue from Madame Blavatsky and her spiritual life, the view gained ground that certain insights about the spiritual world became known because physical letters came from a source that did not lie in the physical world. Such documents were called the "Mahatma Letters." It then became a rather sensational affair when evidence of all kinds of sleight of hand with sliding doors was produced. There are other such examples.

But for the moment let us take another view, ignoring everything outward, and simply examining her writings. Then you will conclude that Blavatsky's works consist largely of dilettantish, muddled stuff, but that despite this they contain material which, examined in the right way, can be understood as containing far-reaching insights into or from the spiritual world, *no matter how they were acquired*. That simply cannot be denied, despite the objections that are raised.

This, I believe, leads to an issue of extraordinary importance and significance in the spiritual history of civilization. Why is it that, at the end of the nineteenth century, spiritual revelations appeared that merit detailed attention, even from the objective standpoint of spiritual science, if only as the basis for further investigation? Why did such revelations that say more about the fundamental forces of the world than anything that has been discovered about its secrets through modern philosophy or other currents of thought become accessible? That seems like a significant question.

This question must be juxtaposed with another not-to-be-forgotten cultural-historical phenomenon, namely that people's ability to discriminate, their surety of judgment, has suffered greatly and regressed in our time.

It is easy to be deceived about this by the enormous progress that has been made. But it is precisely because individual human beings participate in the spiritual life as discerning individuals that we get some idea of the capacity our age possesses to deal with phenomena requiring the application of judgment. . . .

Such things have to be taken into account when taking full stock of the hostile forces opposing the intervention of spiritual movements. It is necessary to be aware of the general level of judgment applied in our time, which is excessively arrogant precisely about its nonexistent capacity to reach the right conclusions.

It was, after all, a very characteristic event that many of the things traditionally preserved by secret societies, which were at pains to prevent them from reaching the public, should suddenly be published by a woman, Blavatsky, in a book called *Isis Unveiled*. Of course people were shocked when they realized that this book contained a great deal of the material they had always kept under lock and key. These societies, I might add, were considerably more concerned about their locks and keys than is our present Anthroposophical Society.

It was certainly not the intention of the Anthroposophical Society to secrete away everything contained in the lecture cycles. At a certain point I was asked to make the material, which I otherwise discuss verbally, accessible to a larger circle. And since there was no time to revise the lectures they were printed as manuscripts in a form that otherwise would not have been published—not because I did not want to publish the material, but because I did not want to publish it in this form. Furthermore, to prevent misunderstanding, there was a concern that only people who had the necessary preparation should read it. Even so, it is now possible to acquire every lecture cycle, even for the purpose of attacking us.

The societies that kept specific knowledge under lock and key and made people swear oaths they would not reveal any of it made a better job of protecting these things. They knew that something special must have occurred when a book (*Isis Unveiled*) suddenly appeared that revealed something significant in the sense that we have discussed. As for the insignificant material, well, you need only go to one of the side streets in Paris and you can buy the writings of the secret societies by the lorry load. As a rule these publications are worthless.

But *Isis Unveiled* was not worthless. Its content was substantive enough to identify the knowledge it presented as something original, revealing ancient wisdom that had been carefully guarded until that moment.

As I said, those who reacted with shock imagined that someone must have betrayed them. I have discussed this repeatedly from a variety of angles in previous lectures.[1] But I now want rather to characterize the judgment of the world, because that is particularly relevant to the history of the movement. After all, it was not difficult to understand that someone who had come into possession of traditional knowledge might have suggested it to Blavatsky for whatever reason, and it need not have been a particularly laudable one. It would not be far from the truth to state that the betrayal occurred in one or a number of secret societies and that Blavatsky was chosen to publish the material.

There was a good reason to make use of her, however. And here we come to a chapter in tracing our cultural history that is really rather peculiar. At the time there was very little talk of a subject that is on everyone's lips today: psychoanalysis. But Blavatsky enabled people of sound judgment who came into contact with this peculiar development to experience in a living way something that made what has been written so far by the various leading authorities in the psychoanalytic field appear amateurish in the extreme. For what is it that psychoanalysis wishes to demonstrate? Psychoanalysis is correct in a certain sense in demonstrating that there is something in the depths of human nature that, in whatever form it exists there, can be raised into consciousness. Psychoanalysis is correct when it says there is something present in the body which, raised to consciousness, appears as something spiritual.[2] It is, of course, an extremely primitive action for a psychoanalyst to raise what remains of past experience from the depths of the human psyche in this way. It is a primitive thing to raise past experience that has been assimilated with insufficient intensity to satisfy the emotional needs of a person, so that it has sunk to the bottom, as it were, and settled there as sediment, creating an unstable rather than a stable equilibrium. But once brought into consciousness it is possible to come to terms with such experiences, thus liberating the human being from their unhealthy presence. . . .

Up to the fifteenth century or thereabouts, it was not an infrequent occurrence for visions of cosmic secrets to be triggered within human beings by some particularly characteristic physical happening. Later, this came to be seen as an extremely mystical event. The tale told about Jakob Boehme having a magnificent vision as he looked at a pewter bowl is admired because people do not know that up to the fifteenth century it was very common for an apparently minor stimulus to provoke in human beings tremendous visions of cosmic secrets.

But it became increasingly rare, due to the increasing dominance of the intellect. Intellectualism is connected with a specific development of the brain. The brain calcifies, as it were, and becomes hardened. This cannot, of course, be demonstrated anatomically and physiologically, but it can be shown spiritually. This hardened brain simply does not permit the inner vision of human beings to rise to the surface of consciousness.

And now I have to say something extremely paradoxical, which is nevertheless true. A greater hardening of the brain took place in men, ignoring exceptions which, of course, exist both in men and women. This is not to say that this is a particular reason for female brains to celebrate, for at the end of the nineteenth century they became hard enough too! But nevertheless it was men who were ahead in terms of a more pronounced intellectualism and hardening of the brain. And that is connected with their inability to form judgments.

This was exactly the same time at which the secrecy surrounding the knowledge of ancient times was still very pronounced. It became obvious that this knowledge had little effect on men. They learned it by rote as they rose through the degrees. They were not really affected by it and kept it under lock and key. But if someone wished to make this ancient wisdom flower once more, there was a special experiment one could try. This was to make a small dose of this knowledge, which one need not even necessarily have understood oneself, available to a woman whose brain might have been prepared in a special way—for Blavatsky's brain was something quite different from the brains of other nineteenth-century women. Thus, material that was otherwise dried-up old knowledge was able to ignite, in a manner of speaking, in these female brains through the contrast with what was otherwise available as culture. It was able to stimulate Blavatsky in the same way that the psychiatrist stimulates the human psyche. By this means she was able to find within herself what had been forgotten altogether by that section of humanity that did not belong to the secret societies, and had been kept carefully under lock and key and not understood by those who did belong. In this way what I might describe as a cultural escape valve was created which allowed this knowledge to emerge.

But at the same time there was no basis on which the knowledge could have been dealt with in a sensible manner. For Madame Blavatsky was certainly no logician, and while she was able to use her personality to reveal cosmic secrets, she was not capable of presenting these things in a form that could be justified before the modern scientific conscience. . . .

Let me illustrate this with an example of how difficult it is in our modern age to make oneself understood if one wants to appeal to wider, more generous powers of judgment. . . .

There was a period at the turn of the century in Berlin during which a number of Giordano Bruno societies were being established, including a Giordano Bruno League. Its membership included some really excellent people who had a thorough interest in everything contemporary that merited the concentration of one's ideas, feelings, and will. And in the abstract way in which these things happen in our age, the Giordano Bruno League also referred to the spirit. A well-known figure who belonged to this League titled his inaugural lecture "No Matter without Spirit."[3] But all this lacked real perspective, because the spirit and the ideas being pursued there were fundamentally so abstract that they could not approach the reality of the world. What annoyed me particularly was that these people introduced the concept of monism at every available opportunity. This was always followed with the remark that the modern age had escaped from the dualism of the Middle Ages. The waffle about monism and the amateurish rejection of dualism annoyed me. I was annoyed by the vague, pantheistic reference to the spirit, which is present, well, everywhere. The word became devoid of content. I found all that pretty hard to take. Actually I came into conflict with the speaker immediately after that first lecture on "No Matter without Spirit," which did not go down well at all. But then all that monistic carrying-on became more and more upsetting, so I decided to tackle these people in the hope that I could at least inject some life into their powers of discernment. And since a whole series of lectures had already been devoted to tirades against the obscurantism of the Middle Ages, to the terrible dualism of Scholasticism, I decided to do something to shake up their powers of judgment. I am currently accused of having been at that time a rabid disciple of Haeckel.

I gave a lecture on Thomas Aquinas and said, in brief, that there was no justification to refer to the Middle Ages as obscurantist, specifically in respect to the dualism of Thomism and Scholasticism.[4] As monism was being used as a catchword, I intended to show that Thomas Aquinas had been a thorough monist. It was wrong to interpret monism solely in its present materialistic sense; everyone had to be considered a monist who saw the underlying principle of the world as a whole, as the *monon*. So I said that Thomas Aquinas had certainly done that, because he had naturally seen the *monon* in the divine unity underlying creation. One had to be clear that Thomas Aquinas had intended on the one hand to investigate the world through physical research and intellectual knowledge but, on the other hand, that he had wanted to supplement this intellectual knowledge with the truths of revelation. But he had done that precisely to gain access to the unifying principle of the world. He had simply used two approaches. The worst thing for the present age would be if it could not develop sufficiently broad concepts to embrace some sort of historical perspective.

In short, I wanted to inject some fluidity into their dried-out brains. But it was in vain and had a quite extraordinary effect. To begin with, it had not the slightest meaning to the members of the Giordano Bruno League. They were all Lutheran Protestants. It is appalling, they said; we make every attempt to deal Catholicism a mortal blow, and now a member of this selfsame Giordano Bruno League comes along to defend it! They had not the slightest idea what to make of it. And yet they were among the most enlightened people of their time. It is precisely through this kind of thing that one learns about the powers of discrimination. One learns, too, about the willingness to take a broadly based view of something that does not rely on theoretical formulations, but seeks to make real progress on the path to the spirit, to gain real access to the spiritual world.

Whether or not we gain access to the spiritual world does not depend on whether we have this or that theory about spirit or matter, but on whether we are in a position to achieve a real experience of the spiritual world. Spiritualists believe very firmly that all their actions are grounded in the spirit, but their theories are completely devoid of it. They most certainly do not lead human beings to the spirit. One can be a materialist, no less, and possess a great deal of spirit. It, too, is real spirit, even if it has lost its way. Of course this lost spirit need not be presented as something very valuable. But having got lost, deluding itself that it considers matter to be the only reality, it is still filled with more spirit than the kind of unimaginative absence of anything spiritual at all, which seeks the spirit by material means because it cannot find any trace of spirit within itself.

When you look back, therefore, at the beginnings you have to understand the great difficulty with which the revelations of the spiritual world entered the physical world in the last third of the nineteenth century. Those beginnings have to be properly understood if the whole meaning and the circumstances governing the existence of the movement are to make sense. You need to understand, above all, how serious was the intention in certain circles not to allow anything that would truly lead to the spirit to enter the public domain. There can be no doubt that the appearance of Blavatsky was likely to jolt very many people who were not to be taken lightly. And that is indeed what happened. Those people who still preserved some powers of discrimination reached the conclusion that here there was something that had its source within itself. One need only apply some healthy common sense and it spoke for itself. But there were nevertheless many people whose interests would not be served by allowing this kind of stimulus to flow into the world.

But it had arrived in the form of Blavatsky, who, in a sense, handled her own inner revelation in a naive and helpless manner. That is already evident in the style of her writings and was influenced by much that was happening around her. Indeed, do not believe that those who wanted to ensure that the world should not accept anything of a spiritual nature had any difficulty in attaching themselves to her entourage. In a sense she was gullible because of her naive and helpless attitude to her own inner revelations. Take the affair with the sliding doors through which the Mahatma Letters were apparently inserted, when in fact they had been written and pushed in by someone outside. The person who pushed them in deceived Blavatsky and the world. Then, of course, it was very easy to tell the world that she was a fraud. But do you not understand that Blavatsky herself could have been deceived? For she was prone to an extraordinary gullibility precisely because of the special lack of hardness, as I would describe it, of her brain.

The problem is an exceedingly complicated one and demands, like everything of a true spiritual nature that enters the world in our time, a quality of discernment, a healthy common sense. . . .

19

Spiritual Truths
and the Physical World

Dornach, June 13, 1923

CONSIDERING A PHENOMENON such as Madame Blavatsky . . . we need
to be concerned first with her personality as such. The other aspect is
the impact she had on a large number of people. It is true, of course,
that this impact was in part quite negative. Those with a philosophical, psychological, literary, scientific—let us say a well-educated—
bent were happy to dismiss this phenomenon in one way or another.
This could easily be done simply by saying that she had engaged in
dishonest practices and that there was no need to spend time on
something where there was evidence of that sort of thing.

Then there were those who were in possession of ancient, traditional wisdom. These were members of one or another secret society.
One must never forget that numerous events in the world are linked
to actions from such secret societies. These societies were concerned
above all with finding a way to prevent such a depiction of the spiritual world from having a wider impact. Because these things could be
read and promulgated, the secret societies had been deprived of a
good deal of the power they wanted to preserve for themselves. That is
why it is members of such societies who are behind the accusations
that Blavatsky engaged in dishonest practices.

More important for our present purpose, however, is that Blavatsky's writings and everything else connected with her personality
made a certain impression on a large number of people. That led to
the establishment of movements describing themselves as Theosophical in one way or another. . . .

Here there is always the question of definition. We must ask, How
did the societies basing themselves on Blavatsky come to use the name
Theosophical Society? One thing that did not happen when the Theosophical Society was founded at the end of the nineteenth century was

to found a society with the aim of propagating theosophy as defined in the dictionary. Nevertheless, a body of knowledge about the spiritual world existed through Blavatsky. Initially, this was simply there. Then it was found necessary to cultivate this knowledge through a society, and a society requires a name. It is pure coincidence that the societies based on that body of knowledge called themselves the Theosophical Society. No one could think of a better name. It's as simple as that. This should never be forgotten. People who have learned about the historical development of their given area of study have likely come across the term *theosophy*. But the term they have come across has nothing to do with what called itself the Theosophical Society.

Within the Anthroposophical Society, at any rate, such things ought to be taken very seriously. There should be a certain drive for accuracy, so that a proper feeling can develop for the subjective scribbling to which these things have gradually given rise.

One question should particularly concern us. Why did a large number of our contemporaries feel the urge to follow up these revelations? Answering this will provide us with the bridge to something of a quite different nature, the Anthroposophical Society.

In considering Blavatsky, it is important that her attitude was what might well be called anti-Christian. In her *Secret Doctrine* she revealed in one large sweep the differing impulses and development of the many ancient religions. But everything one might expect in an objective depiction is clouded by her subjective judgment, the judgment of her feelings. It becomes abundantly clear that she had a deep sympathy for all religions in the world except Judaism and Christianity, and that she had a deep antipathy toward Judaism and Christianity. Blavatsky depicts everything deriving from the latter as inferior to the great revelations of the various pagan religions: in other words, she manifests an expressly anti-Christian perspective, but an expressly spiritual one.

She was able to speak of spiritual beings and spiritual processes in the same way one normally speaks of the beings and processes of the physical world. She was able to discuss aspects of this spiritual world because she had the capacity to move among spiritual forces in the same way that contemporary people normally move among physical-sensory forces.

On that basis she was able to bring to the surface and clarify characteristic impulses of the various pantheistic religions.

Two things might surprise us here. The first is that it is possible at all today for someone to appear who perceives human salvation from this anti-Christian perspective. Second, we might be surprised by the decisive and profound influence exerted by such an anti-Christian perspective on people with a Christian outlook. (Perhaps it is less surprising in those with a Jewish background.) These are two questions we must ponder when we speak about conditions governing the existence of the contemporary life of the spirit among the broader masses in general.

With regard to Madame Blavatsky's anti-Christian perspective, I want only to remind you that someone who became much better known than she in Central Europe, in certain circles at least, had as much of an anti-Christian perspective. That was Nietzsche. It would be difficult to be more anti-Christian than the author of *The Anti-Christ.*[1] It would be adopting a very superficial attitude not to inquire into the reason for the anti-Christian outlook of these two personalities. But to find an answer we need to dig a little bit deeper. . . .

We need to have a clear understanding of the way European peoples and their American cousins have been influenced by the educational endeavors of the last three, four, five hundred years. One need only consider how great the difference really is between today's secular education and the religious impulses of humanity. From the time people enter elementary school, all their thinking, their whole inner orientation, is directed toward this modern, secular education. And then they are also provided with what is meant to satisfy their religious needs. Therefore a dreadful gap opens up between the two. People never really have the opportunity to deal inwardly with this chasm, preferring instead to submit to the most dreadful illusions in this respect.

This raises questions about the historical process that led to the creation of this yawning chasm. For this we have to look back to those centuries in which learning was the province of the few who were thoroughly prepared for it. You can be quite certain that a twelve-year-old schoolgirl today has a greater fund of worldly knowledge than any educated person of the eleventh, twelfth, or thirteenth century. These things must not be overlooked. Education has come to rely on an extraordinarily intense feeling of authority, an almost invincible sense of authority. In the course of the centuries modern education has increasingly come to comprise only the knowledge of what can be demonstrated to the outer senses, or by calculation. By excluding everything else it became possible—because two times two equals four, and the five senses are so persuasive—for modern education to acquire its sense of authority. But that also increasingly gave rise to the feeling that everything human beings believe, everything they consider to be right, must be justified by the knowledge modern learning is so certain of. It was impossible to present in a corresponding fashion any truth from the realms where mathematics and the senses no longer apply.

How were these truths presented to humanity prior to the existence of modern learning? They were presented in ritual images. The essential element in the spread of religion over the centuries lay not in the sermons, for instance, but in the ceremonial, in the rituals. Try to imagine for a moment what it was like in Christian countries in the fourteenth or fifteenth century. The important thing was for people to enter a world presented to them in mighty and grandiose images. All around, frescoes on the walls reminded them of the spiritual life. It was as if their earthly life could reach as high as the tallest mountain, but at that point, if one could climb just a little bit higher, the spiritual life began. The language of the spiritual world was depicted in images that stimulated the imagination, in the audible harmonies of music, or in the words of set forms such as mantras and prayers. These ages understood clearly that images, not concepts, were required for the spiritual world. People needed something vividly pictorial, not something to be debated. Something was required that would allow the spirit to speak through what was accessible to the senses. Christianity and its secrets, the Mystery of Golgotha and everything connected with it, were essentially spoken about in the form of images, even when words were used in story form. The dogmas were also still understood as something pictorial. And this Christian teaching remained unchallenged from any quarter prior to the existence of intellectual learning, and for as long as these things did not have to be justified by reason.

Now just look at historical processes in the thirteenth through the sixteenth centuries, at the urgency with which human beings begin to experience the drive to understand everything intellectually. This introduced a critical attitude of world-historical significance.

Thus, the majority of human beings today are introduced to religious life through Christianity but alongside that to modern learning also. Consequently, both Christianity and modern learning coexist in each soul. And even if people do not admit it, it transpires that the results of intellectual education cannot be used to prove Christian truths. So from childhood people are now taught the fact that two times two equals four and that only the five senses must be used in such a context, and they also begin to understand that such absolutes are incompatible with Christianity.

Modern theologians who have tried to marry the two have lost Christ, are no longer able to speak to the broad spectrum of people about Christ; at most they speak about the personality of Jesus. Thus Christianity itself has been able to be preserved only in its old forms. But modern people are simply no longer willing to accept this in their souls, and they have lost some of their inner security. Why?

Well, just look at the way Christianity has developed historically. It is extremely dishonest to use rationalism to put meaning into Christianity, the Mystery of Golgotha, and everything connected with it. One has to talk about a spiritual world if one wants to speak about Christ. Modern human beings do not have the means in their innermost being to understand Christ on the basis of what they have been taught at school, for rationalism and intellectualism have robbed them of the spiritual world. Christ is still present in name and tradition, but the feeling for what that means is gone; the understanding of Christ as a spiritual being among spiritual beings in a spiritual world has disappeared. The world created by modern astronomy, biology, and science is a world devoid of spirit.

Thus numerous souls have grown up who, for these reasons, have quite specific needs. Time really does progress, and the people of today are not the same as people in earlier ages. You must have said to yourselves, Here I meet with a certain number of others in a society to cultivate spiritual truths. Why do you, each single one of you, do that? What drives you? Well, the thing that drives people to do this is usually so deeply embedded in the unconscious depths of their soul life that there is little clarity about it. But here, where we want to reflect on our position as Anthroposophists, the question has to be asked.

If you look back to earlier times, it was self-evident that material things and processes were not the totality, but that spirits were everywhere. People perceived a spiritual world which surrounded them in their environment. And because they found a spiritual world they were able to understand Christ.

Modern intellectualism makes it impossible to discover a spiritual world, if one is honest, and as a consequence it is impossible to understand Christ properly. The people who try so hard to rediscover a spiritual life are very specific souls driven by two things. First, most souls who come together in the kind of societies we have been talking about start to experience a vague feeling within themselves which they cannot describe. And if this feeling is investigated with the means available in the spiritual world it turns out to be a feeling that stems from earlier lives on Earth in which a spiritual environment still existed. Today, people are appearing in whose souls something from their previous lives on Earth remains active. There would be neither Theosophists nor Anthroposophists if such people did not exist. They are to be found in all sections of society. They do not know that their feeling is the result of earlier lives on Earth, but it is. And it makes them search for a very specific path, for very specific knowledge. Indeed, what continues to have an effect is the spiritual content of earlier lives on Earth.

Human beings today are affected in two ways. They can have the feeling that there is something within them that affects them, that is simply there. But even though they might know a great deal about the physical world, they cannot describe this feeling because nothing that was not of a spiritual nature has been carried over. If, however, I am deprived in the present of everything spiritual, then what has come over from a previous life remains dissatisfied. That is one aspect.

The other effect that lives in human beings is a vague feeling that their dreams should really reveal more than the physical world. It is of course an error, an illusion. But what is the origin of this illusion, which has arisen in parallel with the development of modem learning? When people who have had the benefit of a modern education gather together in learned circles, they have to show their cultural breeding. If someone starts to talk about spiritual effects in the world, people adopt an air of ridicule, because that is what being cultured demands. It is not acceptable within our school education to talk about spiritual effects in the world. To do so implies superstition, lack of education.

Two groups will then often form in such circles. Frequently someone plucks up a little courage to talk about spiritual things. People then adopt an air of ridicule. The majority leave to play cards or indulge in some other worthy pursuit. But a few are intrigued. They go into a side room and begin to talk about these things; they listen with open mouths and cannot get enough of it; but it has to be in a side room because anything else shows a lack of education. The things a modern person can learn there are mostly as incoherent and chaotic as dreaming, but people love it all the same. Those who have gone to play cards would also love it, except that their passion for cards is even stronger. At least that is what they tell themselves.

Why do human beings in our modern age feel the urge to investigate their dreams? Because they feel quite instinctively, without any clear understanding, that the content of their thoughts and what they see depicted in the physical world are all very nice, but do not give them anything for their soul life. They feel that a secret thinking, feeling, and willing lives in them when they are awake, which is as free as their dream life is free when they are sleeping; there is something in the depths of the soul that is dreamt even when they are awake. Modern people feel that, precisely because the spiritual element is missing from the physical world. They can only catch a glimpse of it when they are dreaming. In earlier lives on Earth they saw it in everything around them.

And now those souls are being born who can feel working within themselves not only impulses from their previous lives on Earth, but what took place in the spiritual world in their pre-earthly existence. This is related to their internal dreaming. It is an echo of the life before birth.

But it is not only the historical processes that deny them the spirit; an educational system has been constructed that is hostile to the spirit, that proves the spirit out of existence.

If we ask how people find a common interest in societies such as those we are describing here, it is through these two features of the soul: namely, that something is active both from their previous Earth lives and from their pre-earthly existence. This is the case for most of you. You would not be sitting here if these two things were not active within you.

In very ancient times social institutions were determined by the Mysteries, and were in harmony with the content of their spiritual teaching. Take the Athenians for example. They revered the goddess Athene. They were part of a social community that they knew to be constituted according to Athene's intentions. The olive trees around Athens were planted by her. The laws of the state had been dictated by her. Human beings were part of a social community that was in total accord with their inner beliefs. Nothing the gods had given them had, as it were, been taken away.

Compare that with modern human beings. They are placed in a social context in which there is a huge gap between their inner experiences and the way they are integrated into society. It feels to them as if their souls are divorced from their bodies by social circumstances, only they are not aware of it; it is embedded in the subconscious. Through these impulses from earlier lives on Earth and pre-earthly existence, people feel connected with a spiritual world. Their bodies have to behave in a way that will satisfy social institutions. That their physical bodies no longer really belong to them provokes a persistent subconscious fear. Well, there are modern states in which you feel that your clothes no longer belong to you because the tax man is after them! But in a larger context one's physical body is no longer one's property either. It is claimed by society.

This is the fear that lives in modern human beings, the fear that every day they have to give up their bodies to something that is not connected with their souls. And thus they become seekers after something which does not belong to the Earth, which belongs to the spiritual world of their pre-earthly existence.

All this takes its effect unconsciously, instinctively. And it has to be said that the Anthroposophical Society as it has developed had its origins in small beginnings. To begin with, it had to work in the most basic way with very small groups, and there is much to be said about the ways and means in which work took place in such small groups.

For example, in the first years in Berlin I had to lecture in a room in which beer glasses were clinking in the background. And once we were shown into something not unlike a stable. I lectured in a hall that had no floor in parts, where one had to be careful not to tumble into a hole and break a leg. But that is where people gathered who felt these impulses. Indeed, this movement aimed to make itself accessible to everyone right from the beginning. Thus the satisfaction was just as great when the simplest mind turned up in such a location. At the same time it was no great worry when people came together to launch the Anthroposophical movement in a more aristocratic fashion, as happened in Munich, because that too was part of humanity. No aspect of humanity was excluded.

But the important point was that the souls who met in this way always had the qualities I have described. If such people had not existed, then someone like Blavatsky would not have engendered any interest, because it was among them that she made her mark. What was most important to them and what corresponded to their feelings?

Well, the concept of reincarnation corresponded to the one thing that was active in their souls. Now they could see themselves straddling the ages as human beings, making them stronger than the forces which daily tried to rob them of their bodies. This deep-seated, almost will-like, inner feeling of human beings had to be met by the teaching of reincarnation.

And the dreamlike, out-of-body experience of the soul, which even the simplest country person can experience, could never be satisfied with knowledge based only on matter and its processes. That could only be met by making it clear to people that the most profound aspect of human nature exists as if it is woven out of dreams, if I may put it in this radical way. This element has a stronger reality, a stronger existence than dreams. We are like fish out of water if we are forced to live our soul life in the world that has been conjured up for people by modern education. Just as fish cannot exist in air and begin to gasp, so our souls live in the contemporary environment, gasping for what they need. They fail to find it, because it is spiritual in nature; it is the echo of their experiences in life before birth in the spiritual world. They want to hear about the spirit, that the spirit exists, that the spirit is actually present among us.

You have to understand that the two most important concerns for a certain section of humankind were to learn that human beings live more than a single life on Earth, and that among the natural things and processes there are beings in the world like themselves, spiritual beings. It was Blavatsky who initially presented this to the world. It was necessary to possess that knowledge before it was possible to understand Christ once again.

As far as Blavatsky was concerned, however—and in saying this we should emphasize her compassion for humankind—she realized that these people were gasping for knowledge of the spiritual world, and she thought that she would meet their spiritual needs by revealing the ancient pagan religions to them. That was her initial aim. It is quite clear that this had to result in a tremendously partisan anti-Christian standpoint, just as it is clear that Nietzsche's observation of Christianity in its present form, which he had outgrown, led him to adopt such a strong anti-Christian attitude.

This anti-Christian outlook, and how it might be healed, is the topic I want to address in the next lectures. It remains only to emphasize that what appeared with Blavatsky as an anti-Christian standpoint was absent right from the beginning in the Anthroposophical movement, because the first lecture cycle I gave was *From Buddha to Christ*. Thus the Anthroposophical movement takes an independent position within all these spiritual movements in that, from the start, it pursued a path from the heathen religions to Christianity. But it is equally necessary to understand why others did not follow this path.

20

The Decline of
the Theosophical Society

Dornach, June 14, 1923

IT IS IMPORTANT TO RECOGNIZE the need that existed in the Anthroposophical movement for Christianity to be affirmed, specifically among those who were initially what might be described as the ordinary listeners, for the Theosophical movement under the guidance of H. P. Blavatsky had adopted an expressly anti-Christian orientation. I wish to throw a little more light on this anti-Christian attitude, a perspective that I have also mentioned before in connection with Friedrich Nietzsche.

We must understand that the Mystery of Golgotha occurred in the first place simply as a fact in human evolution on Earth. If you look at the way I dealt with it in my book *Christianity as Mystical Fact,* you will see that I attempted first to understand the impulses underlying the ancient Mysteries. I then tried to show how the various forces active in the individual Mystery centers were harmonized and unified. What humanity initially encountered in a hidden way was presented openly as a historical fact. In this sense the historical reality of the Mystery of Golgotha represents the culmination of the ancient Mysteries. Remnants of the ancient Mystery wisdom were present when the Mystery of Golgotha took place. With the aid of these remnants, incorporated into the Gospels, it was possible to find access to this event that gave earthly development its true meaning.

The impulses derived from ancient wisdom that were still directly experienced began to fade in the fourth century A.D., so that the wisdom was preserved only in a more or less traditional form, allowing particular people in one place or another to revitalize these traditions. But the kind of continuous development that the Mysteries enjoyed in ancient times disappeared, taking with it the means to understand the Mystery of Golgotha.

The tradition remained. The Gospels existed, kept secret at first by the communities of the church and then published in individual nations. The cults existed. As the Western world developed it was possible to keep alive a memory of the Mystery of Golgotha. But the opportunity to maintain the memory ended in that moment in the fifth post-Atlantean epoch when intellectualism, along with what I described yesterday as modern education, made its appearance. And thereby, too, a type of science of the natural world began, which preempted any understanding of the spiritual world as it developed the kind of methodology seen to date. This methodology needed to be expanded in the way that Anthroposophy has sought to expand it. If one does not progress beyond the scientific method introduced by Copernicus, Galileo, and so on, the Mystery of Golgotha has no place within the resultant view of nature.

Now consider the following. In none of the ancient religions was there any division between knowledge of the natural world and knowledge of God. It is a common feature of all pagan religions that there is a unity in the way they explain nature, and in how that understanding of nature then ascends to an understanding of the divine, the many-faceted divinity that is active in nature.

The kind of abstract natural forces we are now aware of, unchallenged in their absoluteness, did not exist. What did exist were nature spirits, which guided the various aspects of nature and with which links could be established through the content of the human soul.

Now Anthroposophy will never make the claim that it somehow wants to become a religion. However, although religion will always need to be an independent spiritual stream in humankind, it is a simple human desire for harmony to exist between cognition and the religious life. It must be possible to make the transition from cognition to religion and to return from religion to cognition without having to cross an abyss. That is impossible, given the structure of modern learning. It is impossible, above all, to discover the nature of Christ on this scientific basis. Modern science, in investigating the being of Christ ever more closely, has scattered and lost it.

If you bear this in mind, you will be able to understand what follows. Let me begin by talking about Nietzsche, whose father was a practicing minister. He went through a modern grammar school education. But since he was not a bread-and-butter scholar but a thinker, his interest extended to everything that could be learned through modern methods. So he consciously and in a radical way became aware of the dichotomy that affects all modern minds, although people do not realize it and are prone to illusion because they draw a veil over it. Nietzsche claims that modern education nowhere provides a direct link to an explanation of Jesus Christ without jumping over an abyss. His uncompromising conclusion is that if one wants to establish a relationship with modern science while preserving some sort of inner feeling for the traditional explanations of Christ, it is necessary to lie. And so he chose modern learning, and thus arrived at a radical indictment of what he knew about Christianity.

No one has been more cutting about Christianity than Nietzsche, the minister's son. And he experiences this with his whole being. One example is when he says—and it is not, of course, my standpoint— that what a modern theologian believes to be true is certainly false. And he finds that the whole of modern philosophy has too much theological blood flowing through its veins. As a result he formulates his tremendous indictment of Christianity, which is of course blasphemous, but is an honest blasphemy. . . . Nietzsche, who was serious about wanting to understand the Mystery of Golgotha, was not able to do so with the means at his disposal, including the Gospels in their present form.

Anthroposophy provides an interpretation of all four Gospels, and these interpretations are rejected decisively by theologians of all denominations.[1] But they were not available to Nietzsche. It is the most difficult thing for a scientific mind—and almost all people today have scientific minds in this sense, even if at a basic level—to come to terms with the Mystery of Golgotha. It is particularly difficult for them to come to terms with what is precisely not in the old Mysteries, but is the discovery of an entirely new Mystery knowledge. The discovery of the spiritual world in a wholly new form is necessary.

Basically Blavatsky's inspiration also came from the ancient Mysteries. If one takes *The Secret Doctrine* as a whole, it really feels like nothing fundamentally new but the resurrection of the knowledge used in the ancient Mysteries to recognize the divine and the spiritual. But these Mysteries are only capable of explaining the events that happened in anticipation of Christ. Those who were familiar with the impulses of the ancient Mysteries when Christianity was still young were able to adopt a positive attitude to what happened at Golgotha. This applied into the fourth century. The real meaning of the Greek

Church Fathers was still understood: how their roots stretched back to the ancient Mysteries, and how their words have quite a different tone from those of the later Latin Church Fathers.

The ancient wisdom that understood nature and spirit as one was contained in Blavatsky's revelations. That is the way, she thought, to find the divine and the spiritual, to make them accessible to human perception. From that perspective she turned her attention to what contemporary traditional thinking and the modern faiths were saying about Christ Jesus. She could not, of course, understand the Gospels the way they are understood in Anthroposophy. . . . That is the origin of her contempt for the way the Mystery of Golgotha was understood by the world. In her view, what people were saying about the Mystery of Golgotha was on a much lower level than all the majestic wisdom provided by the ancient Mysteries. In other words, the Christian God stands on a lower level than the content of the ancient Mysteries.

That was not the fault of the Christian God, but it was the result of interpretations of the Christian God. Blavatsky simply did not know the nature of the Mystery of Golgotha and was able to judge it only by what was being said about it. These things have to be seen in an objective light. As the power of the ancient Mysteries was drawing to a final close in the last remnants of Greek culture in the fourth century A.D., Rome took possession of Christianity. The empirical attitude of Roman culture to learning was incapable of opening a real path to the spirit. Rome forced Christianity to adopt its outer trappings. It is this romanized Christianity alone that Nietzsche and Blavatsky knew.

Thus the souls whom I described as homeless, whose earlier Earth lives were lighting up within them, took the first thing offered because their sole aim was to find access to the spiritual world, even at the risk of losing Christianity. These were the people who began by seeking a way into the Theosophical Society.

Now the position of Anthroposophy in relation to these homeless souls has to be clearly understood. These were searching, questioning souls, and the first need was to find out what questions resided in their innermost selves. And if Anthroposophy addressed these souls, it was because they had questions about things to which Anthroposophy thought it had the answer. Other people among our contemporaries were not bothered by such questions.

Anthroposophy therefore considered what came into the world with Blavatsky to be an important fact. But its purpose was not to

observe the knowledge that she presented, but essentially to understand those questions people found perplexing.

How were the answers to be formulated? We need to look at the
matter as positively and as factually as possible. Here we had these
questioning souls. Their questions were clear. They believed that they
could find an answer to them in something like Annie Besant's book
The Ancient Wisdom, for instance. Obviously, it would have been stupid to tell people that this or that bit of *The Ancient Wisdom* was no
longer relevant. The only possible course was to give real answers by
ignoring *The Ancient Wisdom* at a time when this book was, as it were,
dogma among these people, and writing my book *Theosophy*, which
gave answers to questions I knew were being asked. That was the positive answer and there was no need to do more than that. People had to
be left completely free to choose whether they wanted to continue to
read *The Ancient Wisdom* or whether they wanted to use *Theosophy*.[2]

In times of great historical change, things are not decided in as
rational and direct a manner as one likes to think. Thus I did not find
it at all surprising that the Theosophists who attended the lecture
cycle on Anthroposophy when the German Section was established
remarked that it did not agree in the slightest with what Mrs. Besant
was saying.

Of course it could not agree, because the answers had to be found
in what the deepened consciousness of the present can provide. Until
about 1907 each step taken by Anthroposophy was a battle against the
traditions of the Theosophical Society. At first the members of the
Theosophical Society were the only people one could approach with
these things. Every step had to be conquered. A polemical approach
would have been useless; the only sensible course was hope, and making the right choices.

These things certainly did not happen without inner reservations.
Everything had to be done at the right time and place, at least in my
view. I believe that in my *Theosophy* I did not go one step beyond what
it was possible to publish and for a certain number of people to accept
at that time. The wide distribution of the book since then shows that
this was an accurate assumption.

It was possible to go further among those who were engaged in a
more intensive search, who had been caught up in the stream set in
motion by Blavatsky. I will take only one instance. It was common in
the Theosophical Society to describe how human beings went through

what was called *kamaloka* after death. To begin with, the description given by its leaders could only be put in a proper context in my book *Theosophy* by avoiding the concept of time. But I wanted to deal with the correct concept of time within the Society.

As a result I gave lectures about life between death and a new birth within the then Dutch Section of the Theosophical Society. And there I pointed out, right at the start of my activity, that it is nonsense simply to say that we pass through *kamaloka* as if our consciousness is merely extended a little. I showed that time has to be seen as moving backward, and I described how our existence in *kamaloka* is life in reverse, stage by stage, only at three times the pace of the life we spend on Earth. Nowadays, of course, people leading their physical lives have no idea that this backward movement is a reality in the spiritual realm, because time is imagined simply as a straight line.

Now, the leaders of the Theosophical Society professed to renew the teachings of the old wisdom. All kinds of other writings based on Blavatsky's book appeared. But their content took a form that corresponded exactly to the way things are presented as a result of modern materialism. Why? Because new knowledge, not simply the renewal of old knowledge, had to be pursued if the right things were to be found. Buddha's wheel of birth and death and the old Oriental wisdom were quoted on every occasion. People ignored that a wheel is something that must be drawn as turning back on itself. There was no life in this rejuvenation of ancient wisdom, because it did not spring from direct knowledge. In short, one had to create something through direct knowledge that was also capable of illuminating ancient wisdom.

Nevertheless, in the first seven years of my Anthroposophical work there were people who denied that there was anything new in my material in relation to Theosophy. But people never forgot the trouble I caused in the Dutch Section by filling my lectures with living material. When the congress took place in Munich in 1907, the Dutch Theosophists were seething because an alien influence, as they perceived it, had entered.[3] They did not feel the living present as something different from what was based merely on tradition.

Something had to change. That is when the conversation between Mrs. Besant and myself took place in Munich. It was made clear that the things that I had to represent as Anthroposophy would work quite independently of other things active within the Theosophical Society.[4] What I might describe as a modus vivendi was agreed.

On the other hand, even at that time the absurdities of the Theosophical Society, which eventually led to its downfall, began to be visible on the horizon. For it is clear today that it has been ruined as a society that can support a spiritual movement, however great its membership. What the Theosophical Society used to be is no longer alive today.

When Anthroposophy began its work the Theosophical Society still contained a justified and full spirituality. The things brought into the world by Blavatsky were a reality. People had a living relationship with them. But Blavatsky had already been dead for a decade. The mood within the Theosophical Society, the things existing as a continuation of Blavatsky's work, had a solid historical and cultural foundation; they were quite capable of giving people something. But even at that time they already contained the seeds of decay. The only question was whether these could be overcome, or whether they would inevitably lead to complete disharmony between Anthroposophy and the old Theosophical Society.

It has to be said that a destructive element existed in the Theosophical Society even in Blavatsky's time. It is necessary to separate Blavatsky's spiritual contribution from the effect of the way in which she was prompted to make her revelations. We are dealing with a personality who, however she was prompted, nevertheless was creative and through herself gave wisdom to humankind, even if this wisdom was more like a memory of earlier lives on Earth and restricted to the rejuvenation of ancient wisdom. The second fact, that Blavatsky was prompted to act in a particular way, introduced elements into the Theosophical movement which were no longer appropriate if it was to become a purely spiritual movement.

For that it was not. The fact is that Blavatsky was prompted from a certain direction, and as a result of this she produced all the things that are written in *Isis Unveiled*. But by various machinations Blavatsky for a second time fell under outside influence, namely that of Eastern esoteric teachers who were propelled by cultural tendencies of an egoistic nature. From the beginning a biased policy lay at the basis of the things they wished to achieve through Blavatsky. It included the desire to create a kind of sphere of influence (first of a spiritual nature, but then in a more general sense) of the East over the West, by providing the West's spirituality, or lack of it if you like, with Eastern wisdom. That is how the transformation took place from the thoroughly

European nature of *Isis Unveiled* to the thoroughly Eastern nature of *The Secret Doctrine*.

Various factors were at work, including the wish to link India with Asia in order to create an Indo-Asian sphere of influence with the help of the Russian Empire. In this way Blavatsky's teaching received its Indian content in order to win a spiritual victory over the West. It reflected a one-sidedly egoistic, nationally egoistic, influence. It was present right from the beginning and was striking in its symptomatic significance. The first lecture by Annie Besant that I attended dealt with Theosophy and imperialism.[5] And if one questioned whether the fundamental impulse of the lecture was contained in the wish to continue in Blavatsky's spiritual direction or to continue what went alongside it, the answer had to be the latter.

Annie Besant frequently said things without fully understanding the implications. But if you read the lecture "Theosophy and Imperialism" attentively, with an awareness of the underlying implications, you will see that if someone wanted to separate India from England in a spiritual way, the first, apparently innocuous step could be taken in a lecture of this kind.

It has always spelled the beginning of the end for spiritual movements and societies when they have started to introduce partisan political elements into their activity. A spiritual movement can only develop in the world today if it embraces all humanity. Indeed, today one of the most essential conditions for a spiritual movement whose intention is to give access to the real spirit is that it should embrace all humanity. And anything intending to divide humanity in any way is, from the beginning, a destructive element.

Just consider the extent to which one reaches into the subconscious regions of the human psyche with such things. It is simply part of the conditions for a spiritual movement such as Anthroposophy wants to be that it honestly and seriously endeavor to distance itself from all partisan human interests, and aspire to take account of the general interest of humankind. That was what made the Theosophical movement so destructive, insofar as it contained divisive elements from its inception. And on occasion it also veered in its position; during the war there was a tendency to become very pro-English and chauvinistic. But it is essential to understand very clearly that it is completely impossible to make a genuine spiritual movement flourish if it contains factional interests that people are unwilling to leave behind.

That is why today, in an age deteriorating everywhere into nationalist posturing, one of the main dangers facing the Anthroposophical movement lies in the lack of courage among people to discard these tendencies.

But what is the root cause of this tendency? It arises when a society wants to gain power by something other than spiritual revelation. At the beginning of the twentieth century there was still much that was positive in the way the Theosophical Society developed an awareness of its power, but that awareness had almost completely disappeared by 1906 and was replaced by a strong drive for power.

It is important to understand that Anthroposophy grew out of the general interests of humanity, and to recognize that it had to find access to the Theosophical Society, because that is where the questioners were to be found. It would not have found accommodation anywhere else.

Indeed, as soon as the first period came to an end, the complete inappropriateness of the Theosophical movement for Western life became evident, particularly in its approach to the issues surrounding Christ. Whereas Blavatsky's contempt for Christianity was still basically theoretical, albeit with an emotional basis, the Theosophical movement later turned this contempt into practice, to the extent that a boy was specially brought up with the intention of making him the vehicle for the resurrection of Christ. There is hardly anything more absurd. An order was established within the Theosophical Society that had the aim of engineering the birth of Christ in a boy who was already alive here.[6]

This soon descended into a total farce. A congress of the Theosophical Society was to take place in Genoa in 1911,[7] and I felt it necessary to announce my lecture "From Buddha to Christ" for this congress. This should have resulted in a clear and concise debate by bringing into the open everything already in the air. But the Genoa congress was cancelled. It is, of course, easy to find excuses for something like that, and every word that was uttered sounded uncommonly like an excuse.

Thus we can say that the Anthroposophical movement entered its second stage by pursuing its straightforward course, and it was introduced by a lecture I delivered to a non-Theosophical audience, of which only one person—no more!—is still with us, although many people attended the original lecture. That first lecture, lecture cycle in fact, was entitled *From Buddha to Christ*. In 1911 I had wanted to deliver the same cycle. There was a direct connection! But the Theosophical movement had become caught up in a hideous zigzag course.

Unless the history of the Anthroposophical movement is taken seriously and these things are properly identified, we cannot give a proper answer to the superficial points that are always raised about the relationship between Anthroposophy and Theosophy. These are points made by people who refuse absolutely to acknowledge that Anthroposophy was something quite independent from the beginning, and that it was quite natural for Anthroposophy to provide the answers it possessed to the questions being asked.

Thus we might say that the second period of the Anthroposophical movement lasted until 1914. During that time nothing in particular happened, at least as far as I am concerned, to resolve its relationship with the Theosophical movement. The Theosophical Society remedied that when it expelled the Anthroposophists. It was not particularly relevant to be in the Theosophical Society, and it was not particularly relevant to be excluded. We simply continued as before. Until 1914 everything that occurred was initiated by the Theosophical Society. I was invited to lecture there on the basis of the lectures that have been reprinted in my book *Mystics after Modernism*. I then proceeded to develop in various directions the material contained in it. The Theosophical Society, with its unchanged views, then proceeded to expel me and, of course, my supporters. I was invited in for the same reasons that later caused my exclusion. That is how it was. The history of the Anthroposophical movement will not be understood until the fundamental fact is recognized that it was irrelevant whether I was included in or excluded from the Theosophical movement. . . .

21

The Emergence of
the Anthroposophical Movement

Dornach, June 15, 1923

I HAVE GIVEN YOU some idea of the forces that determined the first two periods of the Anthroposophical movement. But in order to create a basis on which to deal with what happened in the third stage, I still wish to deal with a number of phenomena from the first two.

The first period, up until approximately 1907, can be described as being concerned with developing the fundamentals for a science of the spirit in lectures, lecture cycles, and in subsequent work undertaken by others. This period concludes approximately with the publication of my *An Outline of Esoteric Science*.

Esoteric Science actually appeared some one and a half years later, but the publicizing of its essential content undoubtedly falls into this first period. Some hope was definitely justified in this period, up to 1905 or 1906, that the content of Anthroposophy might become the purpose of the Theosophical Society's existence.

During this time it would have been an illusion not to recognize that leading personalities in the Theosophical Society, and Annie Besant in particular, had a very primitive understanding of modern scientific method. Nevertheless, despite the amateurish stamp this gave to all her books, there was a certain sum of wisdom, mostly unprocessed, in the people who belonged to the Society. This became more marked as the focus of the Theosophical Society gradually moved to London and slowly began to feed, in a manner of speaking, on Oriental wisdom. It sometimes led to the most peculiar ideas. But if we ignore the fact that such ideas were sometimes stretched so far that they lost all similarity to their original and true meaning, such books as Annie Besant's *Ancient Wisdom, The Progress of Mankind,* and even *Christianity* transmit something which, although passed down by traditional means, originated in ancient sources of wisdom.

On the other hand one must always be aware that in the modern world beyond these circles there was no interest whatsoever in real spiritual research. The reality was simply that the possibility of kindling an interest in a truly modern science of the spirit existed only among those who found their way into this group of people.

Yet within this first period in particular there was a great deal to overcome. Many people were working toward something, but it was in part a very egoistic and shallow striving. But even such superficial societies frequently called themselves Theosophical. One need only think, for instance, of the Theosophical branches that spread widely throughout central Europe—in Germany, Austria, and Switzerland—which possessed only an exceedingly anemic version of Theosophical Society tenets, impregnated with all kinds of foolish occult views.

One person who was very active in such societies was Franz Hartmann.[1] But the kind of profound spirit and deep seriousness that existed in these shallow societies will become obvious to you if I describe the cynical character of this particular leader. The Theosophical Society was at one time engaged in a dispute in connection with an American called Judge[2] about whether or not certain messages he had distributed originated with persons who really had reached a higher stage of initiation, the so-called Masters. Judge had distributed these "Mahatma Letters" in America.

While they were both at the headquarters in India, Judge said he wanted some letters from the Masters in order to gain credibility in America, so that he could say he had been given a mission by initiates. Franz Hartmann recounted how he had offered to write some Mahatma Letters for Judge, and the latter had replied that this would not permit him to claim their authenticity. They were supposed to fly toward you through the air; they originated in a magical way and then landed on your head, and that is what he had to be able to say. Judge was a very small fellow, Hartmann told us, and so he said to him, "Stand on the floor and I will stand on a chair, and then I will drop the letters on your head." Then Judge could say with a clear conscience that he was distributing letters that had landed on his head clean out of the air!

That is an extreme example of things that are not at all rare in the world. I do not want to waste your time with these shallow societies. I only want to point out that the close proximity of the Anthroposophical movement to the Theosophical movement made it necessary for the former to defend itself against modern scientific thinking during its first period.

I do not know whether those who joined the Anthroposophical movement later as scientists, and have observed Anthroposophy during its more developed third stage, have gained sufficient insight into the fact that a critical assessment of modern scientific thinking took place in a very specific way during the first period of the Anthroposophical movement. I will only give instances, because this process occurred in a number of different areas. But these examples will show you how the Theosophical movement was strongly influenced by the deference to so-called scientific authority which I described as particularly characteristic of modern education.

Annie Besant, for instance, tried to use in her books all kinds of quotes from contemporary science, such as Weismann's theory of heredity, which bore no relevance to the science of the spirit.[3] She used them as if they provided some sort of evidence. If you recall, at the time when we were in a position to start a center for the Anthroposophical movement in Munich many homeless souls were already organized in the sense that they belonged to various societies. Of course centers for the movement had begun to develop gradually in Berlin, Munich, Stuttgart, Kassel, Dusseldorf, Cologne, Hamburg, Hanover, and Leipzig, and in Vienna as well as in Prague. When we were establishing the branch in Munich it became necessary to assess critically the various larger and smaller groups then in existence.

One group called the Ketterl, consisting of extremely scholarly people, was very much concerned with providing proofs from natural science for the claims made on behalf of the science of the spirit. If Anthroposophy spoke about the etheric body, they would say that science has recognized this or that structure for atoms and molecules. Their formulae and definitions and so on were applied not to processes of the spectrum or electromagnetism but to processes in the etheric or astral field. There was nothing we could do about that. The whole thing dissolved more or less amicably. In the end we no longer had any links with these investigations.

Not so very different were the efforts of a Dr. Hübbe-Schleiden,[4] who played an important role in the Theosophical Society. He was a close friend of Blavatsky, and was the editor of Sphinx for a long time. He, too, was obsessed with proving what he felt was Theosophical subject matter by means of natural scientific thinking. He took me to his home, a little way outside Hanover. It was perhaps half an hour by train. He spent the entire half hour describing the motion of atoms with his index fingers: Yes, it has to happen in this way and that way and then we have the answer. The atoms move in one incarnation and then the wave motion continues through the spiritual worlds; then it changes and that is the next incarnation. He calculated the passage of souls through various incarnations in the same way modern physicists calculate light in terms of wavelengths.

A special version of this way of thinking was evident in the debate about the permanent atom, which took place in the Theosophical Society over a long period. This permanent atom was something awful, but was taken incredibly seriously. For the people who felt the full weight of modern science postulated that while the physical body of course decomposes, a single atom remains, passes through the time between death and a new birth, and appears in the new incarnation. That is the permanent atom, which passes through incarnations.

This may appear funny to you today, but you simply cannot understand the seriousness with which these things were pursued, specifically in the first period, and the difficulty that existed in responding to the challenge: What is the point of Theosophy if it cannot be proved scientifically! During that conversation in the train the point was forcefully made that things have to be presented in a manner that will allow a matriculated schoolboy to understand Theosophy in the same way that he understands logic. That was the thrust of my companion's argument. Then we arrived at his home and he took me into the loft, and up there—I have to repeat that he was an exceedingly kind, pleasant, intelligent man; in other words, a sympathetic old gentleman—were very complicated wire constructions. One of the models represented the atom of a physical entity; the next model, which was even more complex, represented the atom of something etheric; the third model, still more complex, was an astral atom.

If you pick up certain books by Leadbeater,[5] a leading figure in the Theosophical Society, you will find such models in grandiose form. Atomism flourished nowhere as greatly as among those who joined our ranks from the Theosophical Society. And when younger members such as Dr. Kolisko and others are engaged in the fight against the atom in our research institute in Stuttgart, we might well recall that certain people at that time would not have known how to get from one incarnation to the next without at least one permanent atom.[6]

That is something of an image of the way the strong authority of so-called natural scientific thinking exerted its influence in these circles. They were unable to conceive of any other valid way of thinking than the natural scientific one. So there was no real understanding in this quarter either. Only as the Anthroposophical movement entered its second stage did these atomistic endeavors gradually subside, and there was a gradual transition to the subject matter that continued to be cultivated in the Anthroposophical movement. Every time I was in Munich, for instance, it was possible to give a lecture designed more for the group that gathered round a great friend of Blavatsky's. Things were easier there because a genuine inner striving existed.

Within our own ranks, too, there was a call at that time to justify the content of Anthroposophy using the current natural scientific approach. It was less radical, nevertheless, than the demands made by external critics today. A large number of you heard Dr. Blumel's lecture today.[7] Imagine if someone had responded by saying that everything Dr. Blumel spoke about was of no personal concern; that he did not believe it, did not recognize it, and did not want to test it. Someone else might say: See whether it is accurate, examine it with your reason and your soul faculties. The first person says: It is no business of mine, be it right or wrong; I do not want to become involved with that. But I call on Dr. Blumel to go to a psychological laboratory and there, using my psychological methods, I will examine whether or not he is a mathematician.

That is, of course, piffle of the first order. But it is exactly the demand made today by outside critics.

Sadly, it is quite possible today to talk pure nonsense that goes undetected. Even those who are upset by it fail to notice that it is pure nonsense. They believe that it is only maliciousness or something similar, because they cannot imagine the possibility of someone who talks pure nonsense acquiring the role of a scientific spokesman simply as a result of social standing. That is the extent to which our spiritual life has become confused. The kind of things I am explaining here must be understood by anyone who wants to grasp the position of the Anthroposophical movement.

Well, undeterred by all that, the most important human truths, the most important cosmic truths, had to be made public during the first stage. My *Esoteric Science* represents a sort of compendium of everything that had been put forward in the Anthroposophical movement until that point. Our intention was always a concrete and never an abstract one, because we never attempted to do more than could be achieved in the given circumstances.

Let me quote the following as evidence. We established a journal, *Luzifer-Gnosis,* right at the outset of the Anthroposophical movement.[8] At first it was called *Luzifer.* Then a Viennese journal called *Gnosis* wanted to merge with it. My sole intention in calling it *Luzifer with Gnosis* was to express the practical union of the two journals. Of course that was completely unacceptable to Hübbe-Schleiden, for instance, who thought that this would indicate an unnatural union. Well, I was not particularly bothered, so we called it *Luzifer-Gnosis* with a hyphen. People were very sharp-witted and they were keeping a close eye on us at that time!

Of course we started with a very small number of subscribers, but it began to grow at a very fast pace, relatively speaking, and we never really ran at a deficit because we only ever printed approximately as many copies as we were able to sell. Once an issue had been printed the copies were sent to my house in large parcels. Then my wife and I put the wrappers around them. I addressed them, and then each of us took a washing basket and carried the whole lot to the post office. We found that this worked quite well. I wrote and held lectures while my wife organized the whole society, but without a secretary.[9] So we did that all on our own and never attempted more than could be managed on a practical level. We did not even, for example, take larger washing baskets than we could just manage. When the number of subscribers grew we simply made an extra journey.

When we had been engaged in this interesting activity for some time, *Luzifer-Gnosis* ceased publication—not because it had to, for it had many more subscribers than it needed, but because I no longer had time to write. The demands of my lecturing activity and of the spiritual administration of the society in general began to take up a lot of time. To cease publication was a natural consequence of never attempting more than could be managed on a practical level, one step at a time. This belongs to the conditions that govern the existence of a spiritual society. To build far-reaching ideals on phrases, setting up programs, is the worst thing that can happen to a spiritual society. The work in this first period was such that between 1907 and 1909 the foundations of a science of the spirit appropriate to the modern age were put in place.

Then we come to the second phase, which essentially concluded our attempt to come to grips with natural science. The theologians had not yet made their presence felt. They were still seated so firmly in the saddle everywhere that they were simply not bothered.

When the issue of the natural sciences had been dealt with, we were able to approach our other task. This was the debate over the Gospels, over Genesis, the Christian tradition as a whole, Christianity as such.

The thread had already been laid out in *Christianity as Mystical Fact*, which appeared in 1902. But the elaboration, as it were, of an Anthroposophical understanding of Christianity was essentially the task of the second stage up to approximately 1914. As a consequence I gave lecture cycles on the various parts of the Christian tradition in Hamburg, Kassel, Berlin, Basle, Berne, Munich, and Stuttgart.

That was also when, for instance, *The Spiritual Guidance of the Individual and Humanity* was drawn up.[10] It was, then, essentially the time in which the Christian side of Anthroposophy was worked out, following on from the historical tradition of Christianity.

This period also included what I might call the first expansion of Anthroposophy into the artistic field, with performances of the mystery dramas in Munich.[11] That, too, took place against the background of never wanting to achieve more than circumstances allowed.

Also during this time those events occurred that led to the exclusion of Anthroposophy from the Theosophical Society, a fact that was actually of no great significance to the former, given that it had followed its own path from the beginning. Those who wanted to come along were free to do so. From the outset Anthroposophy did not concern itself with the spiritual content that came from the Theosophical Society. But practical coexistence became increasingly difficult as well.

At the beginning there was a definite hope that circumstances, some of which at least I have described, would allow the real Theosophical movement which had come together in the Theosophical Society to become truly Anthroposophical. The circumstances that made such a hope appear justified included the serious disappointment about the particular methods of investigation pursued by the Theosophical Society, specifically among those people who possessed a higher level of discrimination. And I have to say that when I arrived in London both the first and second times, I experienced how its leaders were basically people who adopted a very skeptical attitude toward one another, who felt themselves to be on very insecure ground, which, however, they did not want to leave because they did not know where to look for security.

There were many disappointed people who had great reservations, particularly among the leaders of the Theosophical Society. The peculiar change that took place in Annie Besant from, say, 1900 to 1907 is an important factor in the subsequent course of events in the Theosophical Society. She possessed a certain tolerance to begin with. I believe she never really understood the phenomenon of Anthroposophy, but she accepted it and at the beginning even defended against the rigid dogmatists its right to exist. That is how we must describe it, for that is how it was.

But there is something I must say, which I would also urge members of the Anthroposophical Society to consider very seriously. Certain personal aspirations, purely personal sympathies and antipathies, are absolutely irreconcilable with a spiritual society of this kind. Someone, for instance, begins to idolize someone else, for whatever underlying inner reasons. He (or she) will not acknowledge whatever compulsion it is, and sometimes it can be an intellectual compulsion that drives him to do it. But he begins to weave an artificial astral aura around the individual he wants to idolize. The latter then becomes advanced. If he wants to make an especially telling remark he will say, "Oh, that individual is aware of three or four previous lives on Earth and even spoke to me about my earlier Earth lives. That person knows a lot!" And this is precisely what leads to a spiritual interpretation of something that is human, all too human, to use the expression from Nietzsche.

It would be sufficient to say, "I will not deny that I like that person." Then everything would be fine, even in esoteric societies. Max Seiling,[12] for instance, was very amusing in certain ways, particularly when he played the piano in that effervescent way of his, and he was amusing to have tea with, and so on. All would have been well if people had admitted that they liked that. That would have been more sensible than idolizing him in the way the Munich group did.

You see, all these things are in direct contradiction to the conditions under which such a society should exist. And the prime example of someone who fell prey to this kind of thing is Annie Besant. For example—and I prefer to speak about these things by quoting facts—a name cropped up on one occasion. I did not bother much with the literature produced by the Theosophical Society, and so I became acquainted with Bhagavan Das's name only when a thick typewritten manuscript arrived one day.[13] The manuscript was arranged in two columns, with text on the left side and a blank on the right. A covering letter from Bhagavan Das said that he wanted to discuss with various people the subject matter he intended to reveal to the world through the manuscript.

Well, the Anthroposophical movement was already so widespread at that time that I did not manage to read the manuscript immediately. That Bhagavan Das was a very esoteric man, a person who drew his inspiration from profound spiritual sources—that was approximately the view that people associated with Annie Besant spread about him. His name was on everyone's lips. So I decided to have a look at the thing. I was presented with a horrendously amateurish confusion of Fichtean philosophy, Hegelian philosophy, and Schopenhauer's philosophy; everything was mixed up together without the slightest understanding. And the whole thing was held together by "self" and "not self," like an endlessly repeated tune. The idolization of Bhagavan Das was based purely on personal considerations. Such things demonstrate how the personal element is introduced into impulses that should be objective. The first step on the slippery slope was taken with the appearance of this phenomenon, which became increasingly strong from about 1905 onward. Everything else was basically a consequence of that.

Spiritual societies must avoid such courses of action, particularly by their leaders—otherwise they will, of necessity, slide down the slippery slope. That is, indeed, what happened. Then there was the absurd tale connected with Olcott's death, referred to as the Masters' nomination, which really represented the beginning of the end for the Theosophical Society.[14] That could still be smoothed over, at least, by saying that such foolishness was introduced into the Society by particular people, even if they were acting on the basis of certain principles. It was, however, followed by the Leadbeater affair, the details of which I do not want to discuss just now.[15] And then came the discovery of the boy who was to be brought up as Christ, or to become Christ, and so on.[16] And when people who did not want to be involved in these absurd matters refused to accept them, they were simply expelled.

Well, the Anthroposophical movement followed its set course throughout the whole of this business and our inner development was not affected by these events in any way. That has to be made absolutely clear. It was really a matter of supreme indifference—just as I was not especially surprised to hear recently that Leadbeater has become an Old Catholic bishop in his old age. There was no sense of direction, and everything was going topsy-turvy.

Indeed, there is no particular need to change one's personal relationship with these people. Two years ago a gentleman who had delivered a lecture at the Munich congress in 1907 approached me with the old cordial spirit.[17] He still looked the same, but in the meantime he had become an Old Catholic archbishop. He was not wearing the garments, but that is what he was!

It must not be forgotten that the stream we have been describing also contained precisely those souls who were searching most intensively for a link between the human soul and the spiritual world. We are not being honest about the course of modern culture if these contrasts are not made absolutely clear. . . .

Notes

Prologue

1. Immanuel Kant (1724–1804), the founder of German idealism and the most influential modern philosopher, set the tone and limits for what it is possible for human beings to think and know. His greatness lay in requiring that knowledge be justified; that is, transparent. His weakness lay in his extremely limited view of human experience, which was, in the words of Walter Benjamin, "of the lowest order." Rudolf Steiner likewise contested Kant's limited views. He believed that "present-day philosophy suffers from an unhealthy faith in Kant" and sought to overcome it. See Rudolf Steiner, *Truth and Knowledge* (Blauvelt, NY: Steinerbooks, 1981).
2. J. G. Fichte (1762–1814) and F. W. J. Schelling (1775–1854) are like the two wings of German idealism (Steiner called it "theosophy"). Fichte concentrates on the transcendent function of the Transcendent Ego or "I," while Schelling (the student of Jakob Boehme) introduces a profound, mythological, hermetic cosmology.
3. The "agent" was Felix Koguzki, an herb gatherer. Steiner writes of him elsewhere that he was "a person without any learning but with a deep knowledge and a truly encompassing wisdom. . . . He lived in a remote, isolated mountain village with his rustic family, and his room was filled with mystical and occult literature. . . ." See lecture (Berlin, February 4, 1913) entitled "Self-Education: Autobiographical Reflections 1861–1893" (Spring Valley, NY: Mercury Press, 1985). See also Rudolf Steiner, *Autobiography, Chapters in the Course of My Life: 1861–1907* (Great Barrington, MA: Anthroposophic Press, 2000), pp. 46–48. Steiner writes of the M.: "My Felix was the herald, as it were, of another personality, who served as a means to stimulate in the soul of the boy—who indeed already lived in the spiritual worlds—the regular, systemic qualities one needs to have to gain knowledge in the spiritual worlds. . . . In outer occupation, this excellent man was as inconspicuous as Felix . . ." ("Self Education").
4. G. W. F. Hegel (1770–1831) is the body of the bird of German idealism, the philosopher of pure thinking, the abstract idea. What he contributed to the theosophical picture was above all the understanding of evolution as an evolution of consciousness.
5. See *Nature's Open Secret: Introductions to Goethe's Scientific Writings*, trans. John Barnes and Mado Spiegler (Great Barrington, MA: Anthroposophic Press, 2000).
6. Ernst Haeckel (1834–1919), evolutionary theorist and philosopher, the "apostle of Darwin" in Germany, is best known today for his statement "Ontogeny recapitulates phylogeny." In later life, he became the prophet

of monism, establishing monist associations all over Germany. He was very influential among spiritual thinkers of the time. See Richard Noll, *The Jung Cult* (Princeton: Princeton University Press, 1996).

7. See *A Theory of Knowledge Implicit in Goethe's World Conception* (Spring Valley, NY: Anthroposophic Press, 1978).

8. The key figure here is Steiner's lifelong friend Friedrich Eckstein (1861–1939), whom he met through the man who had introduced him to Goethe, his mentor Karl Julius Schroer. Steiner had read Sinnett's *Esoteric Buddhism* as soon as it appeared in German (1884) and asked Eckstein to explain *The Secret Doctrine*. Eckstein then provided the important office of introducing Steiner to Rosa Mayreder and the Theosophical circle of Edmund and Marie Lang. See Nicholas Goodrick-Clarke, "The Modern Occult Revival in Vienna 1880–1910," in *Theosophical History* 1/5, 1986.

9. See note 5 above.

10. Blauvelt, NY: Steinerbooks, 1981.

11. Hudson, NY: Anthroposophic Press, 1995.

12. See Rudolf Steiner, *Friedrich Nietzsche, Fighter For Freedom* (Blauvelt, NY: Steinerbooks, 1985), and, for more detail, Rudolf Steiner, *Autobiography* (Great Barrington, MA: Anthroposophic Press, 2000), pp. 166–175.

13. See Rudolf Steiner, *The Secret Stream: Christian Rosenkreutz and Rosicrucianism*, ed. Christopher Bamford (Great Barrington, MA: Anthroposophic Press, 2000).

14. *Isis Unveiled: A Master Key to the Mysteries of Ancient and Modern Science and Theology*, 2 vols. (New York: J. W. Bouton, 1877), was Madame Blavatsky's first major work.

15. A. P. Sinnett's *Esoteric Buddhism*, the foundation of much Theosophical teaching, was first published in 1883. It followed publication of the same author's *The Occult World*. *The Secret Doctrine* (1887) was Madame Blavatsky's second major work.

1. Theosophy and Spiritualism

1. Friedrich Albert Lange (1828–1875) was a German philosopher and socialist, important for his refutation of materialism and for establishing the tradition of Neo-Kantianism at Marburg. The phrase "psychology without a soul" comes from his *History of Materialism* (1866).

2. Rudolf Wagner (1805–1864) was an anatomist and physiologist and a zealous opponent of materialism. Karl Vogt was the author of *Koehlerglaube und Wissenschaft* (1855).

3. The Joseph Weber referred to was probably the author *of Metaphysics of the Sensory and the Supersensory* (1802).

4. In German there is only one word, *Spiritismus*, to cover the English words "spiritualism" and "spiritism." As indicated in the Introduction, when the spiritualist movements developed in the mid–nineteenth century,

there was a distinction between the "spiritualism" properly so-called that swept North America and Britain, and "spiritism," the form made popular in continental Europe by Allan Kardec. The chief difference, and a source of much dispute between the two, was that spiritism included a belief in reincarnation, which Anglo-Saxon schools of spiritualism hotly denied. Steiner refers to this controversial difference, which led to immense occult and lethal struggles in chapter 4 below and incidentally in chapter 11. Both spiritism and spiritualism held that mediumistic phenomena are caused by spirits (which spiritualists however limited to the spirits of the dead, while spiritists extended their understanding to include different orders of spirits or spiritual beings). In this sense, Steiner was a "spiritist," not a "spiritualist." However, since "spiritualism" is the most commonly used term in English—and to attempt to interchange the terms depending on context would have been confusing and probably impossible—we have used the terms "spiritualism" or "spiritualist" throughout.

5. Sir William Crookes (1832–1919), renowned English physicist and chemist, discoverer of thallium, and inventor of the radiometer and the Crookes tube, a highly exhausted vacuum tube producing X rays. He was president of the Royal Society, 1913–1915, and also actively engaged in psychical and spiritualist research. He is especially known for his work with the mediums Dunglas Home and Florence Cook, with whom he reported on having witnessed rappings; movement of objects without visible cause; table and chairs raised into the air; human bodies likewise raised; luminous apparitions; automatic writing; ghostlike forms; materializations; and so forth.

6. Alfred Russel Wallace (1832–1913), English naturalist, evolutionist, geographer, anthropologist, social theorist, and spiritualist. He was the co-originator, with Charles Darwin, of the theory of natural selection (around 1856–1857). By 1865, he had begun to doubt materialist models and was investigating spiritualism. The result was a wholly new evolutionary synthesis, in which a material process (natural selection) was understood to rule at the biological level, while a spiritual evolution operated at the level of consciousness. Wallace never recanted his spiritualism and composed more than one hundred writings on the subject.

7. For corroboration of these remarks, see Patrick Deveny's *Astral Projection or Liberation of the Double and the Work of the Early Theosophical Society*, Theosophical Occasional Papers VI (Fullerton, CA: Theosophical History, 1997).

8. Arthur Schopenhauer (1788–1860), leading German philosopher of the will and the unconscious. One of the great "pessimists" and one of first Europeans to be influenced by Buddhism, he was the author of *The World as Will and Representation* (1819). Steiner is quoting, from memory, from an essay entitled "Introduction to the Study of Philosophy."

9. The "Adepts" are the Mahatmas or the Masters of the White Lodge or the Masters of Wisdom and the Harmony of Sensations and Feelings. For Steiner's view, see Rudolf Steiner, *From the History and Contents of the First Section of the Esoteric School, 1904–1914* (Hudson, NY: Anthroposophic Press, 1998).

10. The allegory of the bees derives from the great mythologist Friedrich Creuzer (1771–1858), author of *Symbolik und Mythologie der alten Völker, besonders der Griechen* (1810–1812).

11. Johann Gottlieb Fichte, German idealist philosopher of the "I" and a great influence on Rudolf Steiner; see note 2 to Prologue above. The quotation is from *The Vocation of Man* (1800).

2. Theosophy and Somnambulism

1. Johann Heinrich Jung, known as Stilling, or Jung-Stilling (1740–1817), mystical visionary and pietistic writer who, encouraged by Goethe, overcame poverty to become a physician. Author of a celebrated autobiography in five volumes containing much occult and mystical lore (speaking, for instance, of an esoteric group that meets "in Egypt, on Mount Sinai, in the monastery of Canobin, and under the Temple of Jerusalem"), and also of mystical fiction.

2. Ludwig Laistner, *The Riddle of the Sphinx: Foundations of a History of Myth* (not translated), 2 vols., (Berlin: 1889).

3. Both quotations are from *Faust*, Part One, "Night."

3. The History of Spiritualism

1. See Augustine, *Epistle Against the Manicheans*, 5.

2. See Rudolf Steiner, *Rosicrucianism and Modern Initiation* (London: Rudolf Steiner Press, 1982); *The Secret Stream: Christian Rosenkreutz and Rosicrucianism* (Great Barrington, MA: Anthroposophic Press, 2000).

3. See note 2 above and Ralph White, ed., *The Rosicrucian Enlightenment Revisited* (Hudson, NY: Lindisfarne Books, 1999).

4. Robert Fludd (1574–1637), English metaphysician, cosmologist, doctor, and Rosicrucian. See Joscelyn Godwin, *Robert Fludd: Hermetic Philosopher and Surveyor of Two Worlds* (Grand Rapids, MI: Phanes Press, 1991).

5. See, W. Martin, *Description of the Western Islands of Scotland* (1716). Also, Michael Hunter, *The Occult Laboratory: Magic, Science, and Second Sight in Seventeenth Century Scotland* (Woodbridge and Rochester: Boydel and Brewer, 2001).

6. See Kant, *Dreams of a Visionary Explained by Dreams of Metaphysics* (1766).

7. The place was Göteborg, which is actually four hundred kilometers from Stockholm.

8. Friedrich Christian Oettinger (1702–1782), Swabian pietist theologian, philosopher, cabalist, alchemist, and Rosicrucian.

9. For Jung-Stilling, see note 1, chapter 2.

10. Joseph Ennemoser (1787–1854), author of works on mesmerism, magnetism, and magic.

11. Johann Friedrich von Meyer's main work is *Hades, A Contribution to the Theory of Spirit Exploration* (1810, not translated), written in defense of his friend Jung-Stilling.

12. Justinus Andreas Kerner (1786–1862), poet, physician, medical writer; author of *The Story of Two Somnambulists* (1824) and, above all, his work on Friedericke Hauffe (1801–1829), *The Seeress of Prevorst* (1828), as well as other works on spiritualism, somnambulism, and mesmerism.

13. David Friedrich Strauss (1808–1874), German theologian and philosopher who developed the "mythological" approach to Jesus.

14. Andrew Jackson Davis (1826–1910), "the Seer of Poughkeepsie," also called "the John the Baptist" of modern spiritualism.

15. "Summerland" was A. J. Davis's name for Paradise.

16. Augustus de Morgan (1806–1871), English mathematician and logician, who laid the foundation for modern symbolic logic.

17. Ernst Heinrich Weber (1795–1878), German anatomist and physiologist, known for studies of sensory response; considered a founder of experimental psychology. Gustav Theodor Fechner (1801–1887), the founder of psychophysics, author of *Elements of Psychophysics* (1860).

18. Johann Karl Friedrich Zollner (1834–1882), astrophysicist and researcher into four-dimensionality, which he used for his investigations into spiritualist phenomena. Author of *Transcendental Physics* (1881). Henry Slade (1836–1905) was a well-known American medium.

19. Baron Lazar von Hellenbach (1827–1887), Austrian social thinker and founder of parapsychology in Austria. Author of, among others, *Birth and Death as a Change of Form of Perception* (1886).

20. Allan Kardec (Leon Hyppolyte Denizart Rivail) (1803–1869), educator and founder of spiritualism in Europe. Author of *The Spirit's Book* (1857) and *The Book of Mediums* (1861); also *The Gospel Explained by Spirits* (1864), *Heaven and Hell* (1865), *Genesis* (1867).

21. Eduard von Hartmann, *Der Spiritismus* (1885). Von Hartmann (1842–1906) synthesized the views of Schopenhauer, Kant, and Hegel into a theory of evolutionary history based on conflict of unconscious will and unconscious reason (*Philosophy of the Unconscious,* 1869).

22. Crown Prince Rudolf of Austria (1858–1889); Archduke Johann Nepomuk Salvator of Austria, author of "Insights into Spiritualism" (1889).

23. Oskar Simony (1852–1915), Austrian mathematician and physicist.

24. Carl du Prel (1839–1899), author of *The Philosophy of Mysticism* (1884).

25. Angelus Silesius (1624–1677), mystic, author of *The Soul's Spiritual Delight* and *The Cherubic Wanderer* (both 1657).

4. The History of Hypnotism

1. Athanasius Kircher (1602–1680), German Jesuit scholar and polymath. An expert in geology, astronomy, optics, cartography, mathematics, Greek, Hebrew, and Syriac, among others, he was also an able student of magic and the occult. See Joscelyn Godwin, *Athanasius Kircher: Renaissance Man and the Search for Lost Knowledge* (London: Thames and Hudson, 1979).

2. The text is from *Ars magna lucis et umbrae* (The Great Art of Light and Shadows), 1646. Goethe quoted it in the first part of *Theory of Color*. It was also cited by a contemporary of Steiner, Wilhelm Preyer, in an 1877 lecture "Magnetizing Humans and Animals," published in book form in 1880. Preyer claims it marks the beginning of the scientific study of magnetism. It was first made public by a professor of mathematics and Oriental languages at the University of Altdorf, Daniel Schwenter (1585–1636).

3. Kaspar Schott (1608–1666), Austrian Jesuit and scientist who worked with Kircher in Rome.

4. Jean Leurechon (1593–1670), Jesuit professor of mathematics and philosophy, the author, under the pseudonym H. van Etten, of an epoch-making work called *Mathematical Recreations* (1625).

5. Karl Hansen (c. 1833–1897), celebrated Danish hypnotist.

6. Franz Anton Mesmer (1734–1815), from whom we derive "mesmerism," the earlier word for hypnotism, marks one of the most interesting points of convergence between dynamic psychiatry and theosophy. See Henri F. Ellenberger, *The Discovery of the Unconscious* (New York: Basic Books, 1970); Robert Darnton, *Mesmerism and the End of the Enlightenment in France* (Cambridge: Harvard University Press, 1968); Alan Gauld, *A History of Hypnotism* (Cambridge: Cambridge University Press, 1992); Vincent Buranelli, *The Wizard from Vienna* (New York: Coward, McCann & Geoghan, 1975).

7. Wilhelm Preyer (1841–1897).

8. Steiner is here drawing on the same 1877 lecture of Preyer. See note 2.

9. Justinus Kerner (see note 12, chapter 3), besides writing *The Seeress of Prevorst*, wrote extensively on Mesmer and hypnotic phenomena.

10. Stone, an American, toured England in 1852. Once again, Steiner is here relying on Preyer.

11. Steiner is probably referring to the English doctor James Braid (1795–1860), an early proponent of mesmerism.

12. Faria, a Portuguese priest and hypnotist, gave a course on lucid sleep in Paris in 1813 and published a book on the subject in 1819. The Nancy School later adopted his technique.

13. Moritz Benedikt (1835–1920), professor at Vienna University, very influential pioneer in neurology, electrology, criminology, and psychiatry. He influenced Charcot, Freud, Kraft-Ebbing, and others.

14. August Ambroise Liebault (1823–1904), the spiritual father of the Nancy School, was one of the few mid-nineteenth-century scientists to carry on the hypnotic work. The actual leader of the Nancy School was Hippolyte Bernheim (1840–1919), who became embroiled in controversy with the brilliant neurologist, psychiatrist, and psychologist Jean-Martin Charcot (1835–1893) of the Salpteriere School, with whom Freud studied. See Ellenberger, *The Discovery of the Unconscious.*
15. Wilhelm Wundt (1832–1920), German physiologist and psychologist, founder of experimental psychology.

5. The Return of the Mysteries

1. Cornelius Tacitus (c. 56–c. 120 C.E.), was a Roman politician, orator, and historian.
2. For Steiner on the Greek Mysteries, see Rudolf Steiner, *Wonders of the World, Ordeals of the Soul, Revelations of the Spirit* (London: Rudolf Steiner Press, 1963); also Rudolf Steiner, *Christianity as Mystical Fact* (Hudson, NY: Anthroposophic Press, 1995).
3. The Mysteries of Eleusis, held annually at Eleusis (twenty kilometers west of Athens) in honor of the goddesses Demeter and Persephone, were the most sacred and revered celebrations of Ancient Greece. See Karl Kerenyi, *Eleusis* (Princeton: Princeton University Press, 1991).
4. Hegel sent this poem to his friend the poet Friedrich Hölderlin in 1796.
5. On the importance of devotion for Rudolf Steiner, see the first chapter of *How to Know Higher Worlds* (Hudson, NY: Anthroposophic Press, 1992).
6. The "Stanzas of Dzyan"—metaphysical and cosmological verses from an unknown source—are the foundation of *The Secret Doctrine*, which in some sense is but an extended commentary on them.

6. Remembering Madame Blavatsky

1. Henry Steel Olcott (1832–1907) was born in New Jersey and educated at the College of the City of New York and Columbia University. After his father's business failed, Olcott left the East Coast for Ohio, where he became a farmer. Agriculture became a passion and he returned after two years to pioneer methods of teaching farming. When the Civil War broke out, Olcott enlisted in the Signal Corps and became a surgeon. After the War, he studied law and became a specialist in insurance, customs, and revenue cases. Success allowed him to give full rein to his interest in occult phenomena. He wrote about the beginnings of spiritualist phenomena at the Eddy farmstead for the *New York Sun.* This led to other commissions, which eventually became *People from the Other World* (1872). In October 1874 he met Madame Blavatsky, and a bond was immediately formed. The Mahatmas were delighted: it was as they had

intended! In 1875, at the founding of the Theosophical Society, Olcott was elected the first president. He is the author of, above all, *Old Diary Leaves*, an unmatched account of the events of the time, and *A Buddhist Catechism*.

2. *Isis Unveiled: A Master Key to the Mysteries of Ancient and Modern Science and Theology*, 2 vols. (New York: J. W. Bouton, 1877).

3. See Rudolf Steiner, *The Apocalypse of Saint John* (Hudson, NY: Anthroposophic Press, 1992) and *The Book of Revelation and the Work of the Priest* (London: Rudolf Steiner Press, 1998).

7. Christ and the Further Development of Conscience

1. Primordial teachers of humanity. See Rudolf Steiner, *An Outline of Esoteric Science* (Hudson, NY: Anthroposophic Press, 1997).

2. Arthur Drews (1865–1935), German philosopher and professor at Karlsbad. Author of numerous works on the history of philosophy, Nietszche, Plotinus, logic, and the psychology of the unconscious. *Die Christusmythe* appeared in 1909. For Eduard von Hartmann, see note 21, chapter 3.

8. Ancient Wisdom and the Heralding of the Christ Impulse

1. F. Max Müller (1832–1900), British Orientalist born in Germany. One of those who brought Eastern religions to the West, he edited the 51-volume Sacred Books of the East, translating many key texts himself. He was also the author of *Lectures on the Science of Language* (1861–1864) and *Contributions to the Science of Mythology* (1897).

2. For the letters of the Masters or Mahatmas see A. P. Sinnett, *The Occult World* (1881), *Esoteric Buddhism* (1883); see also *The Mahatma Letters to A. P. Sinnett from Mahatmas M. and K. H.*, transcribed, compiled, with an Introduction by A. T. Barker (1923).

3. Novalis is the pseudonym of the great German Romantic poet, philosopher, and novelist Friedrich von Hardenberg (1772–1801), who was very important to Rudolf Steiner. For the Anthroposophical view, see Sergei O. Prokofieff, *Eternal Individuality: Toward a Karmic Biography of Novalis* (London: Temple Lodge, 1992). On Novalis, see Margaret Stoljar, trans., *Novalis: Philosophical Writings* (Albany: SUNY Press, 1997); Arthur Versluis, trans., *Pollen and Fragments: Selected Poetry and Prose of Novalis* (Grand Rapids, MI: Phanes Press, 1990); Dick Higgins, trans., *Hymns to the Night* (Kingston: McPherson, 1988); Wm. Arctander O'Brien, *Novalis: Signs of Revolution* (Durham: Duke University Press, 1995). For Novalis's life in the form of a novel, see Penelope Fitzgerald, *The Blue Flower* (Boston: Houghton Mifflin, 1995).

9. Materialism and Occultism

1. This lecture cycle should be read in conjunction with C. G. Harrison, *The Transcendental Universe: Six Lectures on Occult Science, Theosophy, and the Catholic Faith* (Hudson, NY: Lindisfarne Press, 1993), which Steiner leaned upon heavily and implicitly refers to frequently. Carl Graf von Leininghen-Billigheim, who had been a friend of Rudolf Steiner in Vienna in the 1880s, translated this work into German as *Das Transzendentale Weltall* (1897).
2. See Rudolf Steiner, *How to Know Higher Worlds* (Hudson, NY: Anthroposophic Press, 1994).
3. The Samothracian Mysteries took place on the Island of Samothrace in the northern Aegean. These Mysteries of the Cabiri (also known as the Dactyls) were reputed by Herodotus to be the most ancient in Greece, originating with the pre-Greek Pelasgian, probably Phrygian, peoples. See Rudolf Steiner, *Mystery Knowledge and Mystery Centres* (London: Rudolf Steiner Press, 1997).

10. The Founding of the Theosophical Society

1. Rudolf Steiner's articles from *Luzifer-Gnosis*, which are known in German as *Aus der Akasha-Kronik* (From the Akashic Chronicle), have been published in English as *Cosmic Memory* (Blauvelt, NY: Garber Communications, 1994).
2. W. Scott-Elliot, *Legends of Atlantis and Lost Lemuria* (Wheaton, IL: Quest Books, The Theosophical Publishing House, 1990).
3. Annie Besant assumed the leadership of the Theosophical Society after the death of Madame Blavatsky. Charles W. Leadbeater, former Anglican clergyman and prominent member of the Theosophical Liberal Catholic Church, was a leading Theosophist and clairvoyant Theosophical spiritual researcher. Both wrote many books.
4. Rudolf Steiner, *Theosophy* (Hudson, NY: Anthroposophic Press, 1994).
5. On occult imprisonment see chapter 15; also Steiner, *Man in the Light of Occultism, Theosophy and Philosophy* (London: Rudolf Steiner Press, 1964); *Earthly and Cosmic Man* (London: Rudolf Steiner Press, 1970).
6. The "pirate" John King is one of the mysteries of Theosophical history. See, on the Internet (blavatskyarchives.com), Maria Cesar Sisson, *Helena Blavatsky and the Enigma of John King*.
7. Henry Steel Olcott, *People from the Other World* (Rutland, VT: Charles E. Tuttle, 1972).
8. A. P. Sinnett, *The Occult World* (London: Trubner and Co., 1881); *Esoteric Buddism* (London: Trubner and Co., 1883).
9. Rudolf Steiner, *Mystics After Modernism* (Great Barrington, MA: Anthroposophic Press, 1999).

10. Rudolf Steiner, *Christianity as Mystical Fact* (Hudson, NY: Anthroposophic Press, 1997).

11. The Significance of the Eighth Sphere

1. Rudolf Steiner, *The Inner Nature of Man and Life Between Death and a New Birth* (London: Rudolf Steiner Press, 1972).
2. On the Eighth Sphere, see primarily C. G. Harrison, the Christian esotericist connected with the "High Church party" in England refered to in this lecture. His book is *The Transcendental Universe* (Hudson, NY: Lindisfarne Press, 1993). See also A. P. Sinnett, *Esoteric Buddhism;* A. T. Barker, ed., *The Mahatma Letters,* in which it is regretted that the topic was ever introduced; and Valentin Tomberg, *Anthroposophical Studies of the Old Testament* (Spring Valley, NY: Candeur Manuscripts, 1985).
3. See Rudolf Steiner, *An Outline of Esoteric Science* (Hudson, NY: Anthroposophic Press, 1996).

13. Some Background to the Role of Madame Blavatsky

1. Hengist and Horsa were two brothers who, according to tradition, led the Jutish invasion of Britain and founded the kingdom of Kent. They are said to have been invited by Vortigern in 449 to help defend the Britons against the Picts and the Scots. They are said to have then fought a battle against Vortigern in 545 in which Horsa was killed.
2. Rudolf Steiner is here again following Harrison in *The Transcendental Universe.*
3. Lecture of March 24, 1916, "Spiritual Research and the Question of Immortality" (not translated).

14. Occult Brotherhoods

1. Master Bertram (c. 1345–1415) was a German painter working in Hamburg. The most important painting attributed to him is the Grabow Altar (1379–1383) now in the Hamburg Kunsthalle.
2. J. W. von Goethe, *Wilhelm Meister,* 6 vols. (London: John Calder, 1977).
3. Éliphas Lévi is the pseudonym of Alphonse Louis Constant (1810–1875), one of the most influential esotericists and occultists of the nineteenth century. It may almost be said that he single-handedly created "esotericism." See Christopher MacIntosh, *Éliphas Lévi and the French Occult Revival* (London: Rider, 1972).
4. Dr. Gerard Encausse (1865–1916), known as Papus, was a Spanish-born French physician, hypnotist, popularizer of occultism, and the author of many books on magic, Cabala, and the Tarot. He joined the French Theosophical Society shortly after it was founded, but soon left it, because of

its "Eastern" flavor. In 1901 he formed the order of Martinists. He visited Russia three times in 1901, 1905, and 1906, serving Tsar Nicholas II as occult consultant.

15. Madame Blavatsky's Occult Imprisonment

1. For a fascinating bird's-eye account of such "training" in Europe, see *Ghostland, or Researches into the Mysteries of Occultism*, by the author of *Art-Magic*, trans. and ed. Emma Hardinge Britten (Chicago: Progressive Thinker Publishing House, 1897).

2. Steiner is referring here to geopolitical machinations and the struggle for power between the Anglo-Saxon and the Germanic cultures for the dominance of the fifth post-Atlanean epoch, especially with regard to Russia—whither the evolutionary center of spiritual-cultural influence is to pass in the sixth post-Atlantean epoch. Later on in this lecture (although not included in the present selction) Steiner says: "I told you some time ago that in the secret brotherhoods, especially those which grew so powerful from the time of James I onward, it was taught as an obvious truth that the Anglo-Saxon race—as they put it—will have to be given dominance over the world in the fifth post-Atlantean period." For all this, see chapter 14 herein and, as always, C. G. Harrison, *The Transcendental Universe*, lecture two and notes.

16. Homeless Souls

1. The *Bayreuther Blatter* was the official organ of the Wagner Association, founded in 1876.

2. See Rudolf Steiner, *Autobiography* (Great Barrington, MA: Anthroposophic Press, 2000), pp. 91–109.

3. Steiner spoke of Dostoyevsky with deep affection in other lectures, for example in the March 20, 1916, lecture given at Munich, published in *Anthroposophic News Sheet*, Dornach, Nos. 7/8, p. 58, and 9/10, p. 67, etc.

4. Marie and Edmund Lang, Franz Hartmann, Friedrich Eckstein, and others had formed a Theosophical study group in Vienna, which Steiner met in 1888. See *Autobiography*, pp. 106–109, and note 8 to Prologue.

5. Goethe's *Fairy Tale*, together with a lecture on it by Steiner, is included in Steiner's *The Portal of Initiation & The Fairy Tale of the Green Snake and the Beautiful Lily* (Blauvelt, NY: Garber Communications, 1981). See also *Autobiography*, pp. 122–125, 255.

6. From 1890 to 1897 Steiner was employed at the Goethe-Schiller Archive in Weimar to edit Goethe's scientific writings within the Weimar edition of Goethe's works. See *Autobiography*, pp. 111–221; also *Nature's Open Secret: Introductions to Goethe's Scientific Writings*, trans. John Barnes and Mado Spiegler (Great Barrington, MA: Anthroposophic Press, 2000).

7. *Mystics after Modernism* (Great Barrington, MA: Anthroposophic Press, 1999). See also *Autobiography,* pp. 256–260.

17. The Unveiling of Spiritual Truths

1. Ralph Waldo Trine (1866–1958), American pupil of Emerson and author of philosophical books. Best known for *In Tune with the Infinite* (1897).
2. Steiner chose this principle, enunciated by Goethe, as the motto for the constitution he gave to the Anthroposophical Society in 1912. From *Sprüche in Prosa: Goethes Naturwissenschaftliche Schriften,* ed. Rudolf Steiner (Dornach: 1975), vol. V, p. 360.
3. Currently available under the title *Intuitive Thinking as a Spiritual Path* (Hudson, NY: Anthroposophic Press, 1995).
4. See note 2 (Fichte) and note 4 (Hegel) to Prologue, above. Karl Wilhelm Ferdinand Solger (1780–1819) was a philosopher and aesthetician.
5. *Encyclopedia of Philosophy,* first published in 1817 (New York: Philosophical Library, 1959), Part One: "Logic."
6. Robert Zimmermann (1824–1912), philosopher and aesthetician, professor of philosophy at University of Vienna from 1861–1895. Cf. Rudolf Steiner, *Autobiography* (Great Barrington, MA: Anthroposophic Press, 2000), pp. 43–45.
7. Franz Hartmann (1838–1912), physician and Theosophist, founded and directed a section of the Theosophical Society in Leipzig, called the "Hartmann-Boehme Society," which was not affiliated with the German Section of the Theosophical Society. He was the author of many books on Theosophy, which according to Steiner "gave the spiritual teaching a completely materialistic form." See *Autobiography,* p. 107; also cf. *The Occult Movement in the Nineteenth Century.*
8. Paul Topinard (1830–1912), French anthropologist. A German translation of his *Anthropology* appeared in 1888.
9. The date and title could not be established.
10. The name *Die Kommenden* (The Coming Ones) was used by a society founded in Berlin by the poet Ludwig Jacobowski that included literary figures, artists, scientists, and others interested in the arts. Steiner delivered twenty-four lectures to the group from October 1901 to March 1902. See *Autobiography,* p. 258.
11. *Christianity as Mystical Fact* (Hudson, NY: Anthroposophic Press, 1997).
12. *Mystics after Modernism* (Great Barrington, MA: Anthroposophic Press, 1999).
13. The reference is to the second major lecture cycle of twenty-seven lectures, titled *From Zarathustra to Nietzsche,* given to Die Kommenden from October 1902 to April 1903. The inaugural meeting of the German Section of the Theosophical Society took place on October 20, 1902, with Annie Besant present.

14. For more on Schelling see note 2 to Prologue above. *Die Weltalter* (The Ages of the World) is a fragment from his unpublished works.

15. *Philosophie der Offenbarung,* 2 vols. (1858); English trans. *Philosophy of Revelation* (New York: Columbia University Press, 1942). Cf. the chapter "The Classics of World and Life Conceptions" in Rudolf Steiner, *Riddles of Philosophy* (Spring Valley, NY: Anthroposophic Press, 1973); cf. also the Dornach, September 16, 1924, lecture in Steiner's *Karmic Relationships,* vol. 4 (London: Rudolf Steiner Press, 1983).

16. Lawrence Oliphant (1829–1888), English writer, traveler, and mystic. He was the author of *Sympneumata; or, Evolutionary Forces Now Active in Man* (1885) and other works. Cf. also the London, August 24, 1924, lecture in *Karmic Relationships,* vol. 8 (London: Rudolf Steiner Press).

18. The Opposition to Spiritual Revelations

1. See chapter 10 above, lecture of October 11, 1915; also Berlin lecture of October 23, 1911, in *Earthly and Cosmic Man* (Blauvelt, NY: Garber Communications).

2. See Rudolf Steiner, *Psychoanalysis and Spiritual Psychology* (Hudson, NY: Anthroposophic Press, 1990).

3. The speaker was Bruno Wille (1860–1928), who began the Giordano Bruno League in 1900. He was a liberal writer on religion and editor of the *Freidenker* (Berlin, 1892) after starting The Free People's Theater in Berlin. He wrote a Faustian, monistic novel, *Revelation of the Juniper Tree.* See Rudolf Steiner, *Autobiography* (Great Barrington, MA: Anthroposophic Press, 2000), pp. 251–252.

4. The lecture referred to is "Monism and Theosophy." See *Autobiography,* pp. 252–253.

19. Spiritual Truths and the Physical World

1. Friedrich Nietzsche (1844–1900), *Twilight of the Idols and The Anti-Christ* (1889), trans. R. J. Hollingdale (London/New York: Penguin Books, 1990). See note 12 to Prologue above.

20. The Decline of the Theosophical Society

1. Rudolf Steiner: *The Gospel of St. John* (Spring Valley, NY: Anthroposophic Press, 1973); *The Gospel of St. John and Its Relation to the Other Gospels* (Spring Valley, NY: Anthroposophic Press, 1982); *According to Luke* (Great Barrington, MA: Anthroposophic Press, 2001); *The Gospel of St. Matthew* (London: Rudolf Steiner Press, 1965); *The Gospel of St. Mark* (Hudson, NY: Anthroposophic Press, 1986); *Background to the Gospel of St. Mark* (London: Rudolf Steiner Press, 1968).

2. *The Ancient Wisdom* was published in 1897, *Theosophy* in 1904.

3. The fourth annual congress of the Federation of European Sections of the Theosophical Society took place in Munich from May 18–21, 1907. Under Steiner's guidance an attempt had been made to create a harmonious correlation between the spiritual activity in and the artistic arrangement of the conference room. There was also a performance of Edouard Schuré's reconstruction of *The Sacred Drama of Eleusis*. See *Autobiography*, pp. 298–301.

4. In the lecture of December 14, 1911, Steiner said: "In front of a witness [Marie von Sivers] who is willing to swear to this at any time, Annie Besant said in Munich in 1907 that she was not qualified to deal with Christianity. And that is why she, as it were, handed the movement over to me, insofar as its Christian aspects were concerned." See *Aus dem Leben von Marie Steiner-von Sivers*, p. 451.

5. "Theosophy and Imperialism" was delivered at the Theosophical Society Congress in London in July 1902.

6. The Order of the Star in the East was organized by Annie Besant and C. W. Leadbeater (see note 3 to chapter 10 above) in 1911 to herald the reincarnated "World Teacher." The boy so designated was Jiddu Krishnamurti (1895–1986), who was "discovered" by Leadbeater in 1909 in Adyar. These events, and their effect on the young Krishnamurti, are described in Mary Lutyens, *Krishnamurti: The Years of Awakening* (New York: Farrar, Straus & Giroux, 1975). Krishnamurti went on to be an influential and paradoxical spiritual teacher who, although he accepted no students and founded no religion, became a beacon of truth for millions around the world.

7. See *Aus dem Leben von Marie Steiner-von Sivers*, pp. 70f.

21. The Emergence of the Anthroposophical Movement

1. See note 7 to chapter 17 above.

2. William Quan Judge (1851–1896) was one of the cofounders of the Theosophical Society. In 1895 he split from the Adyar-based society and became the leader of a secessionist movement in America.

3. August Weismann (1834–1914), German physician and biologist, professor of zoology at Freiburg. He developed a theory of germ plasm and denied that acquired characteristics are passed on to offspring, contending that only variations of the germ plasm are inherited.

4. Dr. Wilhelm Hübbe-Schleiden (1846–1916) first became known for his works dealing with German voyages of discovery and colonial interests. He became acquainted with Madame Blavatsky in 1884 and occasionally worked in the Theosophical Society headquarters in India. He established the Theosophical Society in Germany and edited *The Sphinx* (1886–1895), a monthly magazine for the life of the soul and spirit that was also

the official organ of the Theosophical Union (which he started in 1892) and the German Theosophical Society (founded in 1894). Steiner considered him to be the foremost candidate for general secretary of the German Section when it began, but Hübbe-Schleiden declined. In 1911 Annie Besant nominated him to represent the Order of the Star in the East (see note 6 to chapter 20 above) in Germany, through which he came to oppose Steiner. After the German Section led by Steiner separated from the Theosophical Society in 1913, Hübbe-Schleiden became general secretary of the new German Section. He belonged to the Esoteric School of Theosophy in London and took part in Steiner's esoteric classes. See Rudolf Steiner, *Autobiography,* pp. 271–275.

5. See *Occult Chemistry* by C. W. Leadbeater and Annie Besant, a series of clairvoyant observations abour the chemical elements and atomic theory.

6. Dr. Eugene Kolisko (1881–1939), physician and teacher at the Stuttgart Waldorf School. The scientific institute was one of the sections of Kommende Tag (The Coming Day), a company set up to promote economic and spiritual values, Stuttgart, 1920–1925. The biology department (under Elisabeth Kolisko, wife of Eugene) was transferred to the Goetheanum in Dornach in 1924.

7. Dr. Ernst Blumel (1884–1952), mathematician and teacher, first in further education at the Goetheanum and subsequently (1927–1938) at the Waldorf School in Stuttgart.

8. The journal appeared from June 1903 to 1909. By the time it ceased publication Marie von Sivers had established a publishing company to publish Rudolf Steiner's works. See *Autobiography,* pp. 274–275. Steiner's essays that first appeared in *Luzifer-Gnosis* are available in *How to Know Higher Worlds* (Hudson, NY: Anthroposophic Press, 1992) and *Cosmic Memory* (Blauvelt, NY: Garber Communications, 1994).

9. See *Aus dem Leben von Marie Steiner-von Sivers,* pp. 40f.

10. Rudolf Steiner, *The Spiritual Guidance of the Individual and Humanity* (Hudson, NY: Anthroposophic Press, 1992).

11. Rudolf Steiner: *The Portal of Initiation* (1910), *The Soul's Probation* (1911), *The Guardian of the Threshold* (1912), *The Soul's Awakening* (1913). Available in *Four Mystery Dramas,* trans. Ruth and Hans Pusch (North Vancouver, Canada: Steiner Book Centre, 1973).

12. Max Seiling was a member of the Anthroposophical Society for a time. He turned against it when a book that he wanted to have published by Philosophisch-Anthroposophischer Verlag was turned down.

13. Bhagavan Das was a prominent member of the Theosophical Society. He resigned his office as general secretary of the Indian Section in 1912 because he disapproved of the goings-on within the Order of the Star of the East over the Krishnamurti-Alcyone cult (see note 6 to chapter 20 above) and of the behavior of the president of the Theosophical Society (Annie Besant), who approved of and encouraged these activities.

14. For Olcott, see note 1, chapter 6, above. Olcott had proposed Annie Besant as his successor as president of the Theosophical Society. Some of the circumstances surrounding this nomination had become public, leading Steiner to write in *Luzifer-Gnosis* No. 33 (March/April 1907):

> . . . The deceased president did not merely state that he nominated Mrs. Besant as his successor, but he informed the General Secretaries through a variety of circulars—which then found their way into the Theosophical press and, unfortunately beyond—that the elevated individuals who are described as the Masters, and those in particular who are especially connected with Theosophical affairs, had appeared at his deathbed and had instructed him to nominate Mrs. Besant as his successor.
>
> . . . Now this addition to Mrs. Besant's nomination could simply have been ignored. For whether or not one believes that the Masters genuinely appeared in this case, the source of Olcott's advice has no relevance to the members casting their votes in accordance with the Statutes. Whether he was advised by the Masters or by some ordinary mortals is his business alone. The voters have to adhere to the Statutes and solely ask themselves whether or not they consider Mrs. Besant to be the right choice. An immediate difficulty arose, however, through the fact that Mrs. Besant announced that she had been called upon by her Master to accept the nomination and that for this reason she would assume the burden; indeed, that she considered the order from the Masters as decisive in determining the outcome of the election. Objectively that is a disaster.

This article and other material relating to the Besant nomination are printed in Rudolf Steiner, *From the History and Contents of the First Section of the Esoteric School, 1904–1914* (Hudson, NY: Anthroposophic Press, 1998), part 2, pp. 275–305.

15. C. W. Leadbeater (see note 3 to chapter 10 above) left the Theosophical Society in 1906 after serious differences emerged between him and the Society; this became know as the "Leadbeater affair." (See *From the History and Contents of the First Section of the Esoteric School, 1904–1914*, part 2, pp. 265–274.) In 1909 he was reinstated by Annie Besant, despite her earlier condemnation of his methods.

16. See note 6, chapter 20, above.

17. The person concerned is James Ingall Wedgwood. See Emily Lutyens, *Candles in the Sun* (London: Hart-Davis, 1957).

Sources and Background Reading

Sources

Prologue: A Personal Statement—from *Briefwechsel und Dokumente 1901–1925* (GA 262) [*Correspondence and Documents*, London/New York: Rudolf Steiner Press/Anthroposophic Press, 1988].

Part One: Spiritualism, Somnambulism, and Theosophy—from *Spirituelle Seelenlehre und Weltbetrachtung* (GA 52).

Part Two: White Lotus Day Lectures—from *Ursprungimpulse der Geisteswissenschaft* (GA 96); *Der Christus Impul und die Entwickelung des Ich-Bewusstseins* (GA 116); *Erfahrungen des Uebersinnlichen. Die Wege der Seele zu Christus* (GA 143).

Part Three: The Occult Background of the Theosophical Movement—from *Die okkulte Bewegung in der neunzehnten Jahrhundert und ihre Beziehung zur Weltkultur* (GA 254) [*The Occult Movement in the Nineteenth Century*, London: Rudolf Steiner Press, 1973]; *Gegenwaertiges und Vergangenes im Menschengeiste* (GA 167); *Karma der Unwahrhaftigkeit, Erster Teil* (GA 173) [*The Karma of Untruthfulness*, Volume One, London/New York: Rudolf Steiner Press/Anthroposophic Press, 1988].

Part Four: From Theosophy to Anthroposophy—from *Die Geschichte und Die Bedingungen der anthropsophischen Bewegung im Verhaeltnis zur Anthropsophschen Gesellschaft* (GA 258) [*The Anthroposophic Movement*, London: Rudolf Steiner Press, 1993].

Background Reading

Blavatsky, H. P. *Isis Unveiled*. Los Angeles: The Theosophy Company, 1931.

———. *The Secret Doctrine*. Pasadena: Theosophical University Press, 1970.

———. *The Key to Theosophy*. Pasadena: Theosophical University Press, 1972.

Braude, Anne. *Radical Spirits: Spiritualism and Women's Rights in Nineteenth-Century America*. Boston: Beacon Press, 1989.

Cranston, Sylvia. *H. P. B.: The Extraordinary Life and Influence of Helena Blavatsky*. New York: A Jeremy P. Tarcher/Putnam Book, 1993.

Deveny, John Patrick. *Astral Projection or the Liberation of the Double and the Work of the Early Theosophical Society*. Theosophical History Occasional Papers, vol. VI. Fullerton, CA: Theosophical History 1997.

———. *Paschal Beverly Randolph: A Nineteenth-Century Black American Spiritualist, Rosicrucian, and Sex Magician*. Albany: State University of New York Press, 1997.

Godwin, Joscelyn. *The Theosophical Enlightenment.* Albany: State University of New York Press, 1994.

———. "The Hidden Hand." 1–4 in *Theosophical History,* NS III/2, 3, 4, 5 (1990–1991). London: Theosophical History Center.

Guénon, René. *Le Théosophisme, histoire d'une pseudo-religion.* Paris: Éditions Traditionelles, 1982.

———. *L'Erreur Spirite.* Paris: Éditions Traditionelles, 1991.

Hardinge Britten, Emma. *Ghostland or Researches into the Mysteries of Occultism.* Chicago: Progressive Thinker Publishing House, 1897.

———. *Modern American Spiritualism.* New Hyde Park, NY: University Books, 1970.

Harrison, C. G. *The Transcendental Universe.* Hudson, NY: Lindisfarne Press, 1993.

Kardec, Allan. *The Spirits' Book.* Albuquerque, NM: Brotherhood of Life, Inc., 1989.

Matheisen, Robert. *The Unseen Worlds of Emma Hardinge Britten: Some Chapters in the History of Western Occultism.* Theosophical History Occasional Papers, vol. 9. Fullerton, CA: Theosophical History, 2001.

Olcott, Henry Steel. *Inside the Occult: The True Story of H. P. Blavatsky.* Philadelphia: Running Press, 1975.

Podmore, Frank. *From Mesmer to Christian Science. A Short History of Mental Healing.* New Hyde Park, NY: University Books 1963.

———. *Mediums of the Nineteenth Century.* New Hyde Park, NY: University Books, 1963.

Sinnett, A. P. *Esoteric Buddhism.* Boston: Houghton Mifflin, 1884.

———. *The Occult World.* London: Trubner and Co., 1884.

———. *Some Fruits of Occult Teaching.* London: Theosophical Society, 1896.

Webb, James. *The Occult Underground.* La Salle, IL: Open Court, 1974.

———. *The Occult Establishment.* La Salle, IL: Open Court, 1976.